PRACTICAL TRUTHS
FROM
ISRAEL'S
WANDERINGS

PRACTICAL TRUTHS
FROM
ISRAEL'S
WANDERINGS

by
George Wagner

KREGEL PUBLICATIONS
Grand Rapids, Michigan 49501

Practical Truths from Israel's Wanderings by
George Wagner, Copyright © 1982 by Kregel
Publications, a division of Kregel Inc. All rights
reserved.

Library of Congress Cataloging in Publication Data

Wagner, George, 1793-1870.
    Practical Truths from Israel's Wanderings.

    Reprint. Originally published: The Wanderings of
the Children of Israel. London : J. Nisbet & Co.,
1862.
        1. Christian life. 2. Jews—History—To 1200 B.C.
I. Title.
BV4501.W23   1982   221.9'5   82-18706
ISBN 0-8254-4017-3

Printed in the United States of America

CONTENTS

Contents

ISRAEL AND PHARAOH
(Types of the New and Old Man)

Exodus 6:6, 7

" Wherefore say unto the children of Israel, I am the Lord, and I will
bring you out from under the burdens of the Egyptians, and I
will rid you out of their bondage, and I will redeem you with a
stretched-out arm, and with great judgments: and I will take
you to me for a people, and I will be to you a God: and ye shall
know that I am the Lord your God, who bringeth you out from
under the burdens of the Egyptians."

WE purpose, brethren, if God graciously permit, to preach
a course of sermons on the journeyings of the children of
Israel as typical of the Christian's pilgrimage on earth ;
and to contemplate God's dealings with them, as foreshadows of His still more patient and gentle dealings with
His people now. The subject of such a course begins in
strictness at the passover, but there are a few introductory
points to be considered which will serve to place the following steps of the history in a clearer light. We may
gather up these in three heads: First, Israel's position
in Egypt; secondly, The judgment on Egypt, by means of
which they were delivered ; and thirdly, The bearing of
these on the Christian's life, or, in other words, what part
it is of the Christian's life and experience of which this
part of Israel's history is a type.

First, then, let us briefly touch upon Israel's position
in Egypt. This we all know was one of great and in-

creasing trial. When first Jacob descended into Egypt
with his sons, he was welcomed by a king grateful for all
the wise and effectual services rendered to his dominions
by Joseph. But this period of tranquillity lasted only for
a time. Another Pharaoh ascended the throne who knew
not Joseph, and cared not for the people to which he had
belonged. His conscience, restless and guilty, made him
afraid that this numerous people might join his enemies
in the day of battle, and it seemed to him a matter of
policy to weaken and keep them under. "Come," he
said, (Exod. i. 10,) "let us deal wisely with them; lest
they multiply, and it come to pass that, when there
falleth out any war, they join also unto our enemies,
and fight against us, and so get them up out of the land."
In pursuance of this unrighteous policy, the domestic
happiness of the Israelites was broken up by the murder
of their infant sons; and the massive ruins of Egypt are
witnesses, as well as the language of Scripture, of the
severity of the labours which they were forced to endure.
Their condition is spoken of as a "bondage." "The children of Israel," it says, (chap. ii. 23,) "sighed by reason
of the bondage, and they cried, and their cry came up
unto God by reason of the bondage." And again God
says, (chap. iii. 7,) "I have surely seen the affliction of my
people which are in Egypt, and have heard their cry by
reason of their taskmasters; for I know their sorrows;"
and so again in our text, "I will bring you out from
under the burdens of the Egyptians, and I will rid you
out of their bondage." But why were they thus afflicted?
It was God's appointment, and their affliction was appointed for a special reason. It was never intended that
Egypt should be their home. The time, the *exact* time
of their deliverance from it was fixed. Long before Joseph

went down there God said to Abraham, (Gen. xv. 13,) "Know of a surety that thy seed shall be a stranger in a land that is not theirs, and shall serve them; and they shall afflict them four hundred years." But not merely the number of years generally, but the *very day* of their redemption was predetermined, as we read, (Exod. xii. 41,) "And it came to pass at the end of the four hundred and thirty years, even the *selfsame day* it came to pass, that all the hosts of the Lord went out from the land of Egypt." God was faithful. As year after year passed away, His eye was ever fixed upon His promise. Joseph thought of it in his dying hour, and gave commandment concerning his bones. But many of the Israelites, doubtless, altogether forgot it. Had there been no trial in Egypt, they would have been contented to remain there as their home. Hence, brethren, Pharaoh's cruel policy, hence the iron bondage, hence the bitter cries for deliverance. God never fulfils His promises without first leading His people to *expect* the fulfilment. Whenever, therefore, what St Stephen so beautifully calls "the time of the promise," draws near, it is quite certain that by some means God will prepare His people for its accomplishment—will lead them to feel their need of it, and to desire it with longing hearts. This preparation for the fulfilment of a promise is sometimes brought about by the simple teaching of the Holy Spirit. But in many cases worldliness of mind, and lukewarmness of heart make a *severe* discipline necessary. It was so with Israel on this occasion. They were made to feel that they were in an enemy's territory. Misery and weariness made them welcome the promise of another land and a better home with joy. We have another instance of this at the time of the Babylonish captivity. The seventy years predicted by the prophet Jeremiah were nearly accomplished, but there were no signs of expectation in the people, no waiting for its fulfilment. Haggai's special mission was to awaken them out of their lukewarm state, and *trial* was made to concur with his *words* to produce earnestness in them; "The heaven," says the prophet, (Haggai i. 10,) "over you is stayed from dew, and the earth is stayed from her fruit. And I called for a drought upon the land, and upon the mountains, and upon the corn, and upon the new wine, and upon the oil, and upon that which the ground bringeth forth, and upon men, and upon cattle, and upon all the labour of the hands." Haggai's words, and this discipline produced the desired effect. The people arose and "did work in the house of the Lord of hosts, their God." They felt that the time of the promise was come.

Such then, brethren, was the position of Israel in Egypt. They were under an *iron bondage*, and whilst all their suffering was occasioned instrumentally by the cruelty and jealousy of Pharaoh, it was ordained of God for a special purpose. It was meant to wean them from Egypt, and to make them long for the Promised Land. The trials that reach us *through* man are no less ordained of God than those with which man has nothing whatever to do.

But let us now pass on to the judgments on the oppressing kingdom, which issued in the destruction of its power, and the deliverance of God's people. There is much that is deeply mysterious in this history, and that puzzles earnest and simple-minded readers. We shall scarcely be able to understand Pharaoh's character, or the plagues which were poured out upon Egypt in such awful succession, unless we first gain a true view of the solemn controversy. Was it a contest between Israel and Egypt

merely? You will answer at once, No—between God
and Egypt. But what do you mean by Egypt?—if the
Egyptians only, then the answer is not complete. It is
true as far as it goes, but it is not the whole truth. If
you turn to Exod. xii. 12, you will find an expression
which shews the true nature of the conflict. "And against
all the *gods of Egypt* I will execute judgment." And what
are the *gods* of Egypt? Idols merely? Let St Paul answer, (1 Cor. x. 20,) "But I say that the things which the
Gentiles sacrifice, they sacrifice to *devils*, and not to God."
The real contest, therefore, was between the kingdom of
light and the kingdom of darkness. Of the one kingdom,
the unseen God was the power—Moses and Aaron its
visible and spiritual representatives, and the children of
Israel its subjects. Of the other kingdom, the prince of
the power of the air was king—Pharaoh its earthly, and
the magicians its spiritual representatives, and the people
of Egypt, so far as they were unbelieving, its subjects.
This view of the *contest* will throw some light upon other
perplexing questions. When Moses performed his first
miracles in the presence of Pharaoh, we are told, (chap.
vii. 11,) "The magicians of Egypt, they also did in like
manner with their enchantments." When the waters of
Egypt were turned into blood, we are again told, (ver.
22,) "The magicians of Egypt did so with their enchantments." How, brethren, have you been accustomed
to understand these facts? Perhaps you have thought
that this was all *appearance*. They *seemed* to accomplish these miracles. But you will observe that the
history plainly said, "They *did* so." The true view of
the contest enables us to understand aright this part
of it. Satan has supernatural power; and in order to
deceive Pharaoh, and harden his heart, he gave the ma-

gicians power, as far as he could, (for there is a limit
to his power,) to work miracles of deception in imitation
of miracles of truth. A miracle does not necessarily
prove that a man comes from God ; all it proves is this,
that the person who performs it is connected with some
higher power—with one of two kingdoms. It is the
morality of the miracle, and the holiness of the doctrine
which it is meant to attest, which is the real proof that
he who performs it comes from God. The miracles of the
magicians were *miracles,* manifestations of superhuman
power ; but they were wrought by the power of darkness.

But there is another difficulty on which the same view
of the contest throws some, though certainly less light,—
we mean the awful expression, " The Lord hardened Pharaoh's heart." We have seen already that Pharaoh was
one of the visible representatives of the kingdom of darkness ; yet it would be altogether wrong to suppose that
the kingdom of darkness is ever *so fixed,* that those who
belong to it must of necessity continue so. It was a
solemn moment when Moses first stood before Pharaoh,
and gave proofs of his Divine mission. It was *then* that
his will might, and ought to have been surrendered to the
King of kings—*then* that he might have been translated
from the kingdom of darkness into the kingdom of light.
No eternal decree fixed him where he was,—no everlasting sentence of reprobation set his will against the will of
God ; reprobate he afterwards was, but that reprobation
was not the parent, but the child of his unbelief. God did
not harden his heart, until he had hardened his own. It
is an interesting and striking fact, that after each of the
first five plagues, it is said either as (chap. viii. 22) "that
Pharaoh's heart was hardened," or, as more frequently,
that " Pharaoh hardened his heart." It is not until after

the sixth plague, the plague of boils, that we meet with the solemn expression, (chap. ix. 12,) "The *Lord* hardened the heart of Pharaoh." It was therefore an act of judgment on his previous unbelief. He was unwilling to be translated from the kingdom of darkness, and he was therefore left there, and all the holy influences which might lead to his repentance were removed. The awful sentence was passed upon him, "Let him alone;" hence ten terrible plagues followed, one close upon another. The four first came from below,—two from the water, and two from the earth. The six last from above. Two, the murrain and the boils, from the lower atmosphere. The hail and the locusts from the upper atmosphere. The darkness was a suspension of the light of heaven; and the last plague, the death of the first-born, came down from the actual presence of Jehovah; for it says, (chap. xi. 4, 5,) "Thus saith the Lord, About midnight will *I go out into* the midst of Egypt: and all the first-born in the land of Egypt shall die." If we compare the ten plagues together, we shall see that the four last were more fearful than the preceding six. They were a new series, ushered in by new threatenings, as you will see if you turn to Exod. ix. 14, "For I will at this time send all my plagues upon *thine heart*,"—observe the words, "*upon thine heart*, upon thy servants, and upon thy people; that thou mayest know that there is none like me in all the earth." The six preceding plagues had been the cause of great suffering and loss. The fifth plague, that of murrain, was the first in which there was the destruction of life, but it was the life of beasts. The next plague, that of boils, affected the health of man as well as that of beasts. But the seventh plague was the first in which the life of *man* was taken; we are told expressly (chap. ix. 25) "that the hail smote throughout all the land of Egypt, all that was in the field, both *man* and *beast;*" and thus it was a foreshadow of the last awful judgment which plunged every family in Egypt into deep mourning.   And if you observe the effects of the four last plagues on the heart of Pharaoh, you will perceive, that although it had been rapidly hardening, yet he was more moved for the time by each one of them, than by any of the preceding six.   All, however, failed to turn his hardened heart; and, therefore, as the mercy of God was not glorified in his repentance and submission, the power of God was displayed in his signal destruction; as God himself said, (chap. ix. 16,) " And in very deed for this cause have I raised thee up, for to shew in thee my power; and that my name may be declared throughout all the earth." Pharaoh and Egypt are ever-speaking witnesses of the danger of neglecting the first proffers of mercy, and of the sure end of that presumption which leads sinful man to oppose the will of God.   Having then, brethren, now considered the position of Israel in Egypt, and the judgments poured out in the oppressing kingdom, let us proceed to inquire of what state in the history of the soul this history is typical.

Israel, we think, was a type of the new man; Pharaoh and Egypt, of the old man.   Israel and Pharaoh were very *closely connected,* so that the one suffered from some of the plagues inflicted upon the other, though not from all; yet in other points of view they were quite distinct.   Israel, though oppressed, was soon to be delivered with an everlasting sal-vation ; whereas Pharaoh, though dominant, was soon to be destroyed.   Was, then, this part of the history a type of the old and new man in the true Christian ? We think not, brethren, for two reasons : first, because in the true Chris-tian the new man, and not the old, is dominant ; whereas

in Egypt Israel was oppressed, and Pharaoh, the type of
the old man, supreme : and secondly, because Israel in
Egypt had not yet been cleansed by the blood of the
Paschal Lamb; whereas the true believer is washed from
his sins by the blood of Jesus, as St John says, (Rev. i. 5,)
" Unto him that loved us, and washed us from our sins in
his own blood." If, then, Israel in Egypt cannot be a type
of the true believer, of what state of mind can it be a
type ? of that, brethren, which St Paul describes, Rom.
vii. 9, 24. Perhaps there are many here who have
always taken that chapter as a description of the Christian's conflict. On a former occasion we endeavoured
to shew that this, for many reasons, cannot be the state
which the apostle sketches there : *first*, because that
chapter is progressive,—that is, it does not describe one
fixed state of mind, but the progress of the soul out of a
state of death into union with Christ, which takes place
first, (ver. 25,) " I thank God through Jesus Christ our
Lord ; " secondly, because in the Christian the new man
is conqueror in temptation, as St Paul says, (chap. viii. 37,)
" Nay, in all these things we are more than conquerors
through him that loved us." But in that contest the old
man often prevailed, as he tells us, (chap. vii. 23,) " But I
see another law in my members, warring against the law of
my mind, and bringing me into captivity to the law of sin
which is in my members." What, then, is the state of
mind which the apostle is there describing ? It is the
state of the *awakened* soul,—a state in which there is an
old man and a new man, in which there is a conflict between them, and the new man is often oppressed, as Israel
was in Egypt—the old man often dominant, as Pharaoh
was, though under judgment. It is of this state of conflict that the contest between Israel and Pharaoh is an

exact type, and if you read the history in this light, you
may gain much encouragement and instruction.

For, observe the weakness of Israel at that period.
According to human calculation, it would seem impossible
that a people so feeble, so broken in spirit, and so unac-
customed to war, could escape from so powerful an
oppressor.   But their strength was not in themselves.
Their deliverance was not their own work.   It was God's
work, and His strength was made perfect in their weakness.   So, dear brethren, it may be with you.   Do *you*
begin to see the emptiness of the world, and desire to
escape from its power and pollution?   Do you long more
than ever you did for pardon, and for holiness, and still
feel that you cannot reach Jesus, cannot touch the hem
of His garment?   Be not discouraged.   Who has given
you that desire?   The same God who kindled in Israel
the desire for the fulfilment of His promise.   Wait therefore on the Lord; pray for more faith, and soon, in the
precious blood of our Paschal Lamb, you will find pardon
and rest.   But there is another point in the history which
we ought to observe.   All the terrible judgments on
Pharaoh and Egypt did not issue in their sanctification
and salvation.   Egypt was wasted, and the power of
Pharaoh was broken, but he never gave up his opposition
to the will and purpose of Jehovah.   It is just the same
with the old man—the principle of sin within us.   The
Bible never speaks of its sanctification, but always of its
destruction.   St Paul says of the carnal mind, (Rom. viii.
7,) "but it is not subject to the law of God, neither indeed can be."   We are exhorted to *mortify* it,—"Mortify
therefore," says St Paul, "your members which are on the
earth; fornication, uncleanness, inordinate affection, evil
concupiscence, and covetousness, which is idolatry."   "Put

off," he says, (Ephes. iv. 22,) "concerning the former conversation the old man, which is corrupt according to the deceitful lusts;" and of himself he says, "I am crucified with Christ." Let us then, brethren, present the principle of sin within us to God to be *destroyed*, and the principle of holiness, the new man, to be *strengthened;* and, in all our daily walk, let us constantly ask ourselves what will be the effect of this thing and that thing upon these two principles. We must be jealous over our hearts, for there is a principle of evil there claiming indulgence; we must deny that principle in *little* things as well as in great, for an act of *trifling* indulgence in sin will give great power to its principle. If we cherish in our heart one *little* thought of pride, or vanity, or uncharitableness, or impurity, who can tell the injury that it will do, or whither it may lead us? One little neglect in prayer will prepare the way for another, and thus it is that the plant of grace in the heart grows weak, feeble, and stunted. But if, brethren, you walk with Jesus; if you steadfastly watch against every indulgence of the principle of sin, in thought as well as act; if you fervently pray for more grace, then will the principle of grace become stronger and stronger within you—you will come out of each trial more purified —you will have closer communion with God—your path on earth as a shining light will shine more and more unto the perfect day; and when you reach the valley of the shadow of death, you will find it not gloomy or dark, but resplendent with the presence and the light of the Sun of Righteousness.

THE PASCHAL LAMB

Exodus 12:13

"And the blood shall be to you for a token upon the houses where ye are: and when I see the blood, I will pass over you, and the plague shall not be upon you to destroy you, when I smite the land of Egypt."

LAST Wednesday week, brethren, we contemplated Israel as awakened by sufferings to desire the fulfilment of God's promise, and to long for rest in Canaan. We saw that Egypt, the type of the old man, could not be sanctified, but was given up to judgment; and that Israel, the type of the new man, though utterly weak in itself, was destined to victory by the power of God. But much must be done before this victory could be gained. Israel itself was defiled, both in itself, and by reason of its connexion with Egypt. It was all of mercy that it did not suffer the terrible plagues of Egypt, and that God put a "difference between the Egyptians and Israel." Israel could not put away its own guilt, or roll away, to use the expression which we find in Joshua v. 9, the "reproach of Egypt." The Paschal Lamb met this and other wants. The only way to deliverance from the last desolating plague—the only way of ascent from Egypt to Canaan, was the sprinkling of blood.

Let us proceed to consider, first, The Paschal Lamb itself; secondly, Its connexion with, and application to Israel; and lastly, The manner in which Israel was to partake of it.

First, then, the Lamb itself. You will observe at once that many remarkable rules are given to Moses respecting it ; and these are of great importance, as they mark it out as a beautiful type of the Lord Jesus. The first rule that we may remark was, that "the lamb was to be taken out of the flock on the tenth day of the month, and was to be kept until the fourteenth day before it was killed," as you will see if you will bring the third and the sixth verses together. In the 3d, it says, "In the tenth day of this month they shall take to them every man a lamb ;" and in the 6th verse, "and ye shall keep it up until the fourteenth day of the same month." It is difficult to see the reason of this arrangement, but it may have been twofold. First, in order that the lamb might be carefully examined. It was not every lamb, as we shall presently see, that was fit for this important purpose—not every one that could be a substitute for Israel, or a type of Jesus. It must be very carefully selected, and the number of days during which it was kept evidently would be a great security that it would be a *proper* lamb for so important a purpose. Nothing bearing on redemption should be done in careless haste, though there should be no delay. In this sense, the words of the prophet are true,—"He that believeth shall not make haste." There should be no careless reading of the Bible, no prayers hurried over, no duties thoughtlessly done. Now, in this setting apart of the lamb beforehand, we may see a pre-figuration of the "Lamb of God that taketh away the sins of the world." We often wonder, brethren, if we may reverentially use the expression, at the great *calmness* of God manifested in the work of redemption. There was nothing of that feverish haste which we so often see in men, and which so frequently mars their works. Jesus was set apart before the foundation of the world to be the one great sacrifice for sin. The preparation for that great passover was made, not during four days, but four thousand years; promise after promise, each one more clear and more beautiful than the preceding one, ushered in His coming; and when He *did* appear, He was announced as the true Paschal Lamb. He underwent the strictest scrutiny from friends and foes; and what was the result? St Peter gives it, (Acts ii. 22,) "A man *approved* of God among you by miracles and wonders and signs." And this was beautifully predicted under another image, (Isa. xxviii. 16,) "Behold, I lay in Zion for a foundation a *stone*, a *tried* stone." *Tried* He has been in every way, and by every one—by the Father, by the Church, and by the world. The Father has attested His meetness. The song that fills heaven and is re-echoed by the Church on earth is, "Worthy is the Lamb that was slain;" and the world is silenced, though not saved.

The other reason, which we need only hint at here, because we shall have to return to it in another form, was, that God's people might have "abundant consolation." They knew that another terrible plague, the concentration and consummation of all the other plagues, was about to fall on the already desolated Egypt. They felt that they were sinful and guilty, as well as the Egyptians; but they could look to the Lamb already *prepared* as a pledge that they would be spared. There, they might say, is our *substitute*, the token of God's unchanging love and mercy towards us. And thus it is that the true Christian may look not only at the *actual death* of Jesus, but at all the great preparations for it. He may gaze at beautiful types, and watch unfolding promises, and mark all the works of Jesus, and say to his soul, "Behold all these preparations of mercy, all these gifts of love, all these confirmations of thy faith. In that predicted Lamb is thy salvation, thy rest, and thy security." But, further, we read, (ver. 5,) that the Lamb was to be "without blemish." Nothing imperfect could be offered as a sacrifice, or ever be used in the service of God, (Lev. xxii. 19–22,)—"Ye shall offer at your own will a male without blemish, of the beeves, of the sheep, or of the goats. But whatsoever hath a blemish, that shall ye not offer: for it shall not be acceptable for you. And whosoever offereth a sacrifice of peace-offerings unto the Lord to accomplish his vow, or a freewill-offering in beeves or sheep, it shall be perfect to be accepted; there shall be no blemish therein. Blind, or broken, or maimed, or having a wen, or scurvy, or scabbed, ye shall not offer these unto the Lord, nor make an offering by fire of them upon the altar unto the Lord." And so, amongst the sins committed by the priests in the time of the prophet Malachi, we find this, that they offered imperfect animals as sacrifices to God, as we read, (Mal. i. 8,) "And if ye offer the blind for sacrifice, is it not evil? and if ye offer the lame and sick, is it not evil? offer it now unto thy governor; will he be pleased with thee, or accept thy person? saith the Lord of hosts." The reason of all this is very evident. The lamb must be without blemish; because it was a beautiful type of the perfect, spotless Saviour. Thus it is said of the antitype, (1 Pet. i. 18, 19,) "Forasmuch as ye know that ye were not redeemed with corruptible things, as silver and gold, from your vain conversation received by tradition from your fathers; but with the precious blood of Christ, as of a *lamb without blemish and without spot*." And, again, (Heb. iv. 15,) "For we have not an high priest which cannot be touched with the feeling of our infirmities; but was in all points tempted like as we are, yet without sin." And, once more, (Heb. vii. 26,) "For such an high priest became us, who is holy, harmless, undefiled, separate from sinners, and made higher than the heavens." Our Sacrifice, brethren, is absolutely perfect. Jesus is perfect in Himself, and perfect as a sacrifice. We need nothing else to atone for sin, for our Paschal Lamb has made an *atonement* to which nothing can be added. The very thought of any other atonement *must* be displeasing to God, for it implies that that was imperfect which God has pronounced perfect, and casts a stain upon the spotlessness of Jesus, and the efficacy of His most precious blood.

But there was yet one more point that we must notice, —the lamb was to be a "male of the first year."

This might be because the male was considered more worthy than the female; or because the life of the lamb was meant to be a substitute for the lives of the first-born of the Israelites. It was suitable that, the purpose being to redeem the male first-born, the offering itself should be a male; and in this point of view again, it was a fitting type of our Redeemer. Though, as St Paul says, Eve was "in the transgression," yet it was not by her transgression, but by that of Adam that we fell. Though she was the mother of all living, yet she was not our covenant-head. But Adam was. In him we fell; and it is consequently only by a second Adam, by another covenant-head, that we can obtain life. It is the man Christ Jesus who is the quickening spirit.

Thus far, brethren, we have considered the Paschal Lamb itself as a type of Jesus; its preparation as a type of *His* preparation; its perfection as a shadow of *His* perfection. Let us now view it in its connexion with Israel. And, first, it was evidently meant, as we have already hinted, to be a *substitute* for Israel's first-born. If you have read this and the preceding chapter with care, you must have observed how often God speaks of "putting a difference between the Egyptians and Israel." It was not one founded upon Israel's *merit*, or anything that *naturally* distinguished them from the Egyptians. It was not that Egypt was deservedly given up to destruction, and Israel *deservedly* spared. It was not that God had much against Egypt, and nothing against Israel. It was altogether an act of *grace*. Israel was *sinful* and *guilty*, as well as Egypt. Their first-born might righteously perish, as well as those of the Egyptians. When they were spared as an act of mercy and grace, some life must be given for their life. The Paschal Lamb was therefore a *substitute*. The life of the first-born of Israel was *not* taken, because the life of the Paschal Lamb *was* taken. There was the recognition of sin on God's part, even whilst there was a wonderful display of forgiving love. This point, the *substitution* of the lamb for the first-born, is clearly brought out (chap. xiii.) where the service of the passover was commanded to be kept every year—where it was made perpetual; we read, (ver. 13,) "all the first-born of man among thy children shalt thou redeem." And what was this redemption? It was the *substitution* of a lamb for the first-born. And does not this, brethren, throw a bright gleam of light upon the great atonement? There are many passages of Scripture which virtually speak of Jesus as our *substitute*—of His life being taken for the life of His people—of His suffering in their stead. Then he says Himself, (Matt. xx. 28,) "Even as the Son of man came not to be ministered unto, but to minister, and to give his life a *ransom* for many." Thus St Paul, in allusion to this very type, says, (1 Cor. v. 7,)

"Christ our passover is sacrificed for us,"—that is, in our stead ; and once more, (2 Cor. v. 21,) "For he hath made him to be sin for us, who knew no sin ; that we might be made the righteousness of God in him." And yet, brethren, plain as these and many other texts of Scripture seem to us—clearly as they appear to teach that Jesus is our *substitute*, there are many who cannot receive this truth. There are many who believe, as we do, the doctrine of *incorporation*,—that is, that we receive, and can only receive, life in union with Christ ; but they do not hold this in addition to, but instead of the doctrine of substitution. One with Jesus, brethren, incorporated into Him we must be ; for separated from Him we are *not* justified—apart from Him we can do nothing. But this doctrine of present union with Christ presupposes the fact of His *substitution* as our sacrifice on the cross. On this point the types throw much light. It is a question of the true interpretation of Scripture, of passages in the New Testament, whether Jesus died for our benefit, or in our stead. Interrogate, brethren, the Old Testament. Let the types pour their light into the darkness, if any darkness there be. Does not God answer the question and settle the controversy through them ? Are *not they* a clear commentary on the words "for us ?" Look at the Paschal Lamb. Study Lev. xvi., and see whether it is not as clear as the light, that the Paschal Lamb, the bullock, and the goat, were each of them a substitute—that they were offered, not merely for the benefit of Israel, but *instead* of the offerers. In them, life was given instead of life. Behold, then, brethren, Jesus *your* substitute. His life was given for our life. He suffered that we might live in Him and with Him. His death is your life—His substitution is your salvation. Christ *for* you is your only title to glory—Christ in you is your only hope of glory. But the Paschal Lamb was not *only* a substitute; its blood was to be *applied* as well as shed. It was the *gift* of God to Israel; but it was also to be an *exercise* of faith on their part. "Moses," we read, (chap. xii. 21–23,) "called for all the elders of Israel, and said unto them, Draw out and take you a lamb according to your families, and kill the passover. And ye shall take a bunch of hyssop, and dip it in the blood that is in the bason, and strike the lintel and the two side-posts with the blood that is in the bason; and none of you shall go out at the door of his house until the morning. For the Lord will pass through to smite the Egyptians; and when he seeth the blood upon the lintel, and on the two side-posts, the Lord will pass over the door, and will not suffer the destroyer to come in unto your houses to smite you."

The Israelites, then, were not saved merely by virtue of their circumcision, or because they were descended from Abraham, Isaac, and Jacob; but by the sprinkled blood of the Paschal Lamb. Had any single family disbelieved the judgment which was to be inflicted on Egypt, or neglected on any account to sprinkle the blood on the lintel, then the judgment would have fallen on that family as well as on the Egyptians. What a solemn thought it must have been! With what deep and reverential awe must the head of each family have set about this act of obedience! And when he sprinkled the lintel and the two side-posts with the blood, how much, he must have felt, depended on the act! And can you not imagine, brethren, the happy sense of *security* that he must have felt when all was accomplished? Would he still fear that the destroying angel would pass his threshold? Oh, no. The promise of a faithful and unchanging God was his security. God himself had said, "When he seeth the blood upon the lintel, and on the two side-posts, the Lord will pass over you, and will not suffer the destroyer to come into your houses to destroy you."

Dear brethren, there is a judgment still to fall upon the world. Our Paschal Lamb is already slain, and His precious blood been shed. Is it sprinkled upon our hearts? Of that blood St John says, that it cleanseth us from all sin. Through that blood the beautiful promise in the prophet Isaiah is fulfilled,—"Though your sins be as scarlet, they shall be as white as snow; and though they be red like crimson, they shall be as wool." If your heart is unsprinkled still, oh, what peace have you in this restless world? and what security against judgment, which may fall any moment? You cannot hasten too fast to the fountain, which is still open, still overflowing, but which may, before we think it, be closed for ever. But if your heart *is* sprinkled—sprinkled *every day* with the blood of Jesus, is there anything that you should fear? Then can *you* fear the destroying angel? Oh, no. "There is no condemnation to them that are in Christ Jesus." Should you fear death? No. The sting is drawn, and you may join in the apostle's triumphant exclamation,—"O death, where is thy sting? O grave, where is thy victory?" Should you fear the terrible accompaniments of the second coming?—the signs in heaven and earth,—the melting elements,—the quivering earth,—the trumpet's sound? No. It is to receive *His* sprinkled Israel that Jesus comes. One thing only let us fear, brethren, and that is, sin. One thing let us strive after more than anything else,—to have the token upon our hearts kept *quite* clear—to have the sprinkling of blood renewed there day by day—to have our conscience tender, yet free from accusation.

But there is one thing more that we must note concerning the lamb. It was not only to be killed and its blood sprinkled; it was also to be eaten. "They shall eat," it says, (ver. 8,) "the flesh in that night, roast with fire." The reason is evident. It was not enough for the Israelites to be rescued from destruction. They had a long journey before them, a far more weary way than they anticipated, and they needed *strength* for the journey. The lamb, whose sprinkled blood was a token on their door-posts, was also their *food*. How beautiful a type in this respect also of Jesus, who is the daily food of the believer's soul! To how many a Christian, brethren, may it be said, as the angel said to Elijah, "The journey is too great for thee!" It is a *wilderness* journey, and the way is often steep and narrow. There is many a hill up which you must toil, and many a lonely valley through which you must pass. Your own strength is insufficient; with that alone you will soon faint. But there is strength for you. Jesus is thy food; the nourishment of thy soul. "Arise, therefore, and eat." Eat plentifully; it is a rich banquet. Feed on Him in the Word; feed on Him in the Holy Communion. When Israel left Egypt, not *one* was feeble. But how many of us are feeble now! and why is this, if it be not that we do not sufficiently feed on Jesus?

We can say but little on the manner in which Israel was to eat of it. Observe, first, that it was to be eaten with *bitter herbs*.

There is a traditional interpretation amongst the Jews that the bitter herbs had reference to the sufferings of the Egyptian bondage; and if this be a true interpretation, then here we find the bitterness of suffering combined with the heavenly food which God had provided. This has a meaning also for us, brethren. The bitter herbs signify repentance. When we feed on the Lamb of God, we must not *forget* what we *have* been, and what we *are*. We must not receive that food as an angel would; we must remember our sins—the sins of our unconverted and converted state, our worldliness, our contentedness without God, our impatience and murmurings. We ought never to feed on Jesus without some deep and penitent thought of sin, and never to think of sin without thinking of Jesus too. The lamb and the bitter herbs were to go together. We should notice, also, that it was to be eaten with *unleavened* bread. This was commanded. But if you will refer to ver. 39, you will see that the Israelites were compelled to eat unleavened bread for a time, because they were thrust out of Egypt. The providence of God arranged this. If you ask what this circumstance teaches us, we point to the words of St Paul, (1 Cor. v. 7, 8,) "Purge out therefore the old leaven, that ye may be a new lump, as ye are unleavened. For even Christ our passover is sacrificed for us: therefore let us keep the feast, not with old leaven, neither with the leaven of malice and wickedness; but with the unleavened bread of sincerity and truth."

Lastly, observe that they were to eat it with their "*loins girded*," as we read, (ver. 11,) "And thus shall ye eat it; with your loins girded, your shoes on your feet, and your staff in your hand; and ye shall eat it in haste." They were travellers, and about to commence a long journey. This feast was spread for them at its commencement, and not at its close. Their attitude agreed with this. It was not one of *rest*, but of activity; all was preparation. *We* also, dear brethren, are travellers—pilgrims and strangers on earth. Whatever we may be engaged in, we should ever remember this; we should look around us on the scenes and occupations of the world as on those which belong to the wilderness, not as those of home. And even the refreshments which God has instituted for His people are such as suit pilgrims, and to be received with girded loins, and eaten in haste. Pilgrims, brethren, we all are; we cannot be otherwise. Nothing can convert this world into our home. But if your hearts are sprinkled with the love of Jesus, then you have entered on a journey at the end of which stands a continuing city, the heavenly Jerusalem. March, then, onward. Do not eat and rest; but, like the Israelites, eat and *march*—eat that you may *march*. Then your raiment will not wear out; your strength will not fail; your step will grow firmer and firmer; your eye will discern more clearly the pillar of fire and cloud, until you enter the city where there is no fire or cloud, but God's own unveiled presence.

THE PILLAR OF CLOUD AND FIRE

Exodus 13:21, 22

" And the Lord went before them by day in a pillar of a cloud, to lead
them the way; and by night in a pillar of fire, to give them light;
to go by day and night : he took not away the pillar of the cloud
by day, nor the pillar of fire by night, from before the people."

PREVIOUS to the last desolating plague which fell on Egypt,
the children of Israel must have gathered together to a place
called Rameses, in preparation for the great and arduous
journey before them ; for we read, (chap. xii. 37,) that " the
children of Israel journeyed from Rameses to Succoth."
Rameses was therefore the point from which, at the least,
the largest part of that great multitude—two millions or
two millions and a half—started.   When they had left Rameses, they had really left Egypt; for it says, (chap. xii. 51,)
" And it came to pass the selfsame day, that the Lord did
bring the children of Israel out of the land of Egypt by
their armies," although we all know that Egypt still
threatened them.   Their first station was Succoth, a word
which means tents, a name very probably given to it because the pilgrim Israelites sojourned there for a night.
It must have been very interesting, both to themselves
and the Egyptians, on account of its being the first station
in their new and wilderness life,   The second station was
Etham, which is said (chap. xiii. 20) to be " in the edge of
the wilderness,"—that is, of that great wilderness through
which God afterwards led them.   It has been supposed

that this station was about thirty or thirty-five miles from Rameses.

Nothing remarkable happened to them at either of these stations. Egypt was not yet roused to the pursuit. It was stunned and paralysed by the last heavy plague. But the verses which precede our text, and our text itself, bring before us two interesting points, which we may not omit, as they bear very beautifully upon the Christian's life. The first is, the way along which God led His people. The second is, the manner in which He guided and protected them.

First, then, the way along which God led His people. This was certainly not the one which they would have chosen for themselves. They would naturally have chosen the shortest and most direct route, so as to spend as little time in the wilderness as possible. This way would have been along the north side of the wilderness and through the land of the Philistines. God's plan, however, was very different. We are told expressly, (ver. 17,) that He did not lead them the shortest and most direct route through the land of the Philistines, but that He "led them about," indeed, not seldom a way almost exactly opposite to that which was the end of their journey and the fulfilment of their hopes. And what was the reason of this? There were doubtless many reasons. Had they been allowed to go the most direct way, they would not have met such frequent trials of their faith; they would not have experienced such blessed manifestations of God's presence and love; their hearts would not have been so disciplined and prepared for an entrance into Canaan. That this was one reason why God "led them about," we learn from a passage which must have struck us all, (Deut. viii. 2, 3,) "And thou shalt remember all the way which the Lord thy God led thee these forty years in the wilderness." Wherefore? "To humble thee, and to prove thee, to know what was in thine heart, whether thou wouldest keep his commandments, or no. And he humbled thee, and suffered thee to hunger, and fed thee with manna, which thou knewest not, neither did thy fathers know; that he might make thee know that man doth not live by bread only, but by every word that proceedeth out of the mouth of the Lord doth man live." But this was not the only purpose. Another reason is assigned, (Exod xiii. 17,) "For God said, Lest peradventure the people repent when they see war, and they return to Egypt." See here, brethren, the mercy and gentleness of God. There is a beautiful expression used by St Paul, (Acts xiii. 18,) when speaking of God's dealings with Israel, "And about the time of forty years suffered he their manners in the wilderness."

There is another reading of the passage, the meaning of which you will find in the margin of your Bible, "He bore or fed them as a nurse beareth or feedeth her child." If this reading be the true one, then we have surely a very beautiful instance of God's nursing care of His people at the very commencement of their journey. He knew the power of the Philistines, and saw the weakness of His people's faith. After some experience of Jehovah's faithfulness and power, they might meet them with an undaunted spirit. But now they know but little of the grace and love of Him who led them. Therefore God dealt gently with them, and would not suffer them to be tempted above that they were able to bear. He "led them about," that the enemy might be avoided.

What a picture, brethren, is all this of the way in which God now leads His children to glory! Even now He "leads them about"—leads them all through the long and weary wilderness, and not the short path just skirting it. This has been the case with many of you, beloved in Christ, has it not? When *you* look back to the time when you were first brought out of Egypt—when you solemnly renounced the world with all its attractions, and sin with all its allurements—when the heavenly world broke in upon your astonished and rejoicing heart with all its glory and brightness, and you felt that Christ was very near and very precious, do you not remember times when you have longed to be translated, or even to die, that you might be with Christ, and hold unbroken communion with Him, and serve Him with unfaltering service? Then the world seemed very empty. You thought, " Oh, if I could only skirt the wilderness, and have a speedy as well as an abundant entrance into the presence of Jesus!" But God appointed another path for you. He has led you *through* the wilderness, and not only its edge. Your faith has been often tried, and sometimes severe conflicts with sins which seemed crucified have wearied you. Disappointments have cast many a chill over your spirit. Bereavements have rent the deepest cords of your affections, and have made you feel very desolate. Why has God appointed all this? Why did He not fulfil those intense longings for immediate glory? Why did He send you into all the evils and conflicts of this wilderness life? It was to " humble thee and prove thee,—to know what was in thy heart." Have the dealings of God had this blessed effect in you? Perhaps your joy does not now rise so high as when you first obtained mercy; but is your faith more calm and unwavering, and your experience deeper? Perhaps your consciousness of love is not so powerful and vivid as it then was; but is your love deeper as a principle, leading you to deny your-

self, to mortify sin, and influencing your whole life? Does
it enable you to carry weight, to suffer as Christ did,
without murmuring, to say as Jesus said, " Not my will,
but Thine be done." Oh, then it is not in vain that God
has " led you about." Do you not feel so yourself? Cannot you see, on looking back, that there has been a fitting
adaptation between your trials and your strength? When
you were weak, and yet very unconscious of your weakness, God would not suffer you to encounter the Philistines. It would have been too much for you; you would
have fainted, because you knew not then the full meaning
of that promise, " My grace is sufficient for thee." But,
as your faith increased, and the language of your heart
more and more was, " I know in whom I have believed,"
then heavier trials were appointed you. And what is the
result? If you were asked now, " Would you have God's
way altered? would you have been led in some other
path?" We know what you would answer,—" Oh no!
Chastened me He often has; but He has chastened me in
love. Touched me He often has in the most tender part;
but He has healed by His grace, when He has wounded
me by His providence. Led me He has by a way that I
knew not; but His own presence has gone with me. And
now I leave all my mercies, my trials, my times, my way,
in my Father's hands. Depart I would and be with
Christ, which is far better; but I am willing to journey
onward, if thereby I may glorify Him."

Let us now, brethren, pass on to the second point,—the
manner in which God guided and protected them. " The
Lord went before them by day in a pillar of a cloud, to
lead them the way; and by night in a pillar of fire, to
give them light; to go by day and night; he took not
away the pillar of the cloud by day, nor the pillar of

fire by night, from before the people." The pillar of cloud and fire, then, was the means by which God led His people. But it was only the *means*. Jehovah himself was their true guide. The pillar of cloud and fire was but the symbol of His presence—the visible token that He was amongst them. The language of our text is plain enough,—" The Lord went before them." Compare also the very striking expression in chap. xiv. 24, " The Lord *looked* unto the host of the Egyptians *through* the pillar of fire and of the cloud ; " not, you will observe, from heaven, but from the host of Israel, with whom He was. How full of consolation, brethren, must this fact have been to every believing soul amongst the Israelites ! It must have been a very great comfort to have their way marked out by the moving pillar,—to be freed from all doubts as to their line of march. But this was not their chief blessedness, their chief glory. No, brethren, it was the presence of God. The thing signified was greater than the symbol ; the unseen, more real than the seen. And shall we think, brethren, that God is not so really present with His people as He was with Israel of old ? Have we fewer needs than they had ? or is the Church of the New Testament less precious to God than that of the Old ? Oh no, brethren ; there is more than one assurance that settles this point for ever. Jesus says, " Lo, I am with you alway, even to the end of the world;" and, again, it is written, " I will never leave thee nor forsake thee." Beloved, let us try to realise more this simple but deep truth, that God is with His people. If we have clear and distinct proof that He is ours and we are His—if we can read upon our hearts, sinful as they are, the marks of His adoption, then what decision, blended with humility, will this truth give us ! What calmness in the midst of ex-

citement ! What submission under trial ! What perseverance under difficulties ! What glory does it prove around
the throne of grace, making us feel that it is good to be
there ! What light does it not pour into the varied duties
of daily life! which without it often grow irksome and
monotonous. But we may remark the very striking adaptation of God's method of guidance to the condition and
necessities of the Israelites. We cannot understand the
Bible as a whole, unless we bear in mind that there is
progress in it. The purpose of God's dealing with the
Israelites was gradually to train and prepare them for the
appearance of Christ. They were, so to speak, in a state
of childhood. As St Paul says, (Gal. iv. 1, 2,) " Now I say,
That the heir, as long as he is a child, differeth nothing
from a servant, though he be lord of all; but is under tutors
and governors until the time appointed of the father."
Hence we may perceive in God's dealings with them, all
and more than the gentle and loving condescension which
we sometimes see in a wise mother. They were as yet
carnal, and could not altogether walk by faith ; and consequently there was a blending of faith and sight in the
manner in which they were led. We all know how much
their faith was exercised in the wilderness. They were
called to depend upon God day by day, and yet in another
way they were allowed to walk by sight. By day and by
night there was a manifest and visible token of God's presence. They could not doubt which path to take, when
to start, or when to pause. The pillar of cloud and fire
made all these points quite plain, as we read, (Num. ix.
17–19,) " And when the cloud was taken up from the tabernacle, then after that the children of Israel journeyed :
and in the place where the cloud abode, there the children
of Israel pitched their tents. At the commandment of

the Lord the children of Israel journeyed, and at the commandment of the Lord they pitched : as long as the cloud abode upon the tabernacle they rested in their tents. And when the cloud tarried long upon the tabernacle many days, then the children of Israel kept the charge of the Lord, and journeyed not." Thus, brethren, it is evident that there was no exercise of faith whatever as to what *was* the *will* of God concerning them. The only exercise of faith to which they were called was to do that will made manifest by the pillar of fire and cloud, and follow Jehovah's merciful guidance with unfaltering and contented hearts. It was in *this* that they were so often tried, and in *this* that they so often failed. We, brethren, live under an advanced dispensation,—the dispensation of the Spirit ; and are therefore called to higher exercises of faith,—of that faith which discerns the will of God in circumstances of difficulty, as well as that which walks in it when discerned. Encompassed as we are by helps and privileges, our sinful hearts often fail here—fail through impatience, through want of watchfulness and prayer. When *you*, dear brethren, have been placed in circumstances of difficulty—when you have been obliged to act, and yet have not seen your way clearly, have you never felt a wish that you could see the pillar of cloud or fire going before you ? And yet we need not, and ought not to wish it. It is good for us, brethren, sometimes at least, not to see our way clearly—good for us to feel perplexity, for it seems to make the throne of grace more real. It throws life and earnestness into our prayers. But, difficult as it may sometimes be to discern our path through the wilderness, if you wait upon God in an earnest, patient, and confiding spirit, you will never be allowed to wander. God does go before thee, O believer ;

thy God is with thee. Often, when thou dost not discern it, His gracious hand is leading thee forward. His eye is marking all thy steps. His everlasting arms are underneath thee. You see not the pillar of fire or cloud; but it goes before thee unseen, leading thee onward surely and securely to the rest above. But, you may say, all this is true, and full of comfort. But suppose, now, that some practical difficulties surround my path, how can I best discern the will of God? It is no easy question to answer. It is a point on which deep experience is of great value. But thus much we may safely suggest. The first thing is to pray earnestly for guidance—to cast yourself upon God with humility and confidence, praying Him to direct your path. The next thing is to examine your motives. There may be certain tendencies of disposition which may predispose you to act in a particular way. You must carefully guard against the operation of these tendencies; if not, you may be going your own way, whilst you fancy that you are walking in God's way. After having earnestly prayed for guidance, and carefully examined your own heart, the next step seems to be to weigh well the reasons for and against the step in question, and decide accordingly. Even then you may feel not quite clear; some distressing doubts may yet linger behind. But still you may go forward in hope. It is not until afterwards that you may see that the hand of God has been guiding you through all your difficulties. The pillar of cloud and fire has been moving before you. Have you ever, dear brethren, had reason to regret your decision, after having prayed earnestly to God for guidance, after having carefully examined your own heart, scrutinising all your motives, having well weighed the reasons which ought to influence you? We think not. But one thing is certain, that God will not allow His watchful and dependent children to wander far, or for long. His providence will soon come in to make all clear. The still small voice of His guiding Spirit will whisper, "This is the way, walk ye in it, when ye turn to the right hand, and when ye turn to the left."

And here, brethren, we may point out one more point of adaptation of the method of guidance to the special wants of Israel. One pillar led them forward; but by day it was a pillar of cloud, by night, a pillar of fire. Usually it went before them as their guide; but on one occasion it stood behind them as their protection. It was when the Egyptians were in pursuit, as recorded, (chap. xiv. 19, 20,) "And the angel of God, which went before the camp of Israel, removed, and went behind them ; and the pillar of the cloud went from before their face, and stood behind them : and it came between the camp of the Egyptians and the camp of Israel; and it was a cloud and darkness to them, but it gave light by night to these : so that the one came not near the other all the night." Here then, brethren, is a beautiful variety and adaptation. And thus it is still. There is more than one way in which God guides His praying children through the perplexities of this troublesome world. Most frequently the arrangements of God's providence are like the pillar of cloud, directing our steps. We cannot see our way far beforehand, but just when we reach the place of difficulty, our path is made plain. Sometimes it is the gentle influence of the Spirit of God which, enlightening our judgment, purging our conscience, and purifying our affections, gives us a rapid intuition into the path of duty. Sometimes the voice of a friend, more advanced and more experienced than ourselves, is like the pillar of fire shedding light upon our darkness, and dissipating our previous confusion. Indeed, brethren, when we have a simple and dependent spirit, there is nothing so small that it may not contribute some light to guide our steps. Oh, this then is the great thing,—to have a simple and dependent spirit, to lean altogether on Christ Jesus. Are you still a stranger to Him? Then *you* have no guide to direct your wandering steps—*you* have no pillar of cloud and fire to guide you by day and by night—your eyes are dazzled by an ever-changing mirage—you seem to yourself to see lakes and gardens when there is only a dreary wilderness before you. Oh, seek to be put amongst the children, seek Jesus earnestly, and then, though your path will still lie through the wilderness, you will be happy and joyful in God! He will guide you in every difficulty —He will sustain you in every trouble—He will fulfil to you the gracious promise, (Isa. xlii. 16,) "I will make darkness light before them, and crooked things straight. These things will I do unto them, and not forsake them."

THE FIRST TRIAL OF ISRAEL'S FAITH

Exodus 14:15

"And the Lord said unto Moses, Wherefore criest thou unto me?
speak unto the children of Israel, that they go forward."

"HE led them forth by the right way." Such is the
testimony of the Psalmist to the faithfulness and wisdom
of God in guiding His people. None can look at the
result without feeling the truth and beauty of this testimony; yet to the children of Israel themselves at the
time, God's ways must have appeared very mysterious.
Even at first, we saw last Wednesday, the pillar of cloud
and fire "led them about;" but their faith was still more
tried on the occasion of which this chapter gives us
an account. Their line of route hitherto had carried
them towards the north corner of the Red Sea. But now
they were commanded to journey south, to a place called
Pi-hiharoth. Whatever be the exact position of this
place, which is still a doubtful point, one thing is clear,—
that they were told to go in a direction exactly opposite
to that of the Land of Promise. *That* was north-east; they
were led *south :* and besides this, the Red Sea became a
barrier to them in their onward journey. But just that
which would have led the Israelites to avoid this route,
was the very reason why God chose it. It was a trial in
a twofold way. It was the last trial of Pharaoh and
Egypt. It was the first trial of the faith of the Israelites.

During the infliction of the ten terrible plagues in Egypt, Pharaoh's heart was often moved ; it often seemed under the pressure of suffering, as if he bowed before the will of God ; but when that pressure was removed, he invariably limited God's requirements and claims. At last, however, this spirit seemed to be overcome. The last plague appeared to settle all. His ambition, pride, and rebellion seemed to be laid in the dust. Israel went forth out of Egypt, and their enemies rejoiced at their departure ; but when at God's commandment they journeyed only a few miles south from Etham, all Pharaoh's former feelings revived again. The truth is, his besetting sins had only been kept down for a time by the pressure of judgments. They were never really subdued, and therefore a very little thing was sufficient to call them forth in all their former power. The proud and ambitious king fancied that the prize had again, by some mistake, fallen into his hands. Strange, brethren, that he should have so soon forgotten from whose hand those ten plagues had come, and that he did not yet know that Israel's steps were guided by the Lord ! He was tried once more, and this last trial ended in his utter destruction. We know, brethren, that it is good to be afflicted. Some of the deepest and best remembered lessons are those learnt out in times of disappointment and of suffering. There are few things to which the dying saint looks back with so much thankfulness as to the trials of his path, for he would not for anything be without the blessings that came with them. When he surveys them all, he feels that there has not been one too many, or one too severe. And yet it is not chastisement alone, and of itself, that can produce any one of these blessed effects. Judgments, brethren, may fall— judgments so terrible that they may make the heart quiver

and bleed, and yet its besetting sin may remain as unsubdued as ever. The utmost effect may have been to make
it withdraw itself, like the wary serpent, a little deeper
into the heart. But let the pressure be removed—let
some temptation, perhaps even a very small one, come,
and it uncoils again. It starts into new life, strengthened,
and not annihilated, by the awful discipline it has passed
through. This is one of the solemn lessons which the
history of Pharaoh impresses on our minds. It shews that
judgments may tend to harden, but they never *win* the
heart. It is when it prays for the sanctifying Spirit—
when it sees the hand of a loving Father in the chasten-
ing—when, broken and bruised, it looks to a Saviour's
sympathy and love, and clings the more to His precious
cross; it is *then* that chastisement begins to be blessing.
There are some persons, brethren, who look at affliction as
if some blessing were necessarily lodged in it. They feel
that their hearts are captivated by the influences of this
present world. They are conscious that they do not make
any progress in preparation for heaven, any approach to
Christ. They say within themselves, " I shall be as I am
until affliction comes, and then I shall be changed." This
is a great mistake. True, brethren, it is that we ought to
expect, with Job, to come out of each furnace like gold.
But why? Not because it must of *necessity* purify, but
because the great Refiner sits near. Grace is not *inwoven*
into affliction; it comes from God, and it may come in
such abundance as to pour in through every avenue: but
at whatever time it comes, it is always God's own gift—
always to be distinguished from the affliction, or the
blessing, through which it comes. We cannot, dear
brethren, expect too much from God himself; but if we
place the fountain of grace in the affliction itself, we shall

be sadly disappointed, and find it to be to us "like a brook whose waters fail."

But there is another awful truth which this history very clearly illustrates,—the infatuation of sin. We should have imagined that when the message was brought to Pharaoh of the altered course of Israel, he would have checked at once the rising thought of ambition, and the desire of power. "No; I have suffered enough. I am only thankful that the God of Israel has removed His hand from me and my people." But nothing of the sort entered his mind. The past judgments should have led him to regard this new circumstance as a temptation to be avoided; he viewed it as a grand opportunity, because his heart was blinded by his besetting sin. How terrible are the effects of one besetting sin! It not only overpowers conscience, but it makes a man forget for a time all the sufferings under which he positively writhed before. It obliterates all the lessons of past experience, sets aside even the operations of the understanding, and hurries the sinner on with rapid steps to his own destruction. His ruin may be apparent to all but himself. He hastens to grasp with infatuated mind some new object of pleasure and self-indulgence; but it is the last drop that fills up his cup of iniquity. But let us turn to Israel. This, as we have said, was the *first* trial of their faith. There were evidently two ways in which the country that they had left might prove a snare to them. The attractions of Egypt, such as they were, might induce them in seasons of special hardship to wish themselves back again in it, (we shall meet with instances of this in the course of the history ;) or the *threatening power* of Egypt, which had kept them in bondage so long, might alarm them, notwithstanding their wonderful deliverance, and the presence of God with

them. This was their temptation on the present occasion.
It was the first trial of their faith. It is easy to understand the deep disappointment which they must have felt
when once they had left Egypt, bruised and broken as it
was by judgments. They, doubtless, must have thought
that they should see nothing more of it for ever. We may
imagine their dismay, on looking back, to see their invete-
rate enemies in pursuit, themselves unarmed, their enemies
well armed, provided with chariots of war, and especially
at this *spot* to which they had just moved ; for here the
Red Sea was just before them, on the south was a range
of mountains, which it would be difficult to cross. Behind them were the chariots of their oppressors. To the
eye of sense all must have appeared *very dark*, and their
one day's journey southward a very great mistake. Had
they only looked upward to their covenant God, all would
still have seemed bright ; but it was just here that they
failed. It says, (ver. 10,) " They were sore afraid," and
" cried out unto the Lord."

This, brethren, presents us with a very vivid picture of
the earliest temptations of the young Christian. When
first he looks to Jesus as a Saviour, a change passes upon
his heart, a change in his views, his desires, and his affections. He can understand by the light of his own experience the words of the apostle, " If any man be in Christ,
he is a new creature : old things are passed away ; behold,
all things are become new." The cross of Christ is full
of glory ; the world has lost its attractions. He thinks
that nothing but victory attends him, that he has but to
" go forth conquering and to conquer." But this lasts but
for a short time. The first trial of his still weak faith
soon comes. And what is that trial ? It is not, brethren,
at first that the world becomes attractive again. It is not

that his besetting sins *allure* him. This usually comes at a later stage, just as they did in the case of Israel. At first Egypt put on a *threateniny aspect*. After a season of brightness, of joy and hope, the *guilt* and *power* of past sins begin to lower and to *threaten*. The clouds gather around; new difficulties appear before, and *old* enemies are in pursuit behind; and the young believer, who has hitherto walked more in the strength of his holy and happy feelings than by the power of *faith*, is in dismay. Like Israel, he is sore afraid, and "cries out unto the Lord." But observe the manner in which their want of faith shewed itself. They assumed at once that they would "die in the wilderness." Of the certainty of this assumption they felt no doubt; and miserable as was the bondage of Egypt, they thought it better to be there than to die, especially in the wilderness. "It had been better," they say, (ver. 12,) "for us to serve the Egyptians, than that we should die in the wilderness." Faith, brethren, gives calmness. It elevates the soul so that, as from a lofty eminence, it can survey its difficulties. It is like the eye, with the telescope added. Distant objects, and things otherwise unseen, come into view; and not only is it gifted with far sight, but it enables us to estimate aright the proportion of things. Its calmness and clearness prevent the understanding from forming such assumptions, and forbid the language, "We shall die in the wilderness." It is the property of unbelief to make false assumptions, and to come to wrong conclusions. It is the property of faith to look beyond difficulties to Him who controls all, and to rest upon the promise as sure. "I will not leave thee, until I have done that which I have spoken to thee of," (Gen. xxviii. 15.) It is the property of unbelief to make the heart think any other circumstances *preferable*

to its own. It is the property of faith not to look rest-
lessly for a change of outward circumstances, but for
nearer, deeper communion with God, for "that strength
which is made perfect in weakness."

As the Israelites walked by sight, not by faith, it can
cause us no wonder that they regarded Moses as the
author of their danger and misfortunes. They already
overlooked the glorious fact that God brought them out
of Egypt. They forgot the pillar of fire and cloud, and
said to Moses, "Because there were no graves in Egypt,
hast *thou*" (mark the word)—"*thou* taken us away to die
in the wilderness?" What an unworthy motive, too, to
impute to this faithful servant of God! Nor was this all;
they insinuated that they had foreseen all these difficulties,
and thus intimated that it was owing to Moses's *blind-
ness* that they were brought into all their trials. "Is not
this," they say, (ver. 12,) "the word which we did tell thee
in Egypt, saying, Let us alone, that we may serve the
Egyptians?" Here, brethren, we see the human heart
in one of the most common of all its frequent and varied
manifestations. They forget that God is their guide, and
that all trials—whether they be severe or small—whether
they come without man's intervention or through man—
are His appointment. What is the consequence? They
substitute second causes for the first cause. They put
mere instruments in the place of God; and, as it is more
difficult to be submissive to man than to God, the heart
revolts against the infliction. They say, "This is all *your*
fault; if it were not for *you*, I should not have this trouble."
And their pride lifts itself up, and, entering the unseemly
conflict, adds—"I foresaw it all. Did I not warn you
beforehand?" O brethren, if we would be kept from
these sinful accusations,—and we *must* overcome them,—

then we must look above the instrumentality of man to the guiding and chastising hand of God. We must realise that the trials which come to us *through* man, are not less of God than those in which we cannot but feel " This is the finger of God." It is often difficult to do so. We may have many a hard struggle with the impatience and waywardness of our own sinful hearts ; but we must wait on God until we rise above man, whether he be a Pharaoh or a Moses, and rest in God,—in His will, His strength, and His glory. Moses was calm and patient in the midst of all this danger, and what was still more trying, the accusations of the Israelites. He knew the firmness of the ground on which he stood. What a grandeur there was in his faith ! It raised him above the present, and transplanted him into the future. He foresaw, by the light of promise, the overthrow of their threatening enemies, and anticipated the songs of the now trembling Israelites. " Fear ye not," he says, (ver. 13, 14,) "stand still, and see the salvation of the Lord, which he will shew to you to-day : for the Egyptians whom ye have seen to-day, ye shall see them again no more for ever. The Lord shall fight for you, and ye shall hold your peace." Then follow the words of our text in which God speaks,—" Wherefore criest thou unto me ? speak unto the children of Israel, that they go forward."

We often speak, brethren, of the *power* of prayer. Some of us may have experienced it in our own case, and may have found even mountains subside before it, and the storm become a calm. But whatever we may ourselves have experienced, doubtless its power very far exceeds our very highest thoughts ; and yet, brethren, our text forcibly reminds us that there is a time to *act*, as well as a time to *pray*. We ought to ask counsel of

God, and to cry to Him in difficulty; but so soon as the path of duty is ascertained we should also " go forward." It is wrong to act without deliberation and prayer; but it is also wrong to be deliberating when we ought to be acting. It is sin to " go forward " without prayer; it is scarcely less so to be " crying to God," like the trembling paralysed Israelites, when they ought to be going forward. " Wherefore," said the Lord, " criest thou unto me? speak unto the children of Israel, that they go forward." It is quite certain, brethren, that there can be no progress in the Christian life without prayer,—without real and transforming communion with God; but you may also rest assured, brethren, that very much depends upon our " going forward " at the right moment. Some characters are so constituted as to be prone to the one danger, other characters to the opposite. The energetic character is in danger of neglecting prayer,—of creating a path for himself, instead of walking in God's way. The Red Sea scarcely seems to be an obstacle to him. The meditative and more undecided character dreads mistakes,—betakes himself to God for guidance, and perhaps does not " go forward " when he ought. To one or the other of these dangers all of us must be in a measure prone. To which are you most prone? We must endeavour, by earnest self-discipline and watchfulness, to overcome the evil, and thus have the harmony of our character completed. Are you naturally hasty, imperious? ready to decide upon duty at once? Then you must make it a rule always to *pray*, before you give counsel, and act. Or are you naturally disposed to think, to deliberate and doubt? Then you must try to cultivate decision in action; you must " go forward," as well as " pray." The children of Israel were commanded to " go forward " when their way

was full of perplexity. The Red Sea seemed a complete
barrier to their progress. But there are no barriers with
God—no difficulties limit Him. With Him all things
are possible. At His command they went forward. We
all know the result. We have been familiar with all the
circumstances of this history from our early childhood.
It is summed up in a few words in Heb. xi. 29,—" By
faith they passed through the Red Sea as by dry land :
which the Egyptians assaying to do were drowned." The
waters were to the one a " wall on their right hand, and
on their left;" to the other an overwhelming judgment.
" The Lord saved Israel that day out of the hand of the
Egyptians ; and Israel saw the Egyptians dead upon the
sea-shore. And Israel saw that great work which the
Lord did upon the Egyptians : and the people feared the
Lord, and believed the Lord, and his servant Moses." It
is quite evident that the passage of the Red Sea was a
great crisis in Israel's history, and it must, of course, be
typical of a great crisis in the Christian's life. What
that is St Paul tells us, (1 Cor. x. 1,) " Moreover,
brethren, I would not that ye should be ignorant, how
that all our fathers were under the cloud, and all passed
through the sea." It represents, therefore, just what
baptism represents, and that of which it is one mean,—
the burial of the old man, and the rising of the new man.
As St Paul says, (Rom. vi. 4,) " Therefore are we buried
with him by baptism into death : that like as Christ was
raised up from the dead by the glory of the Father, even
so we also should walk in newness of life." In the passage of the Red Sea, Egypt was typical of the old man ;
Israel of the new. It was then first that Egypt's power
over Israel was completely broken, and that Israel was
altogether freed from its dominion. Henceforth it was

under the guidance of Moses, who, in this respect, was an eminent type of Christ. It now entered on a new life. We see, then, brethren, to what it is that we should go forward. It is to the burial of the old man, and to the putting on of the new man. According to our calling, and the meaning of baptism, this is already accomplished in us. But it must become a great *inward reality;* you must become conscious of it in your own souls. Consecrated we already are, but we must be sanctified. Go forward, then, brethren, in this great work. Perplexities you may feel of various kinds,—difficulties in Scripture, difficulties in the path of duty, and difficulties in yourself. Still go forward ; only fix your eye on Christ Jesus —only seek, through the Spirit, to mortify the deeds of the body, and, one by one, your perplexities will be removed. The Red Sea will divide before you ; and whilst a way is opened for you to walk in newness of life, the power and dominion of sin will be destroyed within you, and that beautiful promise be accomplished—" Sin shall not have dominion over you : for you are not under the law, but under grace."

THE WATERS OF MARAH

Exodus 15:22, 23

"So Moses brought Israel from the Red Sea, and they went out into the wilderness of Shur; and they went three days in the wilderness, and found no water. And when they came to Marah, they could not drink of the waters of Marah, for they were bitter: therefore the name of it was called Marah."

THE early part of this chapter records the song with which Israel celebrated the destruction of their oppressors. No one can read it with any care without feeling how triumphant and elevated its tone is, and how high it rises. But there is a very remarkable allusion to it in the New Testament,—one which invests it with great additional importance, and stamps it with a permanent character. We mean the expressions which occur, Rev. xv. 3,—"And they sing the song of Moses the servant of God, and the song of the Lamb." There can be no doubt whatever but that the "song of Moses" refers to the one recorded in this chapter, and not to that which we read, Deut. xxxii.; but it is surely a very remarkable thing that the "song of Moses" and "the song of the Lamb" should be thus associated together, and that no words should better express the feelings of the saints on that day than those sung centuries ago on the confines of the wilderness. Now, this must, of course, rest upon the typical character of Israel's oppression, and Israel's deliverance. We have seen already that Pharaoh may be

regarded as a type of the old man, which in every true
Christian is given up to destruction ; but the chapter in
which the song of Moses is spoken of teaches us that
Pharaoh and Egypt are typical of something more—of
enemies of the Church as well as of the individual Christian ; for we read, (Rev. xv. 2,) " And I saw as it were a
sea of glass mingled with fire : and them that had gotten
the victory over the beast, and over his image, and over his
mark, and over the number of his name, stand on the sea
of glass, having the harps of God." Pharaoh, then, and
Egypt are types of the beast, to whom it will be given,
according to Rev. xiii. 7, " to make war with the saints, and
to overcome them : to whom power will be given over all
kindreds, and tongues, and nations." And when those
whose names are written in the Lamb's book of life get
the victory over the beast, then will the song of Moses
and the song of the Lamb resound. This first song of
Israel, then, will never grow old. It will reach into eternity. It burst forth from thousands of rejoicing hearts
when first sung over Israel's first enemy ; and it will burst
forth again, in still more triumphant tones, when the
Church's last enemy lies prostrate, and she enters a rest
never more to be disturbed or broken. And thus this
song is evidently suited to express the joyful feelings of
the young Christian in his earliest victory, when the old
man is slain, and in Jesus he finds deliverance from the
body of death ; and it is also suited to the dying saint
who has fought many a conflict, and, in the strength of
his risen head, gained many a victory. According, however, to the typical view which we have hitherto taken of
this history, this triumph is a foreshadow of the young
Christian's earliest victory, this song the note of joy
which rises from his thankful heart, when he first issues

forth from darkness and weary conflict, and lays hold of
Jesus as the all-sufficient Saviour. If you look, brethren,
at a few of the beautiful expressions which it contains,
you will see how suited it is to that passage in the Christian's life. For at its very commencement, you will observe
the utterances of an *appropriating faith.* "The Lord,"
it says, (ver. 2,) " is my strength and my song, and he
has become my salvation : he is my God, and I will prepare him an habitation ; my father's God, and I will exalt
him." Observe, brethren, how very often that little word
"my" occurs in this one verse. That little word, the
language of faith and the spring of all comfort in the
soul—" *my* strength, *my* song, *my* salvation, *my* God."
There is a parallel passage, Isa. xii. 1, 2,—" And in that
day thou shalt say, O Lord, I will praise thee : though
thou wast angry with me, thine anger is turned away,
and thou comfortedst me." And then what follows,—
"Behold, God is *my* salvation ; I will trust, and not be
afraid : for the Lord Jehovah is my strength and my song ;
he also is become my salvation."

And this little word " my " is one characteristic of the
young Christian's faith. Many wearisome doubts, many
agitating fears he *has* had ; long, it may be, has he been
burdened with the weight of sin, and tossed almost hopelessly about, as if there were no anchor for his soul ; but
the Spirit of God has led him forward, and changed the
cry, " O wretched man," into the " I thank God," and the
dreadful feeling of strangeness into the joyful feeling of
confidence : *my* God, *my* salvation, *my* all ! Yes, brethren,
there is such a thing as to rest upon God as *yours*—your
own God—a God who has made Himself over to you in
Christ—a God in covenant. *Then* your soul is brought
out of bondage into liberty, happy and holy liberty, when

by faith in Jesus you can and do say, " My God."
Brethren, have you attained to this appropriating faith?
Are you still agitated with fears? doubtful whether you
have yet touched the hem of Christ's garment? Or can
you say, with the Church, " My Beloved is mine, and I am
his;" and with Thomas, " My Lord and my God." But
there is another beautiful expression here which may and
must be very touching to some; we mean the words, " My
father's God." Imagine, brethren, a child brought up by
holy parents, early consecrated to God, and trained up for
Him. Such training is sure to be followed by some solemn
impressions—impressions which, in some cases, are never
effaced from the soul. But we will suppose them to be
effaced for a season. The temptations of the world creep
in and deaden the soul. The early lessons are forgotten.
The first promises of holiness seem all to pass away as the
morning cloud; but the parent's prayers are recorded in
heaven. The spirit is given—the conscience is awakened
—convictions of sin return—words long forgotten gain
new power in the heart—the wanderer is brought to
Christ; and all this mercy and love is seen to be connected with a father's Christian example, or a mother's
gentle care. In such a case, how touching will be the
expression, " My father's God!" and how thrilling the
desire, " And I will exalt Him!"

But we may also trace in this song the language of
exalted *hope*, especially in ver. 13,—" Thou in thy mercy
hast led forth the people which thou hast redeemed: thou
hast guided them in thy strength unto thy holy habitation." The first clause of this verse was the thankful
announcement of a fact. God *had* indeed "led forth"
His people. The second clause was the language of hope.
They knew not the toils and the dangers of the wilderness

through which they had to pass.   It seemed as if already they had entered into rest—the holy habitation which God had promised.

And thus, brethren, it is pre-eminently a time of hope and anticipation to the young Christian, when he is first brought into marvellous light.   His faith is strong enough to say, "My God," and that is all.   It cannot trust in the dark.   Feeling predominates over faith.   But his hope is bright.   It is not strong enough to carry much weight. It would sink beneath a heavy cross.   But it is a *lively* hope, expanding the whole heart with joyful anticipations of things to come, bearing it forward over the intervening pilgrimage, and placing it so completely in the presence of things promised, that it sometimes seems to be already there.   "Thou hast guided me in thy strength unto thy holy habitation."   "Thou shalt bring me in, and plant me in the mountain of thy inheritance, in the place, O Lord, which thou hast made for thee to dwell in, in the Sanctuary, O Lord, which thy hands have established."   We should have thought, brethren, that Israel's faith would not soon have failed, Israel's hope would not soon have grown dim, and that this beautiful song would have re-echoed again and again in the wilderness, and its sound never have died away before their entrance into the promised rest.   The very reverse really took place.   At the first station in the wilderness their faith completely failed. They sank into despondency, and the song of triumphant thanksgiving was exchanged for sinful murmurings; and from that time forward murmuring predominated over praise, and forgetfulness over gratitude.   Our text records the circumstances of their first trial in the wilderness.   Moses led them into the wilderness of Shur. Three days they journeyed in it without finding any water. This was a much greater exercise of faith than many of us are aware. The sufferings of thirst are amongst the most distressing that can be endured. On the third day, however, there seemed to be the promise of relief. Water was found. We may imagine the eagerness with which they would hasten to it to slake their thirst. What must have been their disappointment to find the waters so bitter that they could not drink them! It would evidently have been much less trying to them not to have discovered water at all. Nothing so thoroughly sifts the heart as disappointment—bright and lofty anticipations suddenly cast to the ground. We know the result in their case. They thought no more of past mercies. The triumphant deliverance of the Red Sea faded away from their memories. They murmured against Moses. But though their faith failed, God did not fail. One at least there was amongst them whose heart was stayed upon God. The golden thread of Divine grace in Israel was not altogether rent asunder. Moses prayed to God ; and in answer to his prayer a tree was shewn him, which, cast into the waters of Marah, made them sweet.

But what is all this, brethren, but a striking picture of human life, and of that which the grace of God can and does effect?

All the waters of human life have been poisoned by sin. There is not one drop that has been left quite pure, —all has been made bitter. Much there is still which at a distance looks beautiful and refreshing ; and those who walk by sense, and not by faith, are *often*, nay, *always* deceived by appearances, just as Israel was. It is not until they taste for themselves that they find out the truth of Solomon's words, that all is "vanity and vexation of spirit." Look, brethren, at the attractions of the

world, which cause so many souls to wander. What are
they all but a vain show, which can intoxicate or lull the
soul for a time, but which leave it, oh, how weary and
restless afterwards! The waters of the world are truly
bitter waters. Or, look at the occupations of life. To
some energetic spirits the very difficulty and toil of
labour are attractive; but after a while, will not the
question thrust itself upon the busy mind, oh, what is the
profit? what the end of all this? Suppose that everything
prospers. Suppose that I have enough to satisfy every
earthly want, to secure me every gratification, to encompass
myself and children with every luxury. What then?
There is a voice, a penetrating voice, that says, "Prepare
to meet thy God!" that proclaims, "It is appointed unto
men once to die, but after that the judgment." And
then, what will become of me? Or, look again at the
relationships of life. Instituted though they are by God,
yet sin has imbittered *them* also. Whence is it, brethren,
that some of the deepest and most certain trials of life
come to us? It is through our relationships and our
friendships. Deep affection, sacred as it is, has always
many anxieties associated with it. How many a mother's
heart is gradually worn out by cares about her children!
How many a father, when surveying the disturbances of
his family, is impelled to adopt the words of the aged
Jacob, "All these things are against me!" And then,
how many a heart is left widowed even early in life,
with a void which nothing earthly can ever fill! Is it,
brethren, too much to say that this world, viewed as it is
in itself, is "Marah?" Its waters are bitter. Have not
numbers who have embraced it as their all, gone down to
the grave restless, discontented, and murmuring? It
may seem to some as if we had invested the world, with

its pleasures, its occupations, and its relationships in too thick a gloom. If so, we would remind you that we have been speaking of the world, as such, as it is in itself,—of pleasures which are far away from God—of business and occupation from which God is excluded—and of relationships which are put in the place of God.

For, brethren, we may thank God that there is a tree which has been cast, and which is evermore being cast, into these bitter waters, and which has power to sweeten them. Do you know, brethren, what that tree is? Has God *shewed* it to you as He did to Moses? It is Jesus, the tree of life,—the tree which St John saw in vision, Rev. xxii. 2, "which bare twelve manner of fruits, and yielded her fruit every month: and the leaves of the tree were for the healing of the nations." When you come to Jesus as an all-sufficient Saviour,—when you depend on Him as your atoning sacrifice,—when you feed on Him as the bread of life,—then *for you* there is no more curse. The waters of human life are no longer bitter waters. Tried you may be, and will be, perhaps, more than ever; but Christ comes with the trial, and fills it with Himself. And then, brethren, can we, ought we, to call it "Marah?" Oh no; everything is different then. The world is different. A new world, with its new joys and heavenly attractions, has cast out the old world from the heart. The occupations of life, be they the great and ever-changing ones of the statesman, or the little daily arrangements of domestic life, are changed then, for a new motive has been introduced. The love of Christ and the glory of God pervade them all, and connect each duty with the cross and with heaven. And then all the relationships of life are penetrated by the healing influences of the tree of life. Our friendships are formed at the foot of the cross, and, cemented by a Saviour's love, shall never die. Death, at the very most, suspends them for a season. It does not, and cannot annihilate them. And of what do all the relationships of life speak to us? They speak to us of God. They are not unhallowed things binding us to the world, but consecrated links binding us to heaven. They speak to us of Him who has taught us to say, "Abba, Father," of Him who is not "ashamed to call us brethren." The tree of life changes the waters of Marah, and makes them all sweet,—"where sin abounded, grace did much more abound."

The next station at which Israel arrived was altogether different from Marah. At the one, everything was naturally barren; there was no supply for their wants. It was only the power of God which could sweeten the bitter waters. At the other, Elim, there was an abundant supply of water, exactly adapted to Israel's wants,—twelve wells of water, a well for each tribe, and a refreshing shade, for there were seventy palm-trees there. We see, then, brethren, here, at the very outset, that Israel's journey through the wilderness was a chequered one; there was a mixture of trial and mercy. Marah, with its bitter waters, intervenes between the triumphant song at the Red Sea, and Elim, with its twelve wells of water. What a picture this of the Christian's life, in which dark hours often follow, and are followed by bright ones! If, brethren, your path is smooth and bright now, if Israel's song of praise finds a response in your heart, you must not think that it will be always so. Some trial of faith will surely be sent you after a season. Rejoice, then, but let it be with a calm and hallowed joy. Sing Israel's song, but take care that it is never exchanged for Israel's discontented murmurings. Thankful we ought to be, but we should take heed of self-exaltation ; for he that "exalt-eth himself," whether on account of his temporal or spiritual blessings, "shall be abased." But if, on the other hand, God is calling you now to taste the waters of Marah, and you are discouraged on account of the weariness of the way, are you ready to think that there will be, there can be no more refreshment for you? Yours may be a lifelong sorrow. The world may appear to you most desolate and most weary ; and yet you may receive comfort and strength from above. It may be very much nearer to you than you suppose. The pillar of cloud may conduct your faltering steps to an " Elim," where you shall sit down under the " shadow of Jesus," and the wells of " living water" shall be opened to you. Remember the beautiful words of Jesus, (John iv. 10,) " If thou knewest the gift of God, and who it is that saith to thee, Give me to drink ; thou wouldest have asked of him, and he would have given thee living water." Remember the gracious invitation, " If any man thirst, let him come unto me and drink." Oh, why should not we, beloved brethren, encamp, like Israel of old, beside the well of living water, and drink abundantly? Our fountain of life is not limited to one spot ; our shelter is not in one place only. As the Christian journeys onward, Jesus, his unfailing shelter, his fountain of life, goes with him ; the pillar of cloud pauses at Elim. Do not encamp beside the broken cisterns of this world, which can hold no water, but pitch your tent beside the waters of life. By daily meditation on the Scriptures, and constant prayer, " draw water with joy out of the wells of salvation," and "my God shall supply all your need, according to his riches in glory by Christ Jesus."

THE BREAD FROM HEAVEN

Exodus 16:15

" And when the children of Israel saw it, they said one to another, It
is manna: for they wist not what it was. And Moses said unto
them, This is the bread which the Lord hath given you to eat."

WE left, you will remember, the children of Israel at
Elim, one of the best stations which they met with in the
wilderness. *There* they found an abundant supply of
water; and what was even still more uncommon in the
wilderness, the refreshing shelter of seventy palm-trees.
If anything was to be found in that weary land to miti-
gate the fierce rays of an eastern sun, it was more frequently the " shadow of a great rock" than the gentler
shade of palm-trees. We are not told how long they
halted at this station. If they could have followed their
own inclinations, it is quite certain that they would have
lingered there; and it is also probable, that He who loves
to deal gently with His people, may have allowed the pillar of cloud to rest at that spot, that the weary Israelites
might recruit their strength, and regain courage and hope.
However this be, one thing is clear, that they must have
paused for some days at some of the stations. We find
the most complete list of the names of these stations in
Numbers xxxiii.; but even there, all the places at which
they stopped are not mentioned. Thus we are told
(ver. 8) that they went " three days' journey in the wilderness of Etham." Omitting those three days, Elim is

the fifth station; and one station intervened between it and the wilderness of Sin, the station which is to occupy our thoughts this morning. Now, it is clear from ver. 1 of the chapter from which our text is taken, that they had been exactly a month in reaching this place; for you will remember that the paschal lamb was slain on the 14th day of the first month. On the following day, they commenced their journey; and it was now the 15th day of the second month that they reached the wilderness of Sin. Thus their marches were not very severe. The pillar of cloud led them gently forward. God often gave them rest by the way,—rest at noon.

A new trial came upon them at this station. Their first trial was the want of water; now it was the want of food. When they left Egypt they took with them herds and flocks, as we read (chap. xii. 38), "And a mixed multitude went up also with them; and flocks, and herds, even very much cattle," and these had sufficed them for food during the first month of their wanderings. But now, in the wilderness of Sin, where nothing could be procured, this provision failed; and with it their faith failed also; and, as before, they murmured. In some respects this trial was greater than the preceding one. Then they found that they must depend upon God for a supply of water, but they had provisions of their own, in their own possession, which they could see with their own eyes. But now they found that they must be completely dependent upon God for everything. This is always difficult for our sinful hearts. It is a blessed thing when such difficulties drive us to prayer, and when prayer rises in proportion to the difficulty. But no prayer arose from the hearts of the Israelites. Their hearts sank deeper in despondency than before, and their murmur-

ings were both more universal and louder. They said,
(ver. 3), " Would to God we had died by the hand of the
Lord in the land of Egypt, when we sat by the flesh pots,
and when we did eat bread to the full; for ye have
brought us forth into this wilderness, to kill this whole
assembly with hunger." What unbelief and sad forgetfulness of God betrayed itself in these words! They quite
forgot the bitter bondage of Egypt, under which they had
sighed and groaned so long. They now thought only of
its " flesh pots " and " its bread." They altogether overlooked the mercy and the grace which had spared them
when the first-born of the Egyptians were slain. The
miracles of love at the Red Sea and at Marah, so great
and so recent, had passed away from their memories.
They thought nothing of the promise of the land flowing
with milk and honey. The argument, so evident and so
comforting, " Can the faithful God, who has brought us
out of bondage, mean to let us perish in the wilderness?"
did not withhold them from the impatient conclusion,
" Ye have brought us forth into the wilderness, to kill this
whole assembly with hunger." And if you watch your
own hearts, brethren, you will find that there is always
this forgetfulness in a murmuring and discontented spirit.
Whenever we are tempted to murmur, there are always
two things at least that we forget. First we forget what
we deserve at the hands of God,—nothing but punishment ;
and then we forget all the mercy and love which He
has shewn us in His acts and His promises. The murmurings of Israel were heard on high—and more than
heard, they were answered too—and answered, not in judgment, but in mercy. In this case, murmuring seemed to
produce the same effects as prayer would have done. But
this will only appear so when we look at the outward

effects. Inwardly it must have been very different. Had they cast themselves on God by dependent prayer, not only would their need have been supplied, but their faith would have been strengthened, their peace deepened, and their hopes increased. Then, too, the gift would have been the crown of their faith, and not its trial. As it was, however, an answer to a murmuring and unhumbled spirit, and not to a praying and dependent spirit, one purpose of the supply was to prove them ; as we will see by referring to ver. 4, " Then said the Lord unto Moses, Behold, I will rain bread from heaven for you ; and the people shall go out and gather a certain rate every day." Why ? " That I may *prove* them, whether they will walk in my law or no." We shall see presently in what way it did shew what was in their hearts. We all know, brethren, what was the nature of the supply given in answer to Israel's murmurings. It was twofold. They longed for the "flesh pots of Egypt," so God gave them " flesh." They thought of the time when they had " eaten bread to the full," so God promised them bread from heaven. We read, (ver. 12), " I have heard the murmurings of the children of Israel : speak unto them, saying, At even ye shall eat flesh, and in the morning ye shall be filled with bread ; and ye shall know that I am the Lord." And in the next verse it is added, " And it came to pass, that at even the quails came up, and covered the camp." But these two kinds of supply were very different. The flesh was quite subordinate to the manna. The quails were sent on this and one other occasion only. The manna was the food of Israel during the space of forty years, and never failed until they were brought into the Land of Promise. The quails had no typical meaning. The manna was a most beautiful type. We shall return, if the Lord permit, on some future occasion to the one, when we have made greater progress in this history. We will now confine our attention, during the rest of this discourse, to the other, the manna, both in its historical and typical aspect.

The name of manna was given to the new kind of food, not by God himself, but by the children of Israel. We are told this more than once, first in the words of the text, "And when the children of Israel saw it, they said one to another, It is manna: for they wist not what it was;" and again in ver. 31, "And the house of Israel called the name thereof manna." And this name appears to have been the one commonly used. Thus Ps. lxxviii. 24, "And had rained down manna upon them to eat, and had given them the corn of heaven." It is not quite certain why they called it manna. Some suppose that it is derived from the Hebrew word "mah," which means "what," and then the emphasis must be laid on the word "what" in the sentence, "They wist not *what* it was." Others think that it signifies "portion," or gift, which is the best interpretation. They called it gift, because it was most evidently the gift of God; and as they did not know its nature, they could not choose any better term whereby to describe it. If, however, we turn from the language of the Israelites to that of God, we shall find that the expression used concerning it is "bread from heaven." Thus, in ver. 4, it is promised, "Behold, I will rain bread from heaven for you." This bread was sent them in the *morning*, whereas the quails were given them at *even*, not ordinarily, but once only. It came down with the silent dew, all unseen, and when the dew was gone up, then the manna became visible. It was with reference to this that the remarkable words are spoken (ver. 7), "And in the morning, then ye shall see the *glory of the Lord.*" In this, the gift bestowed constantly every morning, the glory of the Lord was specially manifested in a way in which it was not seen in the single, isolated gift of quails. We all know, brethren, of what this manna was a type, for we have an interpretation of it in the New Testament, which cannot be doubted or called in question. It is a type of the Lord Jesus himself, for so He tells us in John vi. 32, 33,—"Then Jesus said unto them, Verily, verily, I say unto you, Moses gave you not that bread from heaven; but my Father giveth you the true bread from heaven. For the bread of God is he which cometh down from heaven, and giveth life unto the world;" and again, (ver. 35), "I am the bread of life: he that cometh to me shall never hunger; and he that believeth on me shall never thirst." What, then, the manna was to Israel,—the nourishment of their bodies; that Jesus is to every believer, whether a babe in the divine life, or of full age,—the nourishment of his soul. The manna was Israel's only food during forty years in the wilderness. Christ is the only food of our souls during our journey towards our promised rest; nothing else can nourish them—nothing else can sustain spiritual life, or enable us to put forth spiritual strength. Eloquence may carry our understandings along by its forcible arguments, or make our hearts thrill with its touching appeals; but it requires something more, something else to *feed* the soul. The ordinances of God's house are very solemnising and soothing; yet even these cannot, and do not, *of* and *in* themselves, become its nourishment. They are means, and, as means, are very precious; but the bread of life they are not, they cannot be. This Jesus alone is: He who offers Himself to us in every ordinance,—in prayer, in the Word of God, and most of all, in the Lord's supper.

And does not, brethren, the manner in which this bread descended from above, along with the gentle, silent dew, apply very beautifully to the true bread from heaven? It is not in the bustle of the world, or in the excitements of religion, but in secret and in silence that Jesus descends upon the soul, when the spirit communes with God— when the eye is turned within in earnest searching self-examination—when the heart calmly meditates on the Divine word. And what is the dew on and with which He descends? What but the Spirit of God, of which the dew is the constant symbol in Scripture? When the Spirit falls gently upon our hearts, then Jesus descends there. Where the one is, the other is—yet they are distinct. It is not the Spirit, but Christ in His living person who is the bread of life. The Spirit is as the dew; Jesus as the manna, the bread from heaven. Cherish, then, brethren, we must every gentle influence of the Spirit of God, if we would have our souls nourished. What would the dew descending on the barren wilderness produce? *Nothing*, we might be inclined to answer. Nothing, indeed, was elicited from the barren soil, but it was overspread with food enough to sustain about two millions; and thus, brethren, however sinful your hearts may be, however barren they may appear,—barren as the savage, unculti-vated wilderness,—yet the gentle dew of God's Spirit may descend upon them, and what will follow but this? they will be overspread with the bread of life.

Thus far, brethren, we have viewed the manna as God's gift. Let us now pass on to some of the rules prescribed to Israel concerning it, for from these also we may gather instruction. And first, if you turn to ver. 21 you will find these words, " And they gathered it every morning, every man according to his eating." It was in the early morning that the dew descended ; early in the morning, therefore, they were to go abroad to gather it. This was, therefore, their *first* work. They could do nothing else. They could not journey until they had first of all collected their daily food ; and if any, from sloth or negligence, forbore to go out and gather it, then he would of necessity suffer loss, for " when the sun waxed hot, it melted." And thus, brethren, it is with the true bread from heaven, though many heed it not. It is in the early morning, before the occupations of the day commence, that the gentle dew of the Spirit, and with it the bread of life, descends. It is early in the morning, brethren, that we must go out to gather it. There is no time for gathering so good as that. Then the whole ground is, so to speak, strewed with the bread of life. The mind is more calm and unruffled before the occupations of the day have once set in, and then by feeding on Jesus it is raised above the world. It sets about its occupations as a pilgrim and a stranger on earth. It is enabled more and more to carry Christ into all the duties and occupations of the day, and whatsoever it does, to " do all to the glory of God." Dear brethren, do we go out early in the morning to gather the Divine food ? If we would follow Christ, we must resolutely break through all habits of sloth and self-indulgence. There was no self-indulgence in Christ's life ; there ought to be as little as possible in ours. There can be no vigour without self-denial, and no strength to take our daily march towards heaven unless we first feed upon the bread of life. Watch carefully your own minds, and you will find that whenever you have been self-indulgent in the morning, and given but little time to meditation and prayer, your tone of mind has been lowered throughout the day, the cares and occupations of life have harassed you more—your temper, it may be, has been more easily ruffled—and when you have retired to pray later in the day, you have felt as if the morning dew had all been swept away, and the manna gone. Brethren, let us make it a rule, never to be infringed upon, to gather the bread of life early in the morning. Let the resolution of the Psalmist be ours, "Early in the morning will I direct my prayer unto Thee, and will look up." Again, in ver. 19, we find the command, "Let no man leave of it till the morning." The reason of this is obvious. There is a tendency in our hearts to walk by sight. We naturally like to surround ourselves with possessions, and to see the supply for all our wants. But God was now teaching His people to walk by faith,—to depend not upon what they had, but upon Himself and His own gracious promises. It was evidently to carry out this great principle that the Israelites were to gather day by day just what they wanted, and no more. They were not allowed to "keep it till the morrow," because this would have shewed one of two things,—either their distrust of God's promise and care, or that they did not view this as a part of their daily work, and a fitful spirit which would work hard one day and not at all the next.

It is easy, brethren, to see the application of this to ourselves. We also are called to walk by faith day by day and hour by hour. In everything, whether great or small, we ought to depend fully and completely on God. We cannot lay up a store of grace. The grace of to-day is given us for the day, but it will not suffice for the difficulties and conflicts of to-morrow. To-morrow we must go to God for fresh supplies of grace. You must never, then, brethren, trust to past grace. You ought, indeed, never to forget what you have received. You ought to be thankful for every gift in the past, as well as for every promise of the future. But you must not lean upon grace received, or try to live on old stores of grace. You must not suppose that because your prayers have been very earnest and prolonged, and your soul much strengthened one day, that therefore you may relax somewhat the next. No, brethren; grace, like Israel's manna, cannot be laid up for the morrow. It must come down from heaven each day, and each day be gathered, if our souls are to prosper.

There is one more point which we may briefly notice. So completely was the gathering the manna regarded by God as *a work*, that the Israelites were forbidden to gather it on the Sabbath, and hence we are told (ver. 22) that "on the sixth day they gathered twice as much bread." On the Sabbath no manna was given. "Six days ye shall gather it; but on the seventh day, which is the Sabbath, in it there shall be none." We need not pause now to shew how powerful a sanction this gave to the Sabbath, and how clearly it demonstrates that it was not instituted first at Mount Sinai. But you will observe that it was this command that *proved* and tried the hearts of the Israelites; and many of them did not stand the test, as ver. 27 shews,—"And it came to pass, that there went out some of the people on the seventh day for to gather, and they found none."

But here, brethren, we cannot fail to remark a point of contrast between their manna and ours. Theirs was for the body; ours is for the soul. Theirs did not descend and could not be gathered on their Sabbath; ours does descend and is gathered most richly on the Lord's day.

If on any one day more is gathered than on the rest, it is on that *day* on which the Lord of glory arose, and which is specially consecrated to united worship. Shall we, brethren, call the gathering this Divine manna a *work?* Not certainly as implying any merit,—for nothing can be more free than the gift of Jesus, and of the Spirit, —but as implying importance, and demanding our utmost diligence, we may. And thus Jesus says, (John vi. 27,) "*Labour* not for the meat which perisheth, but for that meat which endureth unto everlasting life, which the Son of man shall give unto you: for him hath God the Father sealed." We call the ministry a "work," and it requires unwearied earnestness ; but there is nothing more important—nothing that requires more diligence, more earnestness, or more watchfulness, than gathering the heavenly manna, for it supplies all strength. It is the life of all other work. Without it we can do nothing aright— nothing to the glory of God.

THE SMITTEN ROCK

Exodus 17:6

"Behold, I will stand before thee there upon the rock in Horeb; and
thou shalt smite the rock, and there shall come water out of it,
that the people may drink."

THE expression, "after their journeys," in ver. 1, would
lead us to expect that there would be at least one station
between the wilderness of Sin and Rephidim. On referring to Num. xxxiii. 12–14, we find that there were two,
—Dophkah and Alush. Nothing of importance could
have happened at these stations. God did not try Israel's
faith, and they did not tempt God. They were never,
however, very long exempted from trial in the wilderness.
If from the wilderness of Sin to Rephidim their path was
comparatively smooth, a twofold trial was appointed them
at the latter place. The first was not a new trial. It was
again the want of water. The second *was* a new trial.
It was a pitched battle with the Amalekites. Before we
proceed to the consideration of the first of these trials, we
may remark that the Israelites were now not far from
Sinai. It was, in fact, the next station to Rephidim, and
according to a very accurate traveller, a march of about
five hours. You have doubtless observed that two names
are given in Scripture to the famous mountain from
which the law was given. Sometimes it is called Sinai,
and sometimes Horeb. In chap. xvi. 1, for example, it is
called Sinai. The wilderness of Sin is spoken of as being

'between Elim and Sinai." In chap. xvii. 6 it is called Horeb, "I will stand before thee there upon the rock in *Horeb*." The question, therefore, arises, whether these two names are exactly identical; and if not, whether Sinai is the name of the whole group of mountains, and Horeb the name of a single mountain, or the reverse. In the first place, it may be confidently asserted that Horeb and Sinai are not absolutely identical. With regard to the next, some very eminent writers have supposed Sinai to be the most comprehensive name, and Horeb to be the designation of a single mountain. Two circumstances seem, however, to favour the opposite conclusion. The one is this, that the name given to it, while the Israelites were still distant from it, is usually "Horeb," whereas it is called "Sinai" when they had actually arrived at the place whence the law was given. This circumstance would, of course, prove that Horeb is the more general, Sinai the more particular name. The other argument is still more conclusive. In the words of our text, God said to Moses, "I will stand before thee there upon the rock in Horeb." The inference from this sentence clearly is, that Rephidim was quite close to Horeb, though it was a day's march from Sinai; and if so, Horeb must have been the name of the whole group of mountains, of which Sinai was the most remarkable. At Marah, you will remember, the people murmured because the water was bitter. *Now* they murmured because there was no water at all. "There was no water," it says, (ver. 1,) "for the people to drink." Did they, in their difficulties, remember how the "bitter waters of Marah were made sweet?" and how God was supplying their wants day by day in a supernatural manner by the gift of manna? Whose was the pillar of fire and cloud that went before them by night and by day? At whose commandment did they journey? God's. Yet all this was again completely forgotten. Again they fastened on Moses as the author of all their sufferings,—"The people did chide with Moses," and used the awful language, implying that he was their only leader, "Give us water that we may drink." Here, then, brethren, we see the danger and the sure result of trusting in man. Moses was, no doubt, a most extraordinary man—most eminent for his meekness and patience, his spirit of prayer, the comprehensiveness of his mind, and the strength of his character. He was just one who was qualified to gain an immense influence over a people like Israel; and had their journeyings been free from trial, and their battles always crowned with victory, they would have given that glory to him which was due to God alone. But the idolatry of the creature is sure to end in disappointment, and disappointment in murmuring. If we lean on any but Jesus, we shall find it, after all, to be a broken cistern; and then, in disappointment, be in danger of throwing away altogether *that* which God has ordained to be an instrument of good—a channel of blessing, and *nothing more*. There ought, brethren, to be deep love and confidence between a minister and his people, for the relationship is a very hallowed one; but there should be no idolatry on either side. Christ should be all to both, —all our rest, all our joy, and all our expectation,—and then there can be no disappointment. There will be no sudden revulsions of feeling when we realise that we are under the guidance of an unchanging God, and that others can be only what He makes them to us. The power of influence we may and must feel; but we should see that it leads us near to Jesus. Influence we may and must exert; but we should do all that in us lies not to call out a spirit of idolatry, such as we see at Corinth,—" I am of Paul, and I of Apollos, and I of Cephas, and I of Christ," and which lays waste many a congregation now, *such* as is sure to lead to divisions of feeling, if not to actual schism, and to a spirit of murmuring such as we see in Israel.

Moses, in success and triumph, gave all glory to God ; and now, in trial and disappointment, he pointed the people to God,—" Wherefore do ye tempt the Lord ? " In what way their murmuring tempted God is clearly explained in ver. 7,—" They tempted the Lord, saying, Is the Lord among us, or not ? " Notwithstanding all the other tokens of God's presence, they thought that their renewed difficulties were a proof that God was no longer amongst them.

And are not our hearts, brethren, far too apt to come to the same conclusion on the same grounds ? We enter on some new path, on some fresh work, because we think that the hand of God is leading us to it, and, almost unconsciously to ourselves, we suppose that His presence will secure us from any great and discouraging difficulties. Our expectations are disappointed—one difficulty after another presents itself—one door after another is closed. What follows ? Too often doubts begin to arise in our minds whether God is really with us. But these doubts should not be encouraged. It is altogether a false inference, that because our path is one of difficulty or trial, therefore the Lord is not among us. The very reverse will usually be found to be the true conclusion. Difficulties and perplexities which come upon us in the path of duty are frequently tokens of God's presence—not the shadows of His frown, but harbingers of the " help of His countenance "—not meant to cast us down, but to

try, and by trial to strengthen, our faith. If, then, brethren, you have now any hidden secret difficulty—if disappointment thickens around you in the path of duty, or
you feel unequal to any work which you have undertaken
—do not conclude from this that God's own presence is
not with you. For this were to walk by sense, and not
by faith. It were to "tempt the Lord." But rather hope
against hope. Depend on the faithfulness of Him with
whom all things are possible. And then will the prayer
be accomplished, (Ps. xc. 16), "Let thy work appear unto
thy servants." In this twofold trial—first the want of
water, and then, and this was the greater of the two, the
murmuring and indignation of the Israelites—Moses cried
unto the Lord, saying, "What shall I do unto this people?
they be almost ready to stone me." A wonderful answer
was given to this prayer. "Go on," said Jehovah, "before the people"—that is, Fear not, but shew this wavering people that you know my power, and trust in my protection. "Go on, and take with thee of the elders of Israel;
and thy rod, wherewith thou smotest the river, take in
thy hand, and go. Behold, I will stand before thee there
upon the rock in Horeb; and thou shalt smite the rock,
and there shall come water out of it, that the people may
drink."

The smitten rock was the answer to Moses's prayer, and
put to shame Israel's murmurings. Yet you will remember that all this recurred again,—the thirst, the murmurings, and the smitten rock; and it recurs with so much
apparent resemblance, that a careless reader, who pays no
regard to chronology, or the more minute details of the
history, might fancy that it was but another account of
the same event. You will find the passage to which we
refer in Num. xx. With very much that resembles the

circumstances to which our text refers, you will find many
points in which the two accounts differ. With regard to
time, nearly forty years intervened between the two temptations. The one took place at the commencement of
their journeyings; the other near their close. It cannot
be an incidental circumstance that twice their wants
should have been supplied out of the smitten rock; but
to this we may return again. With regard to points of
difference, we may notice that there was a difference with
regard to the persons against whom they murmured. At
Rephidim they murmured against Moses alone; at Kadesh
against Aaron as well as Moses. Their murmurings were
somewhat different. At Rephidim their thoughts recurred to Egypt alone; at Kadesh to the destruction of
the Israelites in the wilderness. There was a difference
in God's command to Moses. At Rephidim he was told
to *smite* the rock; at Kadesh to speak to it. And lastly,
there was a difference in the spirit of Moses on the two
occasions. At Rephidim he was strong in faith; at
Kadesh his faith failed, and the solemn words were
spoken, (ver. 12,) "Because ye believed me not, to sanctify me in the eyes of the children of Israel, therefore ye
shall not bring this congregation into the land which I
have given them."

We need scarcely say of what the twice-smitten rock
was a type. St Paul says, (1 Cor. x. 4,) when speaking
of the Israelites, "And did all drink the same spiritual
drink: for they drank of that spiritual Rock that followed
them: and that Rock was Christ." The words are beautiful, and clear enough as to the antitype. But there is one
difficulty. In what manner could the rock be said to follow them? It has puzzled many of the commentators.
Some have said, that inasmuch as the Israelites carried

vessels of water with them, or that the miracle was repeated, it is *as if* the rock accompanied them; others again, as Calvin, say that the rock here signifies the water that flowed from it, and as water never failed the Israelites in the wilderness, the rock might be said to follow them. But the difficulty is completely removed if we only remark that St Paul is not speaking of the *material* but of the *spiritual* Rock, when he asserts that it followed them. It was Jesus who was ever with them in all their journeyings,—" In all their afflictions He was afflicted, and the angel of his presence saved them." We know, then, who it was that spoke the words to Moses, " Behold, *I will* stand before thee there upon the rock in Horeb." It was not the Father who made Himself manifest by some visible sign, but the Son, as St Paul says, " Christ." We now see that there was nothing incidental in the fact that this rock was smitten at the commencement and close of Israel's journeyings. It shews that the Angel of the Covenant was with them all the way that they went, from the beginning to the end. And the more, brethren, we contemplate this rock, the more beautiful it will appear as a type of Christ. We may imagine a believing Israelite in that hour of trial and of murmuring, saying within himself, " This is a time of trouble, but the God of our fathers has not forsaken us, and will never forsake us. He can supply our wants by a thousand channels. Even that hard rock can be made to 'yield water.'" This would be the language of faith; but it was not the language of Israel. They would, and did, look hopelessly around, and doubtless felt that the hard, dry rock would be the very last thing of all to yield water. And such, brethren, are the thoughts of the world concerning Christ. What is He to it practically, but a mere name? a dry, hard rock? Does it think of happiness or of rest? It goes elsewhere to find it. Any cistern, however broken, seems to promise more to the unrenewed heart than Christ does. Nay, more; let the heart be quickened—let it be taught by the Spirit to feel its many wants. It will struggle against its besetting sin—it will try to give up the world; but will it go straight to the Rock? will it say at once, "There is the water of life?" Oh no! It will depend at first upon its own efforts and resolutions. It will hope to turn away God's displeasure by its own doings and earnestness. By degrees the emptiness and hollowness of all that men can do will be felt. Then the thought of Christ will dawn upon the soul. The eye will begin to turn towards the Rock. Jesus Christ, brethren, is not the heart's *first* thought, but the *last*. But when He is once found, then He is all,—Alpha and Omega, beginning and end, first and last. Then there is nothing like that Rock. The language of the heart is, "Yea doubtless, and I count all things but loss for the excellency of the knowledge of Christ Jesus."

But this rock was a *smitten* rock, and it was not until it *was smitten* that it yielded water to the Israelites. And to what, brethren, does this point, but to Him who was "smitten of God," even His Father? as it is written, (Zech. xiii. 7,) "Awake, O sword, against my shepherd, and against the man that is my fellow, saith the Lord of hosts: smite the shepherd, and the sheep shall be scattered: and I will turn my hand against the little ones." And again, (Isa. liii. 10,) "Yet it pleased the Lord to bruise him." *Smitten* Jesus was by the Father whom He loved, and who loved Him with an infinite love, for our sakes and for our sins,—"He was bruised for our iniquities." *Smitten* He was by His own, whom He came to redeem:

smitten in His *spirit* by deep ingratitude, by bitter taunts, by the weight of our sins ; *smitten* in His *body* by the power of suffering, when His sweat was as it were great drops of blood, by the crown of thorns, in His hands and feet by the lacerating nails, in his side by the sharp spear. Thus our Rock was *cleft*. From all eternity it was decreed that Jesus should be the depository of all grace,—the *Rock* on which the Church should be built,— the *Rock* which should cast its sheltering shadow in a weary land,—the *Rock* which should supply living water in the wilderness. But it was not until the rock was *smitten* that the waters of life streamed forth, to bear, like Ezekiel's river, life and refreshment whithersoever they went. But the smitten rock may typify something more than this,—not merely what was accomplished in Jesus once for all—the agony, the crown of thorns, and the cross,—but also what must be and is continually taking place. It may shew not only what God has done, and Jesus has suffered, but also what each individual soul *must* do in order to drink the waters of life. When Moses *smote* the rock with his rod, it was an act of *faith* and obedience. He did it because it was commanded. He did it in a spirit of thankful expectation. Our Rock is ever near. It is full of the waters of life ; but it will only *yield* those waters when struck by the rod of faith. Take, then, brethren, your stand close by the Rock ; never let your encampment be far away from it. Take the rod of faith—ready, simple, childlike faith—smite day by day, and hour by hour, and the waters of life shall never fail.

Are we speaking now to some wearied and distracted heart—to one who has long had an unconscious thirst within, and has tried to satisfy it at cisterns which can hold no water ? You have looked everywhere, it may be, but to the true Rock. The world has said, "Seek it in me." You sought it, but you found it not. Self cried aloud, "Seek it in me." But it led you into a dry land where there was no water. The voice of human love, of domestic affection reached your ear, and the hope revived within you, "Here my thirst can be satisfied." But *this* cistern has turned out to be a broken one, like the rest. And now another voice, unheard before, begins to reach your ear,—the voice of our Rock, which you have forsaken and overlooked. What says it? "If any man thirst, let him come unto me and drink." What a beautiful invitation. It speaks, too, the language of gentle rebuke,— "If thou knewest the gift of God, thou wouldest have asked of him, and he would have given thee living water." Yes, if thou *knewest* the gift of God, thou wouldest not have gone elsewhere to broken cisterns. With the rod of faith in thy hand, thou wouldest have smitten the Rock of Ages, and thy thirst would have been satisfied. For Jesus says, "Whosoever drinketh of the water that I shall give him shall never thirst; but the water that I shall give him shall be in him a well of water springing up unto everlasting life."

Brethren, let it suffice us to have gone so often in childhood and in youth to broken cisterns. Henceforth let us abide by the Rock, which ever follows us, and "drink, yea, drink abundantly."

JEHOVAH-NISSI
(or, Israel's Victory Over Amalek)

Exodus 17:15

" And Moses built an altar, and called the name of it Jehovah-nissi."

Two trials came upon Israel at Rephidim. The one was a want of water, the other was an unexpected conflict. We considered the first in our last sermon. The second is the subject for to-day.

It will naturally fall into two parts. First, Israel's enemy; and, secondly, The manner in which he was overcome.

And first, we may observe that such an attack as this must have been quite unexpected by the Israelites in the wilderness. It was a new trial. True it is that it bore some resemblance to the opposition which they encountered, and the fears which they felt in Egypt. And it must have forcibly reminded them of the past, and have reawakened old feelings. And yet it was in a sense new and unexpected. On that glorious day when they saw the power of Egypt broken, and their enemies destroyed by the power of God, they doubtless thought, " There is the end of our conflict with men. No more opposition awaits us now." Least of all could they expect this in the wilderness. At first, such thoughts seemed to be fulfilled. Their trials arose from want of water and of bread. But now a new era in their destiny commenced. Old conflicts reappeared. They were to learn that though they had been redeemed with a mighty hand, and an out-stretched arm—though they were Jehovah's covenant people—though they had been miraculously preserved again and again—their wilderness-life would be one of opposition. They must expect conflicts as well as trials.

You will not fail, brethren, to see at once what an interesting type Israel is in this respect of the Christian life and experience. Egypt, it has been remarked more than once, was a type of the old man. Of what, then, was Amalek a type? Of the old man also; but with this difference, Egypt is a type of the old man as *dominant* and overpowering the new. Amalek is a type of the old man in its *unavailing opposition* to the new. In other words, Egypt represents the old man before it is crucified. Amalek represents it after redemption has been experienced by the blood of Jesus, and the influence of the Spirit of God. Now, when the young Christian first finds Jesus, and after saying with the apostle, " O wretched man that I am ! who shall deliver me from the body of this death ?" can add, "I thank God through Jesus Christ," he finds peace. He is a new creature—old things have passed away—all things have become new—sinful habits are broken—old tastes are gone—new desires and hopes fill the soul. Where, then, is the old man ? The young Christian could answer, " It is gone, and gone for ever. I shall no more feel its power—no more be conscious of its workings. Trials I expect to have, for we must through much tribulation enter into the kingdom of heaven ; but my enemy, my great enemy, is buried as in the Red Sea." For a little time these anticipations *seem* to be fulfilled. His feelings are all bright, his hopes rise high, and there is much conscious love to the Saviour. But in reality the old man, though crucified, is not wholly extinct—though

weakened, is not unable to struggle again—and after a
while it does renew the conflict. "The flesh lusteth
against the Spirit." Egypt reappears as Amalek. It is a
sad disappointment. A new era in the spiritual life then
sets in—the era of conflict. The advance is more difficult, and seems to be more slow, and hope is often over-
clouded by fears. Should this be the present experience
of any one here, it may be a consolation to you to know
that though this conflict is all *new* to you, and accompanied with feelings of disappointment, yet it is the *appointed* path—along it the footsteps of the flock all lie.
"There hath no temptation taken you but such as is common to man: but God is faithful, who will not suffer you
to be tempted above that ye are able; but will with the
temptation also make a way to escape, that ye may be
able to bear it," (1 Cor. x. 13.) Israel could not enter the
land of promise without overcoming Amalek; and you
cannot enter heaven without again and again overcoming
the old man in you. But this conflict was not only *unexpected* in itself, but it came from an unexpected *quarter*.
If you refer to Gen. xxxvi. 12, you will see that Amalek,
the father of this people, was the son of Eliphaz, and the
grandson of Esau. In the 16th verse he is called "Duke
Amalek." The relationship, therefore, between Israel
and Amalek was a very close relationship, and unity and
love ought to have existed between them. But the old
and reckless enmity of Esau against his brother Jacob descended to his posterity, and Edom and Amalek are always
represented in Scripture as Israel's irreconcileable enemies.
Thus, to quote one passage out of very many, (Amos i.
11,) "Thus saith the Lord; For three transgressions of
Edom, and for four, I will not turn away the punishment
thereof; because he did pursue his brother with the sword,

and did cast off all pity, and his anger did tear perpetually, and he kept his wrath for ever: but I will send a
fire upon Teman, which shall devour the palaces of Bozrah." It was at Rephidim that this unnatural opposition on the part of Amalek first shewed itself, and on
this account it was reckoned as the first among the heathen, as we read, Num. xxiv. 20, "And when he looked
on Amalek, he took up his parable, and said, Amalek was
the first of the nations; but his latter end shall be that
he perish for ever." On this account it was consigned to
complete destruction, as we read, ver. 14 of our chapter,
"I will utterly put out the remembrance of Amalek from
under heaven;" and again, ver. 16, "Because the Lord
hath sworn that the Lord will have war with Amalek
from generation to generation." Such opposition must,
we think, have been altogether unexpected from *such a
quarter*. Israel would have looked for an opponent anywhere but in Amalek.

And thus, also, brethren, in the Christian life, we often
meet with enemies where we do not expect to find them.
As a rule, we may say that the indulged sins of the unrenewed man are the snares and temptations of the renewed
man. From them we may fully *expect* opposition and
conflict. Still these will not be our *only* dangers. As
we advance, new and more hidden evils of our hearts will
come to light. We may have to combat with some new
form of selfishness which we have not discovered yet.
Different circumstances may bring it out to view. And
we may feel quite as much surprise as Israel must have
felt when the Amalekites stepped out of their conceal-
ment at Rephidim. The heart, brethren, is a very deep
thing, and is not known at once. The more deeply we
are taught of God, and in His light see light, the more

we shall discover secret and unexpected evils within. But when we make these new discoveries, we ought not to be thrown into too deep consternation, or count it a strange thing—for even in Israel's history we see this foreshadow, and are thus prepared to expect it. But there is one more point that we may notice before we leave this head, —the difference between Israel's conflict in Egypt, and that which they had to sustain now. In Egypt their enemies came openly upon them. At Rephidim the Amalekites attacked them in a treacherous manner, as we learn from Deut. xxv. 17, 18, "Remember what Amalek did unto thee by the way, when ye were come forth out of Egypt ; how he met thee by the way, and *smote* the hindmost of thee, even all that were feeble behind thee, when thou wast faint and weary; and he feared not God." In Egypt the Israelites were completely passive. The command was, " Stand still and see the salvation of the Lord, which he will shew you to-day." " The Lord shall fight for you, and ye shall hold your peace." At Rephidim Moses said to Joshua, " Choose us out men, and go out, fight with Amalek." And if you turn, brethren, to the Christian life, you will find the same points of contrast there. The temptations of the unrenewed and worldly heart, like the attack of the Egyptians, are the more *open* and *daring*. The temptations of the sanctified heart are more subtle and refined ; like Amalek, they attack our *weak* points, and perhaps do not threaten us with entire destruction, but weaken us little by little. We must beware of refined temptations,—temptations to hard thoughts of God, to self-confidence, to want of love and courtesy towards others. The other point of contrast is nearly as evident. When God first quickens us by His Spirit, we are passive. Life is God's gift, and

must be *received*. We cannot do *living* acts before we
are made alive—cannot *walk* in the Spirit before we *live*
in the Spirit. In the *first* crucifixion, that of the old
man, we simply receive—we are passive. The power of
God effects it. But afterwards the Christian life is *active*,
as well as receptive. The graces wrought in us by the
Spirit must be exercised. The Christian armour must be
taken, put on, and vigorously used,—we must "fight the
good fight of faith," but all through the strength of
Christ and in the power which His Spirit gives.

But let us pass on to the second point,—the manner in
which Amalek was overcome. This was very striking.
Joshua, in accordance with the instruction of Moses, went
out and fought with Amalek. But Moses himself, with
Aaron and Hur, went up to the top of the hill, and there
held up his hand with the rod of God in it. We cannot
doubt what this meant. It signified prayer. We see
here, then, brethren, the beautiful combination of active
energy with prayer. One part of Israel is fighting, the
other is praying—both at the same time. Which, it
might be asked, gained the victory? Both contributed
towards it. To have prayed alone without fighting would
have been presumption. To have fought without prayer
would have been still worse; it would have been self-de-
pendence. It is easy, however, to see which contributed
most towards the victory. Which was felt to be the most
important? It was prayer. Moses himself, Israel's great
leader, did not go into the battle. He gave himself to
prayer. This of itself proves its great importance; but
besides this we are distinctly told (ver. 11) that "when
Moses held up his hand, Israel prevailed: and when he
let down his hand, Amalek prevailed." And if anything
else is wanted to shew it, you have it in this, that so

little comparatively is said of Joshua's part in the conflict, so much of Moses's. Prayer weakened the force of Amalek ; prayer gave power to Israel. The whole Bible is full of proofs of the *power* of prayer, but nothing can shew it more forcibly than the result of this conflict. "When Moses held up his hand, Israel prevailed : and when he let down his hand, Amalek prevailed." And what may we see here, but the Christian's privilege and duty ? His *privilege,* for in one point of view Joshua's force is a type of the Church militant. And of what is Moses a type, but of Him who is gone up to the right hand of God, there to make intercession for us? His uplifted hand bears no staff as Moses's hand did, but it bears something far more precious, even the marks of the crucifixion. Who knows the power of His prayers? Every victory gained, every difficulty removed, the first change of our hearts, all growth in grace, every advance in holiness, all consolation in suffering, all skill in conflict, all strength to overcome *may,* and *must,* be traced up to His intercessions. What words interpret so beautifully His unceasing act as these, "I have prayed for thee, that thy faith fail not ?" Are you, then, weary ? Yet you need not faint. In difficulties ? Yet you need not despair. Do you feel your weakness ? Yet you may go forth to meet the enemy. And why ? Because your Saviour intercedes for you—because His strength can, and will, be made perfect in your weakness.

But here, too, we see the Christian's *duty,* as well as privilege. It is to aim at the combination of a spirit of prayer with a spirit of energy. Labour we ought without weariness ; but it is prayer that moves the arm of God, and thus gives wonderful power to the feeblest instruments, wonderful hope to support under difficulty, wonderful perseverance to continue in well-doing, and wonderful success in efforts for God's glory; and thus St Paul, after describing the different parts of the Christian's armour, adds, (Eph. vi. 18,) "Praying always with all prayer and supplication in the Spirit, and watching thereunto with all perseverance and supplication for all saints." Whatever, then, brethren, we do, whether it appear to be something small, or it be something evidently great, let us go up to the mount, and lift up our hands to God. We cannot fight the good fight of faith, we cannot visit the poor, or comfort the afflicted aright, without a spirit of prayer; for we are not sufficient to think even a good thought of ourselves. All strength, all wisdom, all love, all gentleness, all true sympathy, come down from above, and are bestowed upon the praying heart. *Strength* is promised, (Isa. xl. 29,) "He giveth power to the faint; and to them that have no might he increaseth strength." *Wisdom* is promised, (James i. 5,) "If any of you lack wisdom, let him ask of God, that giveth to all men liberally, and upbraideth not; and it shall be given him." And these promises fulfilled, the praying heart becomes, like "Naphtali, satisfied with favour, and full with the blessing of the Lord."

But though Moses prayed, the conflict lasted long; though Israel prevailed, the victory was not gained at once. The consequence was that "Moses's hands became heavy," and the battle might still have been lost, had not Aaron and Hur stayed up his weary hands, and kept them steady until the going down of the sun.

There are times, brethren, when those whose faith is usually strong and example bright are conscious of weariness. Their hands grow heavy. Job was far in advance of his friends in the divine life, yet the pressure of long-continued trial seemed to place him below them, though in reality it did not. Moses, the great leader of Israel, was far stronger in faith, and more steadfast in temptation than Aaron, yet now *his* hands are weary; and Aaron and Hur, the one on the one side, and the other on the other side, can and do stay them up. In ordinary cases, it is the strong members of Christ's body who encourage the weak, and help them by their example and their prayers to pursue, though faint; but there are times of weakness and of weariness when the youngest Christian, even a little child, may stay up the heavy hands of the advanced believer. If we realized more, dear brethren, our union with Christ, and with each other in Him, should we not desire more fervently to strengthen each other's hearts, especially in hours of sorrow and of weakness? We know the effect of co-operation, how the hopefulness of one mind will help to banish the despondency of another. The strength and perseverance of *one will* will carry forward the weak and the faltering. But no less mutual assistance may be rendered each other by the members of Christ's body in *prayer*—in *prayer*, that highest of privileges, and yet sometimes most difficult of duties. What, brethren, can be a greater blessing than to be the means of leading some discouraged brother or sister in Christ to the throne of grace in a more hopeful and expectant spirit? It is the Spirit of God alone that can accomplish this—can strengthen faith, animate hope, and deepen love; but the Spirit produces these fruits through the instrumentality of sympathy and love in the members of Christ's body, and sustains our hands by leading some Aaron and Hur to place their hands underneath us.

By the going down of the sun the victory was gained.

" Joshua discomfited Amalek ; " and Moses, full of thankfulness to God for the mighty help granted to his people, built " an altar," both to render thanks and also for a memorial, "and called it 'Jehovah-nissi'—'Jehovah my banner.'" This name evidently had reference to the past and to the future. Israel had just won its first victory in God's strength; but Amalek, though discomfited, was not utterly destroyed ; and, as it says, (ver. 16,) that " the Lord had sworn that the Lord will have war with Amalek from generation to generation," it is clear that the people of God had many more conflicts before them. But God had manifested Himself to Israel in a new character in this first conflict,—as their *banner ;* and when they looked forward to a conflict which was to last " from generation to generation," this was their hope and consolation, that "Jehovah would be in every conflict " what He had just proved Himself to be. After each they would be able to raise an altar with the same beautiful inscription, " Jehovah-nissi " —" The Lord my banner." And we, too, brethren, if we are Christ's, have entered on a conflict which will never altogether cease until we are landed in glory. The " old nature" within us may be weakened by many victories, and kept down by the power of the Spirit of God ; but so long as we are in the body the "flesh will lust against the spirit." Amalek will vex Israel. What, then, is our consolation ? Oh, it is this, that Jehovah is our banner. We may say with the Psalmist, (Ps. lx. 4,) " Thou hast given a banner to them that feared thee, that it may be displayed because of the truth." We may say with the Church, (Song of Sol. ii. 4,) " His banner over me was love." We may take this as our motto before conflict, in conflict, and after conflict, — " Jehovah-nissi " — " The Lord my banner ! "

THE GIVING OF THE LAW
(A Type of Pentecost)

Exodus 19:4-6

" Ye have seen what I did unto the Egyptians, and how I bare you
on eagles' wings, and brought you unto myself. Now therefore,
if ye will obey my voice indeed, and keep my covenant, then ye
shall be a peculiar treasure unto me above all people : for all the
earth is mine : and ye shall be unto me a kingdom of priests, and
an holy nation."

WERE it, brethren, our purpose to enter fully into the
history of the Israelites, we should not have omitted the
meeting between Jethro and Moses, recorded in the former
chapter, full as it is of interesting lessons ; nor should we
fail to dwell on the details of the ceremonial law, which
were so important for Israel, and, in many respects, such
beautiful types of Christ. But we are engaged, you will
remember, in viewing Israel's history, under *one special
aspect*, as typical of the Christian life ; and therefore it is
not every event in their history, or every feature of the
ceremonial law, that we are called upon to notice.

Omitting, therefore, the 18th chapter altogether, we
proceed this morning to contemplate the arrival of the
Israelites at that station which was the most important
to them of any, and to consider the greatest of all the
events of their history,—the giving of the law on Mount
Sinai. When Moses was first called to bring forth Israel
out of Egypt, Jehovah said to him, (Exod. iii. 12,) " Cer-

tainly I will be with thee; and this shall be a token unto thee, that I have sent thee: When thou hast brought forth the people out of Egypt, ye shall *serve* God upon this mountain." Whereas then, as we have already seen, the characteristic of other stations now passed was on *God's part* the supply of Israel's temporal wants, and on *Israel's part, murmurings,*—the characteristic of this station was on God's part the gift of the *moral* law, the bringing of His people into a solemn and conscious covenant with Himself; and on *their part, service,*—"Ye shall *serve* God upon this mountain." Sinai was, so to speak, Israel's first and great temple, where God manifested Himself to His people, and they consecrated themselves in works, if not in heart, to Him; and with this promise made to Moses, the retrospective words of our text beautifully agree. "Ye have seen," said the Lord, "what I did to the Egyptians"—how I overthrew and destroyed them,—"and how I bare you on eagles' wings"—carried you through all temptations, and over all difficulties—and, what is added? —carefully observe the words—"and brought you to myself." Here then, at Sinai, Israel was brought into special nearness to Jehovah, into the bonds of the covenant, —"brought to Himself." At the publication of the law Israel *met* God, as we read, (ver. 17,) "And Moses brought forth the people out of the camp to meet with God." And all the accompaniments of that meeting rendered it very solemn and impressive. The season of previous preparation, (ver. 10,) "And the Lord said unto Moses, Go unto the people, and sanctify them to-day and to-morrow, and let the people wash their clothes, and be ready against the third day: for the third day the Lord will come down in the sight of all the people upon Mount Sinai." The scene itself, which must have been one of surpassing grandeur, the barren mountains rising up from the surrounding wilderness, and then the thunders and lightnings, the thick cloud upon the mount, and the voice of the trumpet, which shewed that Jehovah was the Lord of hosts, and explains what so many other passages of Scripture allude to—the presence of angels at the giving of the law—as, for example, (Ps. lxviii. 17,) "The chariots of God are twenty thousand, even thousands of angels : the Lord is among them, as in Sinai, in the holy place." And in the New Testament, (Acts vii. 53,) "Who have received the law by the disposition of angels, and have not kept it ; " so also, (Gal. iii. 19,) "Wherefore then serveth the law ? It was added because of transgressions, till the seed should come to whom the promise was made; and it was *ordained by angels* in the hand of a mediator." And once more we find the apostle deducing an argument from this fact for the greater glory of the gospel, and therefore the greater danger of its rejection, (Heb. ii. 2, 3,) "For if the word *spoken by angels* was steadfast, and every transgression and disobedience received a just recompense of reward, how shall we escape, if we neglect so great salvation ; which at the first began to be spoken by the Lord, and was confirmed unto us by them that heard him." And then the bounds set to the mount must have filled them with reverential awe, (ver. 12,) "And thou shalt set bounds unto the people round about, saying, Take heed to yourselves, that ye go not up into the mount, or touch the border of it : whosoever toucheth the mount shall be surely put to death ; " and, (ver. 21,) " Go down, charge the people, lest they break through unto the Lord to gaze, and many of them perish." And the words of the law itself, the terms of the covenant, deepened the solemnity of this great meeting. The com-

mandments were all moral, even the fourth having a
moral element in it, and must every one of them have
been responded to by every conscience. They reversed
man's order. The world recognises the importance of the
relationship between man and man, and hopes that the
performance of relative duties will knit up our broken
relationship to God, and secure our entrance into heaven.
But this law laid down Israel's relationship to God as the
first and most important of all relationships, the foundation on which every other rests, and shewed that it is
only when we are restored to God that we can be restored
to each other ; and this law is spiritual as well as *moral*.
It affects the heart, its state and its motives, as well as
the outward life.

It is beside our purpose, brethren, to comment upon
its separate commandments ; but it bears directly upon it
to remark that when it was spoken by the voice of God,
it was also written on two tables of stone, as we read,
(Exod. xxxii. 15, 16,) " The tables were written on both their
sides ; on the one side and on the other were they written. And the tables were the work of God, and the writing was the writing of God, graven upon the tables."
Now, this writing proved two things. It shewed the condescension of God towards Israel. He knew that the
impressions of this solemn meeting would soon pass away
from their hearts and memories, and if left to the uncertainty of mere tradition, the law would vanish altogether.
It was therefore *written,* written on tables of stone, that
its testimony might never pass away. But this also
proved its imperfection ; not its imperfection in itself,
or as a means of preparation for the gospel, but that it
was not, and could not be, a final dispensation. It was
written on tables of stone, but not on the fleshly tables

of Israel's heart. Though "holy, just, and good"—though perfect in itself, it could not bring Israel once and for ever to God. It commanded, but did not transplant itself into their hearts.

But of what was Sinai and the giving of the law a type? Of the day of Pentecost, and of the outpouring of the Holy Spirit, whereby the work of the law was and is written upon the hearts of believers. There is more than one proof of this.

And, first, it is interesting to notice that agreement between the two events in point of time. We are told (ver. 1) that it was in the *third month* that the children of Israel came into the wilderness of Sinai, and, according to a Jewish tradition, which in all probability is correct, it was on the sixth day of that month that the law was given, and, if so, it must have been the fiftieth day after the day of the Passover ; and, secondly, we cannot fail to be reminded of the promises of that new covenant predicted by the prophet Jeremiah, and quoted by St Paul, Heb. viii. 10, and which he calls (ver. 6) "a better covenant, established on better promises." And what was the special promise of that covenant, connected in its nature with the giving of the law, and yet far higher and better. It was the promise of the illumination of the mind, "I will put my laws into their mind," and the transfer of the law into the heart, "and write them in their hearts ; " and this illumination and transfer is effected by the influence of that Spirit which was first poured out in His fulness on the day of Pentecost, and under whose dispensation we now at this moment live. Thus St Paul says, (2 Cor. iii. 2, 3,) "Ye are our epistle written in our hearts, known and read of all men ; forasmuch as ye are manifestly declared to be the epistle of

Christ ministered by us, written not with ink, but with
the Spirit of the living God; not in tables of stone, but
in the fleshly tables of the heart." How great, brethren,
is the gift which was typified by Sinai!—so great that
he that is least in the kingdom of God is greater than
John the Baptist; so great that whereas Israel, though
a kingdom of priests, was obliged to teach every man his
neighbour, and every man his brother, saying, Know the
Lord—under this covenant the promise is, All shall know
me, from the least to the greatest. And all this arises
from the *effective* teaching of the Holy Spirit. At Sinai
a perfect rule was given; but our darkened understandings and corrupted hearts require more than a perfect
rule of obedience. We want also the *spirit* of obedience.
We require not only an object to be placed before us,
but the eye to be created which shall discern the object;
not only the pattern to be given according to which we
must be moulded, but the power to be exercised which
shall mould us according to that pattern.

You see, then, brethren, what this great event in Israel's
history typifies in the history of the Christian Church,
and what it typifies in the life of each individual Christian. In the one, the day of Pentecost; in the other, the
writing of the law of God upon the heart. We may as-
sume that these Israelites had been circumcised, and had
thus been brought into covenant with God in their infancy—for circumcision was the sign of that covenant;
yet at Sinai we find them subsequently brought into a
natural and *conscious* covenant with their God. And
thus, brethren, have we also been brought into covenant
with God in our infancy by a better sacrament than that
of circumcision; and yet now that our consciousness is
developed, we ought consciously to lay hold, through the

influence of the Holy Spirit, of the precious promises of our covenant, and consciously to experience the gradual transcribing of the law upon our hearts. Do we often feel that our comprehension of the things of God is dull and weak? The promises of God encourage us to pray that the "eyes of our understanding may be enlightened," not once for all only, but day by day, that we "may know what is the hope of His calling, and what the riches of the glory of His inheritance in the saints, and what is the exceeding greatness of His power to us-ward who believe." Do we often feel that our hearts are hard, and our affections cold and earthly? The promises of the covenant encourage us to pray that our hearts may be renewed, and that the Spirit of God may transcribe His law in clearer, deeper characters there, and may add one feature after another of the beautiful image of Jesus.

This, then, brethren, is the great point to which Sinai and its law direct our thoughts; but there are other points which are instructive, and chiefly by way of contrast. The need which the law awakened, the gospel has satisfied; and, to use the apostle's words, " What the law could not do, in that it was weak through the flesh, God sending his own Son in the likeness of sinful flesh, and for sin, condemned sin in the flesh; that the righteousness of the law might be fulfilled in us, who walk not after the flesh, but after the Spirit." Let us notice a few of these points :—

And, first, remark that although our text speaks of Israel being brought to God, "brought to Myself," yet even when brought near, they were, in many respects, left at a distance from God. Their nearness was only such compared with what it had been, not with what it might be. The regulations respecting the Mount—the bounds set to it, prove this. What does it all shew, but that Israel, though nearest of all nations, was still kept at a distance, as a servant, and not yet brought near as a child? The tendency of all these regulations was evidently to check the curiosity of undisciplined hearts, and to produce reverential awe. And what, brethren, does the gospel do? It brings us *near* to God—it places no bounds around His presence, but encourages us to draw nigh to Him. "For through him," says St Paul, (Eph. ii. 18,) "we both have access by one Spirit unto the Father." "Ye are not come," he says, (Heb. xii. 18–24,) "unto the mount that might be touched, and that burned with fire, nor unto blackness, and darkness, and tempest, and the sound of a trumpet, and the voice of words ; which voice they that heard entreated that the word should not be spoken to them any more : (for they could not endure that which was commanded, And if so much as a beast touch the mountain, it shall be stoned, or thrust through with a dart : and so terrible was the sight, that Moses said, I exceedingly fear and quake.) But ye are come unto Mount Sion, and unto the city of the living God, the heavenly Jerusalem, and to an innumerable company of angels, to the general assembly and church of the first-born, which are written in heaven, and to God the Judge of all, and to the spirits of just men made perfect, and to Jesus the Mediator of the new covenant, and to the blood of sprinkling, that speaketh better things than that of Abel."

How strikingly do the words of Jesus spoken to His disciples, when contrasted with the regulations respecting the Mount, shew the difference between the two dispensations, and the greater *nearness* into which the true Christian is brought now,—(John xv. 15,) " Henceforth I call you not servants; for the servant knoweth not what his lord doeth: but I have called you friends; for all things that I have heard of my Father I have made known unto you;" and so again, St Paul says, (Rom. viii. 15,) "For ye have not received the spirit of bondage again to fear; but ye have received the Spirit of adoption, whereby we cry, Abba, Father." Reverence, brethren, the deepest reverence, we ought to feel now; but it is reverential love and confidence that the promises of the New Testament produce, and not the trembling awe of Sinai. We cannot draw too near to God. Those who live nearest to Him may live nearer still. Those who enjoy the deepest communion with Jesus may know still more of it, and be more transformed into the same image. Again, observe another deep want, which all the solemnities of the law, its words, and its sanction created, and which found its utterance in their petition to Moses, (chap. xx. 19,) "Speak thou with us, and we will hear; but let not God speak with us, lest we die." It was the want of a Mediator—of a "daysman who should lay his hand upon them both." The law had already taught them to feel the contrast between God's character and their own—His exalted holiness and majesty, and their own sinfulness, although they had "sanctified themselves;" and whatsoever heart feels this contrast must also feel the necessity of a Mediator. What a beautiful adaptation, then, there is in Jesus to all our need! He is the one and only Mediator between God and man; not a temporary mediator, as Moses, but one who will never lay down His office until the "number of the elect is accomplished," and His Church presented, "without spot or wrinkle, or any such thing, unto the Father;" not an imperfect mediator, but Himself God and man, bearing the nature of both parties be-

tween whom He mediates. Brethren, we may and ought
to go to Jesus with the language of Israel, " Speak thou
with us ;" but ought we to add, " Let not God speak
with us, lest we die ?" Oh no. These words seem to
indicate a sort of contrast between God and the mediator. But there is no contrast between the Father and *our*
Mediator. When we draw near to God through His blood
and intercession, then we can listen to the Father's voice,
and be conscious of the Father's love. " At that day,"
said Jesus to His disciples, (John xvi. 26, 27,) " ye shall
ask in my name : and I say not unto you, that I will pray
the Father for you : for the *Father himself loveth* you,
because ye have loved me, and have believed that I came
out from God." In Christ, brethren, we are reconciled
to God, are brought near to Him, are carried into the
fulness of His love, and therefore can listen to His voice
and live, yea, live because we listen to His voice.

But there is yet one more point connected with this
feeling which we may notice. God said to Israel, (chap.
xx. 22,) " Ye have seen that I have *talked with you* from
heaven." But in order that He might talk with them
again, and that there might be constant communion between Him and them, something more than the mediation of Moses was needed. They were not only in themselves at a *distance* from God, which required mediation,
but they were guilty, and therefore required sacrifices ;
hence God commanded them (ver. 24) to make " an altar
of earth, and to sacrifice thereon burnt-offerings and peace-
offerings," and then He added the beautiful promise, " In
all places where I record my name I will come unto thee,
and I will bless thee." And here, again, we are pointed
to Jesus, the one great and all-sufficient Sacrifice, as well
as Mediator of the New Covenant. As in Him we can

listen to the voice of God and live, and know that the distance between God and us is removed, so also in Him the guilt of our sins is removed—the purged conscience is set at rest—peace is restored to the heart. In Him, as Sacrifice and Mediator, the Father fulfils the promise, " I will come unto thee, and I will bless thee."

We cannot conclude without the expression of the earnest wish and prayer that wheresoever we are we may depend with more simple faith upon the one great Sacrifice, may know more of the glory of our one great Mediator, may have deeper communion with the Father in Him, and may seek increasing measures of that Spirit who will write the law in its great principles on our hearts, and enable us to exemplify it in our lives, and so, following Him who was obedient to the law for our sakes, to glorify God the Father, Son, and the Holy Ghost, to whom, &c.

THE GOLDEN CALF

Exodus 32:1

"And when the people saw that Moses delayed to come down out of the mount, the people gathered themselves together unto Aaron, and said unto him, Up, make us gods, which shall go before us; for as for this Moses, the man that brought us up out of the land of Egypt, we wot not what is become of him."

WE left Israel, you will remember, brethren, at the foot of Sinai, trembling at the presence of God, and exclaiming, with apparent earnestness and sincerity, "All that the Lord hath spoken will we do." But, alas! their words were soon forgotten—their resolution soon passed away. Moses was afterwards summoned up into the mount, as we read Exod. xxiv. 12, "And the Lord said unto Moses, Come up to me into the mount, and be there: and I will give thee tables of stone, and a law, and commandments which I have written; that thou mayest teach them." "And Moses," we are told, (ver. 18,) "went into the midst of the cloud, and gat him up into the mount: and Moses was in the mount forty days and forty nights." What a hallowed season of communion with God must that have been to Moses! How different from the toils and anxieties of his usual life! His mind was instructed by what he saw and heard in that mount, his affections deepened, and his will still more moulded and strengthened; his whole being braced for the new difficulties and trials which he had to encounter. But whilst he was

engaged in this sacred service, the people below grew
impatient. Whether it was that they thought some evil
had befallen him, or that they wished to proceed on their
journey at once, without any further delay, we are not
told. "We wot not," they said, "what is become of him."
But however this be, Moses's delay upon the mount not
only shewed their impatience, but brought out the idolatry
of their hearts. "Up," they said to Aaron, "make us
gods, which shall go before us." There is something very
awful in this idolatry; yet it is quite evident that they
were idolaters before in heart, foolishly and sinfully leaning upon an arm of flesh. You will observe how completely they seem to have forgotten Him who had led, and
was leading them still, with a pillar of cloud, the symbol
of His own presence. They said, "This Moses, the man
that brought us up out of Egypt." Their first idolatry
was more refined and less glaring. The last was very
gross. But the point, brethren, to observe is, how very
close the connexion is between the two—how one, if outward circumstances permit, leads on to the other. We
marvel at the request, "Make us gods, to go before us;"
but the root of that request lay deeper,—it was the previous departure of their hearts from their covenant God,
and their leaning too much on him who was but an instrument in God's hands. The human heart is prone to
idolatry. When it is surrounded by outward darkness, and
its way is not hedged up, it often falls into outward and
palpable idolatry; when surrounded by light, its idolatry
is of a more hidden and refined kind. This latter, brethren,
is our danger. We may almost shudder at the request,
"Make us gods, to go before us;" and yet we may trust
too much in the guidance and judgment of some beloved
friend who has been a help to us. The graces which we

admire in some fellow-Christian may be the means of
leading us nearer to God, and of making us confide more
in His guidance; and then it is well. But they may be
made by our sinful hearts a shadow, as Moses was to
Israel, and intercept the rays of light which should warm
and enlighten us. And what will be the consequence of
this spirit, if not discerned and overcome? In one case it
will lead to a murmuring and discontented spirit; in another to something worse, perhaps the entire shipwreck of
faith and a good conscience. Brethren, God is jealous;
let us be jealous over the affections of our hearts, the
thoughts of our minds, and the words of our lips, that we
never in word or thought give that glory to another which
belongs to Jehovah, and Him alone. But some one, on
reading the words of our text, may be disposed to ask,—
Is it possible that the Israelites could be so debased as to
suppose that gods made with their own hands could go
before them and guide them? We do not think that they
intended to leave Jehovah altogether out of account, or
that they could mean that the golden calf, just now made,
had *really* brought them up out of Egypt; for, remark
the words of Aaron, (ver. 5,) "And Aaron made proclamation, and said, To-morrow is a feast to the *Lord*,"—to
the *Lord*, not to their new gods, but to the *Lord*. It is
much more likely that they regarded the golden calf as
representing Jehovah. Moses had been Jehovah's *representative* to them before; and now, in their impatience
and sinful idolatry, they had chosen another and a forbidden *representative*,—a golden calf. And if they viewed
it as *representing* Jehovah, we can better understand how
they could say, "These be thy gods, O Israel, which
brought thee up out of the land of Egypt." And this,
brethren, is the view which all intelligent idolaters have

ever taken of their own idols. Ask the intelligent member of the Church of Rome how he can worship an image or a picture. He will answer at once,—We do not worship it; we worship Him whom it represents. The image or picture which we can see, serves to fix our thoughts on that which we cannot see. But pass away, brethren, from the member of a fallen church to an intelligent heathen, and ask a Cicero of ancient Rome, or an educated Hindu of modern India, the same question, and you will get precisely the same answer. Does, then, this answer clear the Hindu of the sin of idolatry? or could Aaron and backsliding Israel have boldly denied their idolatry, because they did not worship the golden calf *itself*, but God *through* it? Oh no. Of the heathen, St Paul says, (Rom. i. 23,) "And changed the glory of the uncorruptible God into an image made like to corruptible man;" and, (ver. 25,) "Who changed the truth of God into a lie, and worshipped and served the creature more than the Creator, who is blessed for ever." And how did He who had given the command, "Thou shalt not make unto thee any graven image, or any likeness of any thing that is in heaven above, or that is in the earth beneath, or that is in the water under the earth: thou shalt not bow down thyself to them, nor serve them; for I am a jealous God"— how did He view Israel's sin? Did He recognise any such distinctions? No, brethren. He said to Moses, (ver. 7, 8,) "Thy people have corrupted themselves: they have turned aside quickly out of the way which I commanded them: they have made them a molten calf, and have worshipped it, and have sacrificed thereunto."

Never then, brethren, let the Romanist argument, so often dinned into our ears, deceive any of you as to the real sin of idolatry. If his argument justifies his practice, it also justifies the heathen ; and thus justifying too much, justifies nothing. God is a jealous God; and His jealousy requires in *individuals* the entire consecration of the undivided heart to Him, and in His Church *purity* and simplicity of worship, as the expression of purified and simple hearts.

It is very painful to see how quickly Aaron yielded to the sinful request of the people, " Make us gods, which shall go before us." He had been greatly honoured of God. He was led by the Spirit of God to meet his brother Moses when he was on his way to Egypt to become the leader of the Israelites. On account of his gift of eloquence, he was made Moses's spokesman, and was present at all his interviews with Pharaoh and with the elders of the people. He was one of those who held up Moses's hands in prayer when Israel and Amalek were engaged in conflict ; and at this very time God was saying to Moses on the mount, (chap. xxviii. 1, 2,) "Take thou unto thee Aaron thy brother, and his sons with him, from among the children of Israel, that he may minister unto me in the priest's office, even Aaron, Nadab and Abihu, Eleazar and Ithamar, Aaron's sons. And thou shalt make holy garments for Aaron thy brother for glory and for beauty." On his heart was to be the breastplate of judgment, (ver. 29,)—" And Aaron shall bear the names of the children of Israel in the breastplate of judgment upon his heart, when he goeth in unto the holy place, for a memorial before the Lord continually." On his forehead was to be the mitre, bearing a plate of pure gold with this inscription, " Holiness to the Lord." It is, brethren, when we look at his conduct by the side of his privileges and gifts bestowed upon him, and in the light of God's gracious thoughts concerning him, that we see how sinful and unworthy it was. But what was his sin? A wavering spirit arising from fear of the people. When Moses descended from the mount and said to Aaron, (chap. xxxii. 21,) "What did this people unto thee, that thou hast brought so great a sin upon them? Aaron said, Let not the anger of my lord wax hot: thou knowest the people, that they are set on mischief." In a moment of weakness he yielded to the pressure of temptation, and seemed anxious to conceal his fear in his readiness to fulfil their desire. He suggested what they should do: "Break off the golden ear-rings which are in the ears of your wives, of your sons, and of your daughters, and bring them unto me." He built an altar before the golden calf which he had fashioned with his own hands. Oh, had he been faithful and firm, might he not have turned back the people from their sinful purpose? We know the power of eloquence; and how often an infuriated mob has been quieted, and diverted from some dreadful purpose, by words of truth and power! Aaron was gifted with eloquence; but the fear of man palsied his heart, and made *him*, who ought to have stemmed the torrent of their corruption, the instrument of their sin. What a warning this, brethren, against a vacillating spirit! How it shews that where the fear of man prevails, faithfulness to God must be wanting! And then what will the highest and most commanding natural gifts avail? Nothing. It is easy to see what Aaron ought to have been and done. Yet, are our hearts unlike his? If we have been thrown either with relations or strangers to whom the cross of Christ has been foolishness, have we, with gentle firmness without ostentation, confessed Christ? Have we never been silent when we ought to have spoken, or taken part in conversation when we ought to have been silent? And

how much more resemblance may there be between ourselves and Aaron than we *suppose,* simply because our
hearts have not yet been placed in circumstances which
could thoroughly sift them !

The character of Moses stands out in striking contrast
to that of his brother. He had held deep communion
with God on the mount ; and whether we view his feelings
before his descent from it, or his conduct afterwards, we
cannot but see the hallowed and sanctifying effects of that
communion. We may trace it in his two beautiful intercessory prayers, and in his conduct and mode of dealing
with the children of Israel between the two. Look at his
first prayer recorded in the 11th and two following verses.
It was occasioned by the solemn words of Jehovah in 9th
and 10th verses : " I have seen this people, and, behold, it
is a stiffnecked people : now therefore let me alone, that
my wrath may wax hot against them, and that I may
consume them : and I will make of thee a great nation."
Had these words fallen on an ambitious or selfish heart,
or one that was not tenderly compassionate, no intercessory prayer would have followed. But Moses sought not
his own things, but the glory of God ; and deeply as the
Israelites tried his spirit, still he loved them. Hence it
was that he took no notice of the words which would have
attracted all the notice of many a heart, " I will make of
thee a great nation," and was only occupied in his prayer
with God, His glory, and His faithfulness. His *glory,* in
the argument, (ver. 12,) " Wherefore should the Egyptians
speak, and say, For mischief did he bring them out, to slay
them in the mountains, and to consume them from the
face of the earth ?"—and His faithfulness, in the earnest
petition, " Remember Abraham, Isaac, and Israel, thy servants, to whom thou swarest by thine own self, and saidst

unto them, I will multiply your seed as the stars of heaven, and all this land that I have spoken of will I give unto your seed, and they shall inherit it for ever." How clear it is that God, not self,—God's honour and the fulfilment of His promises, not his own personal aggrandisement,—occupied the first place in his heart. Dear brethren, it is at this that we ought to aim. It is a long and difficult work to crucify self. It is only by the blood of Jesus and the power of the Spirit of God that it can be accomplished. The destruction of *self* is God's great work in us ; a work which nothing less than Divine power can accomplish, and yet one which is not accomplished without watchfulness on our parts to discern the workings of self, without earnest prayer for victory, without habits of self-control.

So beautiful and elevated was Moses's spirit when he was with God. Now let us descend with him from the mount, and see him—and this was a greater trial of his heart—amongst men.

He went down from the mount with Joshua, bearing in his hands the two tables of testimony. Joshua heard the noise of the people as they shouted, and said to Moses, "There is a noise of war in the camp." But no. It was not the voice of them that shout for mastery, nor was it the cry of those who are overcome,—though they were indeed overcome,—but the noise of them that sing, not songs of praise, calm and elevated, but tumultuous songs. It was at this critical and very trying moment that Moses descended. His position was one of far greater difficulty than that of Aaron, when the Israelites said to him, "Make us gods, to go before us." What did he do? He acted with that straightforward simplicity, and with that calm firmness and decision, which communion with God gives. In the deep emotion of his heart he " cast the tables out

of his hands, and brake them beneath the mount," thus
shewing Israel how awfully they had broken the law of
their God. Then he took the calf which they had made,
and burnt it in the fire, and ground it to powder, and
strawed it upon the water, and, most remarkable of all,
he made the children of Israel drink of it. Now, whatever was the meaning of this last act, it shews most
strikingly the power of earnest conviction and faithfulness to God. Here was one man standing alone amongst
an idolatrous and excited people, yet he acts without any
hindrance in direct opposition to all that they had been
doing. He destroys the calf which they had just made.
We hear of no protest. The idolaters witness it in silence. He makes them drink the polluted water. They
all obey. How was it that they could act thus? For
one simple reason,—" He acted with God, and for God."
Every guilty conscience felt this, and was abashed. Moses
was possessed of invincible strength, simply because he
acted for God ; all the Israelites were perfect weakness,
because they had forsaken God, and were condemned by
their own consciences. Brethren, let us endeavour to
walk with God, and to act and speak for Him, and then
there will be true power in our acts and words, a power
derived from the life of God in them, whereas self-willed
acts only provoke, and never can touch, the guilty conscience. Such, brethren, was the immediate result of the
consecration of the gold ear-rings of wives, sons, and
daughters,—their possessions utterly lost, and they themselves compelled to undergo humiliation. And such must
be the end of every vain and sinful use of our possessions. How readily they broke off their golden ornaments
to make a golden calf, which could profit them nothing !
Should we be less ready to deny ourselves to give to

Jesus, and profit souls for whom Christ died? What they gave only hardened their hearts, and was sure to be lost; what we give to Jesus in faith and love enlarges our own hearts, and never can be lost. Look at the *golden* calf, the fruit of sinful idolatry in a journeying people; and what ought not faith and love to produce in us, encompassed as we are with the blessing of homes and quietness?

We can say but few words on Moses's second intercessory prayer on this occasion, recorded in verses 31, 32 of this chapter,—"And Moses returned unto the Lord, and said, Oh! this people have sinned a great sin, and have made them gods of gold. Yet now, if thou wilt forgive their sin—; and if not, blot me, I pray thee, out of thy book which thou hast written." The former prayer shewed the place which the glory of God, and His faithfulness to His promises, occupied in Moses's heart; this shews the strength of His love to a troublesome and disobedient people. You will remember that St Paul makes use of similar language, (Rom. ix. 3,) "For I could wish that myself were accursed from Christ for my brethren, my kinsmen according to the flesh." Both passages have puzzled many. It has been asked, " Could Moses really desire to be blotted out of God's book, or Paul desire to be accursed from Christ?" The answer is, It is the language of fervent love, a love that was willing to do and suffer everything for its objects. A world that bows down before the idol of expediency, that knows nothing of self-sacrifice, cannot understand such language. But there are some loving hearts, some who ponder much the cross of our Redeemer, and learn there to love the souls for whom Christ died, who *can* understand it. There are times when in secret prayer they get vivid views of the

glory of heaven, and of the misery of that place into
which no hope can enter. They think of the souls whom
they love, and if ministers, of the souls committed to their
charge. Oh, if only all could be brought there! As a
devoted minister once expressed it, in a forcible, though
quaint way, "Your heaven would be two heavens to
me." But how dreadful the thought that one—if only
one—should be missing at the right hand of God,—one
be lost! Is it too much for love, a love agitated by these
solemn thoughts, to say, "Yet now, if thou wilt forgive
their sin—; and if not, blot me, I pray thee, out of thy
book which thou hast written." Jesus said it, not in
word only, but in act. He bore the terrific curse due to
us. He cried, "My God, my God, why hast thou forsaken me?" Oh, brethren, that God may give us more
of the mind of Christ, more deep and self-sacrificing love,
a love that can labour without weariness, that can suffer,
if need be, with cheerfulness, in seeking to save the precious souls for whom Christ died !

THE RESTORED PRESENCE

Exodus 33:14, 15

" And he said, My presence shall go with thee, and I will give thee
rest.   And he said unto him, If thy presence go not with me,
carry us not up hence. "

ISRAEL'S sin of idolatry had caused a separation between
God and His people.   The golden calf was destroyed—
the people deeply humbled—three thousand men were
slain by the swords of the Levites.   A plague still consumed them, but the separation still lasted.   God is a
jealous God, and cannot suffer alienated affections ; He
is a holy God, and cannot dwell in the midst of wilful
abominations.   And so when He commanded Moses to
" depart and go up " from Sinai, and gave the beautiful
promise, (ver. 2,) " And I will send an angel before thee ;
and I will drive out the Canaanite, the Amorite, the
Hittite, and the Jebusite," He added, (ver. 3,) " for I
will not go up in the midst of thee."   Here, then, brethren,
you will observe that a distinction is made between the
presence of Jehovah himself, and the presence of the
angel that was to go before them ; whereas, if you turn
to Exod. xxiii. 20, 21, you will perceive that no such distinction was made when the same promise was first given.
" Behold, I send an Angel before thee, to keep thee in
the way, and to bring thee into the place which I have
prepared.   Beware of him, and obey his voice, provoke
him not ; for he will not pardon your transgressions : for

my name is in him." Remark the last words, "my name
is in him." What is God's *name* but His Being and
nature? So that His *Being* was *in* that promised Angel.
We know, then, brethren, who that Angel was. It was the
Son of God, before He became the Son of man, called
(Isa. lxiii. 9) "the Angel of His Presence." To have that
"Angel" go before them, keep them in the way, and bring
them into the place prepared for them, was to have Jehovah himself "in the *midst* of *them.*" But now their back-
slidings had separated between themselves and God. The
angel that went before them had not Jehovah's name "in
him." God said, "I will not go up in the midst of thee;
for thou art a stiffnecked people." This moved them;
for when they heard these evil tidings, they mourned,
and stripped themselves of their ornaments. But this
was not enough. The breach was not yet healed. Moses
followed out God's purpose. He took the tabernacle, we
read, (ver. 7,) and pitched it not *within* the camp, but
without the camp, *afar off* from the camp. Why was
this, but to shew that God was a holy God, and that their
camp was in His eyes a defiled and polluted place—a
place where He could not dwell—a place where He could
not be found? *If* any heart in Israel, convinced of sin,
and wearied with its burden, wished to find Him, he
must *go forth* from that polluted place. "It came to
pass, that every one which *sought* the Lord went *out* unto
the tabernacle of the congregation, which was *without* the
camp," (ver. 7.) It has been thought by some that this
tabernacle, though called the "Tabernacle of the congregation," was nothing else than Moses's tent, and thus that
Moses himself and Joshua dwelt afar off from the camp
of Israel, and *his* tabernacle, and not *their* camp, was the
place where God communed with Moses. But however

this be, it is clear that Israel felt how different Moses was from itself—how different the tabernacle from their camp; for when Moses went out into the tabernacle, all the people rose up with reverential awe, and looked after Moses until he was gone into the tabernacle.

Terrible, indeed, must this conscious separation have been to Israel. It was sad for Moses too. Though none of Israel's guilt rested on him—though "God spake unto Moses face to face, as a man speaketh unto his friend"— yet that meek servant of God, that loving leader of dis- obedient people, could not bear this separation. Again he betakes himself to intercessory prayer—again, to use the words of the Psalmist, (Ps. cvi. 23,) "Moses his chosen stood before him in the breach." The manner of his intercession on this occasion is very beautiful and instructive. He begins by reminding Jehovah of the difficult charge he had received. "See, thou sayest unto me, Bring up this people." But Moses knew that this command virtually implied the promise of grace to enable him to fulfil it, and so he adds, "And thou hast not let me know whom thou wilt send with me." But how, it may be asked, could Moses speak thus after the promise recorded in ver. 2, "I will send an angel before thee?" The answer seems to be, that this promise did not *satisfy* Moses. It was not the presence and guardianship of a *created* angel, but the presence of *Jehovah* with his people, as well as with himself, that he desired. And so he says, (ver. 13,) "Shew me now *thy* way;" as if he had said, "It is with Thee in Thy way that I desire to walk, with Thee that I desire to commune—Thy presence that I long to enjoy." And this desire, you will observe, is not rudely and roughly stated, but brought forward, if we may use the expression, with delicate skill. Throughout this prayer, we cannot fail to notice how each point that Jehovah grants is not accepted by Moses as something *final*, but is made the step whereby to ascend higher. So, in his longing for the removal of all separation, in his desire for God's presence, he says, (ver. 12,) "Yet thou hast *said*, I know thee by name, and thou hast also found grace in my sight." He rests upon the word of Jehovah and pleads the grace already experienced. God loves to grant importunate prayer. The breach was closed up. "My presence," says Jehovah, "shall go with thee, and I will give thee rest." But even this promise, full and satisfying as it is, does not seem to be *all* that Moses desires. His expectations rise higher; and he prays, (ver. 18,) "Shew me thy glory." This also was granted, as we read, chap. xxxiv. 6, 7, "And the Lord passed by before him, and proclaimed, The Lord, the Lord God, merciful and gracious, long-suffering, and abundant in goodness and truth, keeping mercy for thousands, forgiving iniquity and transgression and sin, and that will by no means clear the guilty; visiting the iniquity of the fathers upon the children, and upon the children's children, unto the third and to the fourth generation." Two things cannot fail to strike us here,—first, the grace and condescension of Jehovah, in allowing His children thus to plead with Him; and, secondly, the faith and persevering earnestness of Moses, who the more he got, the more he sought.

Having thus endeavoured to trace the course of this history, let us now pause a little on the promise itself,— "My presence shall go with thee, and I will give thee rest."

What a promise, what a provision, brethren, God's presence on our way, God's rest at its end!

The world's way, brethren, is always dark ; the Christian's way is occasionally so. But God's presence is light. When you journey amongst lofty Alps, it often happens that the mountains are covered with thick clouds, and the sun's rays are altogether intercepted,—amongst the pouring rain, the wild and savage rocks, the melting snow, the cold and chilly air,—the imagination, too, portraying to itself scenes of danger,—the way lost amidst the fog on the approach of a dizzy snow-storm, how desolate every thing is ! Let but the clouds pass away, and the sun pour out its beams, and all seems changed. The magnificence of the scenes around rivets the mind and elevates the feelings. The more so if it be the early morning, when the loftiest mountain-tops catch the first streaks of light, and one peak after another is lighted up with a golden hue. Even the cold snow looks warm in its tented brilliancy. But the most desolate scene in nature is but a faint picture of the desolation, the awful desolation, of a *dark* soul,—a *soul without God*. Its brightest scene is but a faint picture of that light, that *warm* light, which the presence of God gives. It was a dark day to Jacob when he was compelled to leave his home, and his aged father and mother, on account of his brother's anger. His conscience must have been full of *accusations*. He had taken advantage of his father's infirmities to deceive him, and had wronged his generous though worldly-minded brother. And thus all was dark within and without,—within, because he could not realize God's presence, —*without*, because he was homeless and in danger. But God met him at Bethel, and from the top of the prophetic ladder gave him the promise of His presence,—" Behold I am with thee, and will keep thee in all places whither thou goest." How speedily must the light of God's gracious presence have chased away the darkness from his heart! Dark, again, brethren, awfully dark *in itself,* and of *itself,* is the valley of the shadow of death; for death is the penalty of sin, and one proof of the inflexible righteousness of God. Its sensations, too, are all unknown. Its way is all lonely. Whose heart does not naturally recoil from it as something dark? But the presence of God in the soul can light up this valley, and remove its loneliness and separation. Let but faith cling with unfaltering grasp to the promise, "My presence shall go with thee," and it can understand the feelings of the Psalmist, "Yea, though I walk through the valley of the shadow of death, I will fear no evil: for thou art with me; thy rod and thy staff they comfort me"—and the triumphant language of St Paul, "But thanks be to God, which giveth us the victory through our Lord Jesus Christ." For God's presence is light, and in His light we see light.

Is there any heart here dark and lonely? Do doubts and fears agitate you? Does memory recall past sins, and conscience accuse you? Are your thoughts all confused? What can remove all this? Not the reasonings of your own mind,—not worldly arguments of consolation, but the presence of God, diffusing light in the conscience, warmth to the affections, and order to the thoughts. "Light" (we read, Ps. xcvii.) "is sown for the righteous;" and again, (Ps. cxii. 4,) "Unto the upright there ariseth light in the darkness," because God's presence will not fail to meet the seeking soul. "The Lord shall be unto thee an everlasting light, and thy God thy glory."

And again, "Here we have no continuing city." Like Israel of old, we are on a journey. Our life is a broken one: part of it spent here, and part there; one part comparatively bright, another crowded with trial. It almost seems as if it were made of several lives, instead of being the life of one person. We want, then, brethren, something that will give it unity,—something that will continue the same and unchangeable amongst all the changes in our outward circumstances and our inward feelings; and where shall we look for this but in the PRESENCE of *God*,—in the fulfilment of this promise, " My presence shall go with thee." Imagine, brethren, the deathbed of some worldly man, on whom many afflictions have been expended in vain. In his long life he has never been suffered to settle quietly down, but has been moved from place to place. He has sought diversion, sometimes in one way, and sometimes in another. One by one, children and friends have been removed from him ; and with all this his feelings have changed too, often torn and distracted, his hopes often disappointed, yet all unsanctified. Suppose him to look back at its solemn close upon his past life. Where is its unity ? What is it there that has connected all its periods and circumstances together ? Nothing.

But turn to the Christian's deathbed. Suppose *him*, too, to be aged, and one who has passed through as much bereavement and as many changes. Suppose his life to have been outwardly as broken as that of the other. Yet how different will be his retrospect ! Changes, he will say, great changes and many bereavements, there have been in my life. I have been emptied from vessel to vessel. But one thing has never failed—one thing makes me feel that my life has been *one ;* it has calmed my joys ; it has soothed my sorrows ; it has guided me in difficulty ; it has strengthened me in weakness. It is the *presence* of God—a faithful and loving God. Yes, brethren, the presence of God is not only *light,* it is *unity.* It gives *unity* to the heart that believes it—*unity* to the life that is conformed to it. It was the presence of God in David's soul that enabled him to say, "*One* thing have I desired of the Lord;" and in St Paul's that enabled him to say, "This one thing I do."

But once more. The Christian's life is one of conflict. It is a constant warfare with his three great enemies,—the devil, the world, and the flesh. The first, an invisible, but personal, being; the second, a powerful influence around him; the third, an enemy within the camp, deep in his own heart—all in league with each other, all bent on one end,—the alienation of our hearts from God. It is a *tremendous* conflict. What shall give us strength for it? It is a *ceaseless* conflict. What shall sustain our hope? The presence of God, brethren: for the presence of God is not only light and unity; it is also *power*. It produces and keeps alive in the soul all those Christian graces which, together, constitute the Christian armour, and enables the believer to stand fast in the day of battle; so that the Christian, when he looks around upon present temptations, or forward to future conflicts, and asks himself the question, where shall I gain strength? where have my hope renewed? may reply, and say with Moses, "Is it not, O God, in that thou goest with us?" In Thy presence is *light, unity,* and *power*.

But what is the end of the Christian's way? *Rest*. "I will give thee *rest*." In one sense this is a distinct promise. It does not run, My presence shall go with thee, and *it* shall give thee rest; but I will give thee rest. Yet, in another point of view, it is but the development of the former one; for where is rest to be found but in the presence of God?

There is a twofold rest; or, perhaps, it is more true to

say, two different degrees of rest. There is a *rest* for us
on our way, however difficult and painful ; and there is a
rest for us at its *end.* The first is true, but imperfect;
the second is true and perfect. To the enjoyment of the
first Jesus invites the weary and heavy laden, in the well-
known words, " Come unto me, all ye that labour and are
heavy laden, and I will give you rest. Take my yoke
upon you, and learn of me : for I am meek and lowly in
heart : and ye shall find *rest unto your souls.*" And so
also St Paul says, (Heb. iv. 3,) " For we which have believed *do* enter into rest "—observe, not *shall* enter, but
do enter, into rest. There is, then, a *present* rest in this
troublesome world—a rest in Jesus, a rest from the guilt
of sin in His forgiving love, from the accusations of conscience in His precious blood, a rest from disappointment
in Him who " sticketh closer than a brother." And yet,
brethren, a simple and strong faith is required to enable
us to enjoy this rest; for everything around us and within
us—the power of Satan, the deceitful influences of the
world, the treachery of our own corrupt hearts—try to
rob us of it. But this rest is but a feeble anticipation
of that *rest* which is reserved for the *end* of the Christian's journey. *There,* brethren, the presence of Jesus, and
of the Father in Him, will be far more to us than it is
now, for " now we see through a glass, darkly ; but then
face to face." There no painful doubt can enter our
perfectly enlightened minds, no sin can burden the clear
conscience, no care can distract the heart. The storms
which have so often agitated us will be all hushed, and
no angry billow can fall upon that calm shore. Of this rest
St Paul speaks in the beautiful words, " There remaineth therefore a rest to the people of God ; " and again to
the Thessalonians, (2 Thess. i. 7,) " And to you who are

troubled, rest with us." The presence of God, then, is not only light, unity, power, but also *rest*—a *rest* upon our way in proportion to our faith—a rest at the end of our way, where faith will issue in sight. And now, brethren, let me recall your thoughts to the history, and remind you how it was that the promise was given, "My presence shall go with you, and I will give thee rest." There was, we have seen, a separation between God and Israel. Their iniquities separated between them and their God, and their sins hid His face from them; but they had a mediator, and through the faithfulness and persevering prayers of Moses, God's presence was restored to them, and the covenant was renewed. Brethren, are you conscious of a separation between God and your souls? Are you unable to feel "God is with me, and I am with Him?" Is there some rent still between the light of His countenance and your spirit? What is the reason of this? It must be the consciousness of sin, and the power of unbelief. But this separation need not continue. There is a Mediator between us and God. Jesus has stood in the breach, and, Himself God and man, has reunited sinful man to God. Cast yourself, then, with all your sins, and all your wants, on Christ Jesus, and this promise will be yours,—"My presence shall go with thee." You may walk in the happy consciousness that God is with you now, and in the joyful hope that He will be with you for ever. You may find that presence, light, unity, power, and rest to your soul, and may be able to use the words of Asaph, which seem to be an echo of our text, —"Thou wilt guide me with thy counsel, and afterward receive me to glory," (Ps. lxxiii. 24.)

THE SILVER TRUMPET

Numbers 10:12

" And the children of Israel took their journeys out of the wilderness of Sinai ; and the cloud rested in the wilderness of Paran."

THE children of Israel spent one year all but ten days at the foot of Sinai. For we are told that they arrived there (Exod. xix. 1) in " the third month." And in the verse preceding our text we are informed that it was " on the twentieth day of the second month, in the second year, that the cloud was taken up from off the tabernacle of the testimony." That short year was a very eventful one in their history. At the foot of Sinai they were brought afresh as a people into covenant with God. They received the law written with the finger of God. They beheld and heard its solemn sanctions,—the lightnings and thunders which re-echoed about the mount. And then, too, in forgetfulness and sad impatience, they worshipped the golden calf, and were severely chastened for their awful idolatry. How much mercy and affliction, grace and correction, forbearance and severity on God's part—how much trembling awe and bold declension, hasty resolution and speedy departure from it on theirs, were crowded into that one year ! For Moses it was a time of special anxiety, and special nearness to God ; to Israel, a time of special declension and correction. And may we not see something like this, brethren, in our own lives ? Sometimes years pass away without any great changes around us,

or any great changes within us, and then a whole throng
of events is crowded into a short space of time,—sorrows
and consolations, fearful conflicts and encouraging victories, terrific doubts that rack the soul, and that calm
hope which is its anchor, keeping it in the midst of the
storm—seasons of special communion with God, and times
of deadness and unprofitableness of spirit, and, still worse,
of backsliding. These seem a life in themselves, blessed
if they bear us nearer to the throne of God.

But now God's presence was restored to Israel, and
they were to move forward. It was not granted that they
might rest where they were, but that they might journey
onward through all difficulties and all opposition, to the
promised land. This chapter gives us an interesting
account of the arrangements that preceded and accompanied the moving of the camp. The arrangement that
preceded it was the preparation of the silver trumpets;
the arrangements that accompanied were the adjusted
work of the three Levitical families. Let us look at them
in order. We all know well that there was a symbol of
God's presence which appealed to the eyes of the children
of Israel,—the pillar of fire and cloud. It pleased God
now to add another sign, one that appealed to their ears,
—the silver trumpets. In number they were to be two,
in construction to be formed of a "whole piece of silver,"
(ver. 2.) But it is far more important to observe the
occasions when they were to be used. We can scarcely
fail to be struck with the *frequency* and *variety* of these.
When Israel rested, and it was the will of God that they
should assemble at the tabernacle of the congregation to
worship, the blast of *one* trumpet summoned the princes,
the heads of the thousands of Israel. The notes of the
two summoned the whole of Israel. When the move-

ment of the pillar of the cloud shewed Israel was to journey onward, the silver trumpets set them rapidly in motion, and shewed the *order* in which they were to march. Thus we read, (ver. 5, 6,) "When ye blow an alarm, then the camps that lie on the east parts shall go forward. When ye blow an alarm the second time, then the camps that lie on the south side shall take their journey : they shall blow an alarm for their journeys." If, too, they were obliged to go to war with their enemies, then also the trumpets were to be blown, and the promise, the beautiful promise, was given, "Ye shall be remembered before the Lord your God, and ye shall be saved from your enemies." Nor was this all. The most remarkable use of them still remains to be mentioned. These trumpets were also to be blown, (as we read, ver. 10,) over their burnt-offerings, and over the sacrifices of their peace-offerings ; that they might be a memorial before their God. The sound of the silver trumpets was, then, no *uncommon* thing. It entered into all the important events of Israel's life. It summoned them to worship at the tabernacle, and to journey in the wilderness. It called them to battle, and it consecrated their offerings. It ought, too, specially to be noticed that it was not any Israelite, or any head of the thousands of Israel, that could blow these trumpets. Even when the summons was to war, it was reserved to the priests to blow them, (as we read, ver. 8,) "And the sons of Aaron, the priests, shall blow with the trumpets." And why was this, if not to teach the Israelites to regard the sound of these silver trumpets on every occasion, whatsoever it might be, as the *voice* of God? Whether they summoned to worship, or to journeys, or to battle, or consecrated some offering, they were not the call of a mere man invested with some

authority. They were the *voice* of God, indicating the
will of Him who led and guided all Israel's steps.

The promises, too, connected with the blowing of the
trumpets on some occasions, and doubtless implied in the
others, are very remarkable. Observe the one in ver. 9,
—" Ye shall be remembered before the Lord your God."
The sound, then, of that trumpet calling them to war would
be something more to them than mere *sound*. It would
bear the promise to their hearts. It would do more ; it
would make them feel that it spoke to God as well as
them. It reminded Him as well as them of the promise
which could never fail. You remember, brethren, that
when God made His covenant with Noah, and set His
bow in the cloud as a token of His covenant, He said, " I
will look upon it." Observe, it was not " Ye shall look
upon it, and remember my covenant," but " *I* will look
upon it, that *I* may remember the everlasting covenant."
What, then, would those acquainted with this promise
feel when gazing upon the bow in the threatening cloud ?
Would they not feel " God's eye as well as mine is upon
that bow. It puts *Him* as well as *me* in remembrance
of the promise ? " Just so, brethren, would the believing
Israelite feel as he was listening to the sound of the silver
trumpet. " It is the voice of God to me," he would say,
" but it also reaches the ear of God, and pleads, as it were,
His own promise."

And to what does all this lead our thoughts ? Surely
to this, that those two silver trumpets must, like the other
ceremonies of that ritual, have been typical. As there
is something in this dispensation which corresponds to
the sacrifices and the priesthood of that earlier covenant,
so there must be something which corresponds to the
varied use of the two silver trumpets ; and what that is,

brethren, it is not difficult to discern. It is the *voice* of
Him who came preaching peace, the proclamation of those
of whom the prophet speaks, (Isa. lii. 7,) " How beautiful
upon the mountains are the feet of him that bringeth
good tidings of good, that publisheth salvation ; that
saith unto Zion, Thy God reigneth ! " For just as the
two silver trumpets entered into every part of Israel's
life, and their varied notes were always adapted to Israel's
wants and position, so it is with the gospel. Its
awakening power, its soothing promises, its sanctifying
influence, is meant to consecrate every act of our lives,
and move every thought of our hearts.

Did the sound of the silver trumpets call the slothful
or backsliding Israel to the tabernacle of the congregation, either to hear the will of God announced by Moses,
or to worship ? So, brethren, does the voice of Jesus in
the gospel invite us into the presence of God. It says
to the slumbering heart, " Awake, thou that sleepest, and
arise from the dead, and Christ shall give thee light." It
says to the fearful and desponding, " Come boldly unto
the throne of grace, that you may obtain mercy, and find
grace to help in the hour of need." It says to the backsliding and to the guilty conscience, " Return unto the
Lord thy God ; for thou hast fallen by thine iniquity.
Take with you words, and turn to the Lord : say unto
him, Take away all iniquity, and receive us graciously :
so will we render the calves of our lips," (Hosea xiv. 1, 2.)
It says, again, " Behold, I stand at the door, and knock :
if any man hear my voice, and open the door, I will come
in to him, and sup with him, and he with me."

Did the sound of the silver trumpets bid Israel arise
and follow the pillar of fire and cloud which went before
them ? So does the voice of Jesus bid us arise and jour-

ney onward. When our hearts are entangled by the secret influences of the world—when we begin to take up our rest in the love of the creature—when the ease and comforts of life engross our thoughts, and render the heart lukewarm, then there is a still small voice full of warning, " Arise ye, and depart, for this is not your rest ; it is polluted." Whensoever we rest contented with low attainments, losing sight of Him to whose image we ought to be conformed, the silver trumpets sound, bidding us press toward the mark for the prize of our high calling in Christ Jesus. As, too, Israel of old was called to engage in warfare with their enemies and God's, and one use of the silver trumpets was to summon them to preparation and to the field of battle, so, brethren, has the Israel of God now a great conflict to engage in—a conflict with enemies seen and unseen, and the unseen more powerful than the seen; " For we fight not against flesh and blood, but against principalities and powers, against the ruler of the darkness of this world, against spiritual wicked-ness in high places." Yet, brethren, how seldom do we realize as we ought the greatness of the conflict, and the power of our spiritual enemies ! and, consequently, we are too often *off our guard*. Hence it is that the silver trumpets are needed to summon *us* too to the conflict. We require to be called to " take the whole armour of God, that we may be able to withstand in the evil day ; and having done all, to stand." We require to be sum-moned to " endure hardness," as good soldiers of Christ Jesus, (2 Tim. ii. 3,) that we may not, like Israel of old, turn back in the day of battle, but may feel and exclaim with David, (Ps. xviii. 32, 34, 35,) " It is God that girdeth me with strength, and maketh my way perfect,"—" He teacheth my hands to war, so that a bow of steel is broken in mine arms. Thou hast also given me the shield of thy salvation : and thy right hand hath holden me up, and thy gentleness hath made me great."

And, once more, were the silver trumpets needed to consecrate all Israel's offerings, that they might be a memorial before the Lord? Oh, still more is it the gospel of Christ that does and can consecrate all acts of life and of worship! St Paul, speaking of those who have departed from the faith, and who command others to abstain from meats, says, (1 Tim. iv. 4, 5,) "For every creature of God is good, and nothing to be refused, if it be received with thanksgiving : for it is *sanctified with the word of God* and prayer." It is the word, too, of the gospel which explains to us the means of approach to God, and, still more, prepares *our hearts* for that communion. We should listen to the sound of the silver trumpet in every act of life, in every prayer, and over every offering. With this everything will become a memorial before the Lord. But let us pass on from the arrangements that *preceded* to those that *accompanied* the moving of the camp ; and in doing so we shall not pause to shew the place which each tribe occupied in the march, but fix our exclusive attention upon the tribe of Levi.

This tribe, we are all aware, was in a special sense consecrated to the service of God. It was taken from among the children of Israel instead of all the first-born, who were spared on that fearful day when the first-born of the Egyptians perished. Thus (Num. iii. 13) we read, " Because all the first-born are mine ; for on the day that I smote all the first-born in the land of Egypt I hallowed unto me all the first-born in Israel, both man and beast: *mine shall they be :* I am the Lord." In consequence of

this consecration, they encamped, not in the same line
with the other tribes, but "round about the tabernacle."
And for this there was a twofold reason; one, the very
obvious reason, that the service of the tabernacle, when
it rested, and the carrying the different parts of it during
the march, was entrusted to them. The other was a very
remarkable reason; it was that Levi might be a spot of
mediating shelter for other tribes. Thus we read, (Num.
i. 53,) "But the Levites shall pitch round about the tabernacle of testimony, that there be *no wrath upon* the congregation of the children of Israel."

And here, brethren, you will not fail to notice in pass-
ing, two great principles on which God dealt with Israel.
The principle of substitution—for Levi was taken *instead*
of the first-born; and the principle of mediation—for Levi
encamped round about the tabernacle, and sheltered the
other tribes from the wrath of God. Both instances are
beautifully illustrative of the work of Jesus. For He is
our Substitute, through whom the believer is spared; He
is our Mediator, through whom the believer is sheltered
from the displeasure of God due to sin. You are doubtless aware that the tribe of Levi was made up of three
families,—the family of Gershon, that of Kohath, and that
of Merari. Each of these had a special charge allotted to
them in the moving of the camp.

The first and most honoured were the sons of Kohath.
They were appointed to carry the "most holy things,"
(chap. iv. 4). The ark of testimony, covered with badgers'
skins and blue cloth, the table of shew-bread, the candle-
stick, the golden altar, with all its vessels—all these being
previously covered by Aaron and his sons. The sons of
Gershon carried all the hangings and curtains of different
kinds, the curtains of the tabernacle, and those of the

courts. And lastly, the sons of Merari had the heaviest work. They had to carry all the boards, pillars, and bars of the tabernacle. Such was the distribution of their work in point of *honour*. But this was not the order of their march. In this Gershon and Merari preceded Kohath ; and naturally, for the outer parts of the tabernacle would be the first to be taken down, and the first to be set up. These, therefore, marched in advance of the Kohathites, and in the rear of Judah and Issachar. Then marched Simeon and Gad, followed by the Kohathites, and then the other tribes. Thus, brethren, there was beautiful order in the camp of Israel. All had their appointed work, and each his appointed place; and so long as they faithfully and contentedly did that work, and kept that place, there was no confusion. It was the rebellion of their wills which so spoiled the beauty of order, and marred the word of God.

God is a God of order, and it must be His will that there should be order in His Church now ; yea, a more beautiful order than amongst Israel of old, for now it should be developed from unity within, and not merely be imposed from without. Each true Christian now has his place in the body of Christ,—a place assigned him as truly, though not as visibly, as the place assigned to each tribe in the camp of Israel. No member of Christ's body is overlooked on account of weakness, and none able to do without the other members of Christ's body, by reason of strength. And as the place of each in the body is assigned by the grace of God, so is work appointed for each by the providence of God. True it is that this is not always made as plain to us as it was to the three families of Israel. We may have to wait for work, and may have many doubts what that work will be. Still, if there

be the desire to work for Christ, and a willingness to
do that work which God appoints, it is sure to be made
plain.   Our difficulties in this matter arise chiefly from
our own hearts; we often mark out in our minds the
work that we should like, and generally it is Kohath's
path.   God almost invariably appoints work which is
not altogether to our minds.   Sometimes he bids us carry
the boards and pillars of the tabernacle.   We begin to
doubt whether this is God's appointed work, or perhaps
to fret, if we cannot help seeing that it is.   If, brethren,
we had more faith, more simplicity of spirit, more simple
desire to please God, and not ourselves, we should generally see our way more clearly, for self-seeking and self-
will are the mists which obscure our path; and if there
were more contentment with our appointed work, whatsoever it be, even if we have to do, like the sons of
Merari, with the boards and stock of the tabernacle,
and not with the ark of testimony and the golden altar,
we should have much more real enjoyment in our work.

   Brethren, let us not be slothful followers of Him who
went about doing good, and counted it His "meat to
do the will of Him that sent Him."   Let us seek to live
more to Christ, and for the members of His body.   And
let us never forget that the only state of mind in which
we can really be fellow-workers with God is brokenness
of heart on account of our sins, and past and present
unprofitableness, love to Jesus, and a desire not to gra-
tify self, but to glorify God.   It is a noble work, brethren, which is set, not before ministers only, but before
the whole Church of the living God now.   It is not to
bear the vessels of the sanctuary, or the boards and hangings of the tabernacle, but to seek living stones for the
living temple of God,—that temple which is the habita-

tion of God, and against which the gates of hell shall not prevail. We do not think, brethren, that any usefulness, or any success which may have been granted to us in God's work, can give any comfort to us in a dying hour. One thing, and one alone, can sustain us then,—"the blood of Jesus." Everything else must be put on one side. But we do think that, next to those exalted thanksgivings which will issue from the hearts of the redeemed around the throne when they review God's mercy to themselves, those will be the loudest and most heartfelt which they offer when they think of some soul rescued from death, by the grace of God, through their insignificant instrumentality. Oh that our hearts were more impressed now, brethren, with the blessedness of *living* to God, and that we felt the meaning of those words, " He that winneth souls is wise." Surely then there would be more resemblance between our camp below and the Church above, where there is perfect *order*, and perfect holiness, and perfect fulfilment of the will of God.

TABERAH: OR, THE SIN OF COMPLAINING

Numbers 11:3

" And he called the name of the place Taberah : because the fire of the
Lord burnt amongst them."

WE have now entered upon a new portion of Israel's history,—their journey from Sinai to the confines of the land
of promise. Was it brighter than that which lay between
Egypt and Sinai ? Did they manifest more submission to
the will of Him who led them ? Alas ! quite the reverse.
To trace their history henceforth is little else than to trace
the history of their final fall, which, we shall see, did not
break in upon them all at once, but came on by degrees.
You will remember, brethren, that we remarked at the
very outset of this course of lectures that Egypt might be
regarded as a type of the old man, and Israel as a type of
the new man, in the true Christian. But Israel now as a
whole had become almost as Egypt. It had fallen under
the power of unbelief. It is in Moses and a few others
alone that we can see true types of the new man, foreshadows of those who in Christ Jesus are become new
creatures. Let us view, then, Moses and Israel in this
portion of their history as types of the new and old man ;
Moses inviting Hobab to accompany them, Israel complaining at Taberah ; and that which is necessary in order
to see the full meaning of the latter, the ark of the covenant, the searcher of Israel's resting-place. It is evident,
brethren, that this portion of Scripture, (extending from

chap. x. 29 to chap. xi. 5,) is much more than enough for
one lecture. All that we can attempt is to suggest thoughts
to be worked out elsewhere.

We begin with Moses and his beautiful invitation to
Hobab, (chap. x. 29,) "We are journeying unto the place
of which the Lord said, I will give it you: come thou
with us, and we will do thee good: for the Lord hath
spoken good concerning Israel." These words afford us
more than one glimpse into Moses's state of mind.

More than forty years had now elapsed since he had
"refused to be called the son of Pharaoh's daughter, choos-
ing rather to suffer affliction with the people of God, than
to enjoy the pleasures of sin for a season." What enabled
him to make this difficult choice? The apostle tells us,
"faith." But faith is a grace that does not stand alone.
It soon becomes the parent of other graces. God has told
us what He is; and it is the characteristic of faith to rest
in Him as a *present* God—to enjoy Him as an all-sufficient
and present portion. But God has spoken about His
people's future—told them not only what He *is*, but what
He *will* be to them. He hath spoken "good concerning
Israel." These promises kindle and sustain "hope." The
heart is enlarged with the joyful anticipation of things to
come. Moses's invitation to Hobab shews that "hope"
was *one*, it may be the prevailing, characteristic of his
state of mind at this time. There was something, too, in
his outward circumstances which might give an impulse
to this expansive feeling. Hitherto they had been march-
ing almost *away* from the land of promise; now their
steps were turned, and they were about to move in a direct
line for it. This had no effect whatever on the minds of
the carnal and discontented Israel; present inconveniences
and trials completely thrust all the promises out of their

minds. But Moses pondered the promise; he anticipated the "good which God had spoken concerning Israel." Hope rose high in his expecting heart, rendering more bearable the heavy burden which he had to carry,—a disobedient and gainsaying people. Hope, brethren, is a very important grace. Far more is said concerning it in the New Testament than in the Old, and for obvious reasons; for the covenant under which we are is a "better covenant, established upon better promises," and hope should be in proportion to the fulness of the promise. St Peter speaks of an "inheritance incorruptible, undefiled, and that fadeth not away;" and St Paul (Col. i. 5) calls it "The *hope* which is laid up for us in heaven." The effect of this grace in keeping the heart "steadfast and unmoveable" amidst the temptations and storms of life, is beautifully described by the same apostle, (Heb. vi. 19,) where he compares it to an anchor: "Which hope we have as an anchor of the soul, both sure and steadfast." It is productive of *patience* in tribulation, and so we meet with the expression, (1 Thess. i. 3,) "the patience of hope" and of joy, when we are in heaviness through manifold temptations; and thus we are exhorted (Rom. xii. 12) "to rejoice in hope." Why is it, brethren, that our hearts do not *abound* more in hope? Is it not that they are not occupied enough with God's *promises?* That they do not realize, as Moses did, the good which God hath spoken concerning Israel? We live too much in the *present* or the *past,* and not enough in the *future.* Let us meditate, brethren, more on what we shall be,—like Jesus, for "we shall see Him as He is;" more on that glory which will be revealed: and hope will rise higher and higher; our walk will be more elevated, as Moses's was; our patience will have her perfect work.

Hope, then, brethren, was a feature of Moses's spirit. But *another* is very apparent in this invitation to Hobab,— his holy *benevolence*. He was anxious that one related to him, though not *of* Israel, should share in the "good" promised to Israel: "Come thou with us, and we will do thee good: for the Lord hath spoken good concerning Israel." It is true, indeed, that this was not the *only* reason for the invitation. The 31st verse assigns another: "Leave us not, I pray thee; forasmuch as thou knowest how we are to encamp in the wilderness, and thou mayest be to us instead of eyes." Even though Israel was guided by the pillar of cloud and fire, this Midianite, well acquainted with the country, might be of much use. Still there was a deeper and more unselfish desire in Moses's heart: it was that Hobab might share in the blessings promised to Israel. And this, brethren, is the more beautiful, when we bear in mind that Israel of old was not called to *impart* to others the truths which they had been taught. The Church of the Old Testament was not in any sense, to use a common expression, a "missionary Church." Its duty was to keep the oracles of God, and to live in *complete separation* from all the other nations of the earth; so that Moses went beyond the spirit and requirements of the law when he gave utterance to the benevolent desire of his heart, "Come thou with us, and we will do thee good: for God hath spoken good concerning Israel." But we, brethren, who live in the latter times, when the fulness of Divine love has burst through the barriers which for a time confined it, when the gracious command has been given, "Preach the gospel to every creature," *we* ought to say, by the holiness of our lives, by the sympathy of our hearts, by the words of our lips, to those around us, "Come with us, and we will do thee good." We see this compassionate love in Paul, (Rom. x. 1,) "My heart's desire and prayer to God for Israel is, that they might be saved." And perhaps even more in the words, (1 Thess. ii. 8,) "So being affectionately desirous of you, we were willing to have imparted unto you, not the gospel of God only, but also our own souls, because ye were dear unto us." We see it in the beloved John, (3 John 4,) "I have no greater joy than to hear that my children walk in truth." But, most of all, we see it in Jesus, the fountain of all grace—" For when he was come near, he beheld the city, and *wept* over it, saying, If thou hadst known, even thou, at least in this thy day, the things which belong unto thy peace ! but now they are hid from thine eyes." And how full of love are His repeated invitations—" Come unto me, all ye that labour and are heavy laden." "Him that cometh unto me, I will in no wise cast out." Oh, we, brethren, ought to be more like-minded with Jesus ; and if we realized more the good which God has spoken concerning Israel, we should surely desire that relations and friends might "come with us ;" that what goodness the Lord shall do unto us, the same He might do to them.

Moses, then, in striking contrast to Israel, manifested his *hope* in God's promises, and his *love* to the soul of his Midianite relative. We know not for certain what effect this invitation produced. At first, Hobab seemed resolute in declining it. He said, (ver. 30,) "I will not go ; but I will depart to mine own land, and to my kindred ;" and the history says nothing more. But there is one fact which may lead us to think that Hobab changed his mind. The Kenites were his descendants ; and where do we find them settled afterwards ? Not at Mount Sinai, but in the land of promise with the Israelites, (Judges i.

16,) " And the children of the Kenite, Moses's father-in-
law, went up out of the city of palm trees with the children of Judah into the wilderness of Judah ; and they
went and dwelt among the people." And if this conclusion be true, how encouraging it is ! *Long*, it may be,
some loved soul may withstand the influence of a holy
life, and the force of gentle invitations—*long*, it may say
in words and by acts, " I will not go ; " yet afterwards,
when we have almost ceased to hope, it may think of the
" good spoken concerning Israel." It may arise through
grace and go. But let us pass on from Moses ; and
before we contemplate Israel at Taberah, there are one or
two things connected with the *ark* which we ought to
notice. We all know that the pillar of cloud went before
Israel to *guide* them ; but ver. 33 shews us that the ark
of the *covenant* was not carried *with* the other sacred
things in the camp, but *before* it. And why ? " To search
out a resting-place for them." And so, you will remember,
that when Israel reached Jordan, the ark of the *covenant*
went down first into the waters of Jordan, and kept them
divided, whilst Israel passed through. Now, what was
the ark ? It was the centre of the holy of holies—the
place where the tables of the covenant, revealing the will
of God, were kept—the place where God met Israel, and
Israel met God, in the person of the high priest. Of
what, then, was it a type ? Of Jesus, brethren, *in* whom
is established an everlasting union between Godhead and
manhood—*through* whom we may have access to the
Father. Is there not something beautiful in the expression with reference to the ark, " to search out a resting-
place for them ? " It was a very *temporary* resting-place,
sometimes palms only for a night ; still the ark, the symbol of the Divine presence, " searched it out." And are

the steps of God's Israel left unguided now? Oh no. Christ Jesus has gone before His people to prepare a rest for them in heaven, and He goes before them *now* to *search* out for them *little* resting-places on earth. Forget not, brethren, that these are *short*, for we are on a journey; but remember, too, that if you are walking in a dependent spirit, those resting-places, short as *they* may be, are *chosen* for you by Christ. It is promised, (Isa. lviii. 11,) "The Lord shall guide thee continually," *always* in *all* thy steps, *small* and *great*. The places to which He will lead thee will often be the very last that you would have chosen. When this is so, let this thought quiet thy heart, "It is Jesus that has *searched* it out for me."

But notice also what is said of the pillar of cloud. It not only went before them, but is said (ver. 34) to be *upon them*. It must have stretched back, therefore, over the whole camp. Thus also it is written, (Ps. cv. 39,) "He spread a cloud for a covering;" and St Paul says, (1 Cor. x. 1,) "All our fathers were under the cloud." That *cloud* was, therefore, the symbol of God's *protection* —a protection so beautifully promised under another image, (Ps. xci. 4,) "He shall cover thee with his feathers, and under his wings shalt thou trust." Moses, therefore, was but expressing the meaning of these Divine symbols of guidance and protection, when he prayed so beautifully on the ark setting forward, "Rise up, Lord, and let thine enemies be scattered, and let them that hate thee flee before thee;" and when it rested, "Return, O Lord, unto the many thousands of Israel."

Having thus noted, brethren, Israel's privilege in having such a leader as Moses, a man of such unwavering *hope* in God's promises, and of such *holy benevolence*, and, still more, in having such guidance and protection, we shall be better able to estimate aright their conduct at Taberah. This is spoken of, chap. xi. 1: "The people complained." It might seem to some almost needless to pause on this, as already we have seen their "murmur" so often. But if you look more carefully at the passage, you will find something *new* and very *instructive* in it. For, you will observe that it does not say that the people "murmured," but "complained," or, as it is in the margin, "were as it were complainers;" by which it is evidently meant that there was a feeling in their minds of *scarcely expressed* dissatisfaction. There was no sudden outbreak of murmuring, but the *whispers* and *looks* of discontent. There is no special mention of any particular *reason* for it. It does not say that their manna failed, or that any hostile army was arrayed against them. Doubtless the journeying was always wearisome, and on its wearisomeness and fatigues they suffered their minds to dwell, forgetful of all the mercies vouchsafed them, and "complained." Now, we must all feel that *right-down* murmuring is very sinful, and in its *worst* forms most Christians overcome it; but not so *complaining*, for this seems to many to be scarcely wrong, and it often grows upon them so gradually, that they are seldom conscious of it. The causes of complaint are manifold. *Little* difficulties in our circumstances—*little* acts of selfishness in our neighbours; but complaining is most of all a danger with persons who have *weak health*—for weakness of body often produces depression of spirits—and this is the soil in which a complaining spirit takes deepest root. Then, too, it often grows into a *habit;* a tinge of discontent settles on the countenance, and the voice assumes a *tone* of complaint. And though this, like most habits, soon becomes *unconscious*, yet it is not the less mischievous on that account.

It is mischievous to our own souls, for it damps the work of the Spirit of God in our hearts, and enfeebles the spiritual life. It is mischievous in its effects upon others ; for when Christians complain, it gives the world altogether wrong impressions of the strength and consolation which the love of Christ affords, and it frequently generates the same spirit ; one complains, and another, having the same or other causes of complaint, sees no reason why he should not complain too. And this was probably its history in Israel. It is scarcely likely that all began to complain at the same moment. Doubtless there were some who set the sad example, and then the hearts of all being *predisposed*, it spread like an epidemic. Brethren, we should settle it well in our hearts that *complaining*, no less than *murmuring*, is a fruit of the flesh. David complained in Ps. lxxvii. 3, "I complained, and my spirit was overwhelmed ;" but he soon felt that the root of the evil was in himself. "This," he adds, (ver. 10,) "is my infirmity." Asaph complained when he saw the prosperity of the wicked. He said, (Ps. lxxiii. 13,) "Verily, I have cleansed my heart in vain, and washed my hands in innocency ;" but he soon felt ashamed of his spirit, and his words. "So foolish," he says, (ver. 22,)—"so foolish was I, and ignorant." Job, wonderfully patient as he was, gradually fell into a spirit of complaint, when his trials lasted long ; but how deeply he afterwards felt it to be a work of the flesh, we may see in the striking words which he spoke when he was brought up out of the depths,—"I have heard of thee by the hearing of the ear : but now mine eye seeth thee. Wherefore I *abhor myself*, and repent in dust and ashes." But no part of Scripture proves more strikingly than the events at Taberah, how displeasing to God, and how dangerous in its results, a complaining

spirit is. The punishment which followed, and which gave
the name to the place, proves the first point. Patient and
long-suffering as God ever was with Israel, we are told,
(chap. xi. 1,) that "His anger was kindled; and the fire of
the Lord burnt among them, and consumed them that
were in the uttermost parts of the camp." The severity
of the punishment shews that this was no *little* sin, encompassed as they were with mercy, and guided by Jehovah himself through the wilderness.

It was no less dangerous in its result, for the subsequent history shews how "complaining" ripened into
"murmuring," and murmuring was at last the cause of
Israel's final fall. Let us endeavour, then, dear brethren,
to watch against a "complaining spirit." In heavy and
stunning afflictions we glorify God, when, like Aaron, we
are enabled to "hold our peace." Like David, we can
say, "I was dumb, and opened not my mouth, because
thou didst it;" or, as in Ps. cxxxi. 2, "Surely I have
behaved and quieted myself, as a child that is weaned of
its mother: my soul is even as a weaned child." Still
more if we can, through grace, rise to the elevation of the
afflicted Job, and say, "The Lord gave, and the Lord
hath taken away; blessed be the name of the Lord;" or,
if anything, to the still higher elevation of the apostle
Paul, (Phil. iv. 11–13,) "I have learned, in whatsoever
state I am, therewith to be content. I know both how
to be abased, and how to abound: everywhere and in all
things I am instructed both to be full and to be hungry,
both to abound and to suffer need. I can do all things
through Christ which strengtheneth me." In the lesser
and more ordinary trials of daily life, its difficulties and
its duties, we glorify Him by Christian *cheerfulness;* and
how can we maintain this spirit but by tracing the hand

of a Father in them all, carrying them all to God in prayer, and leaving them at the foot of His throne, and, most of all, by looking above present things to the "everlasting covenant ordered in all things and sure?" For the things which are seen, our difficulties and our trials, are temporal; but the things which are not seen, our strength and our crown, are eternal.

KIBROTH-HATTAAVAH
(or, The Graves of Lust)

Numbers 11:4

" Who shall give us flesh to eat ? "

NOTHING is said after ver. 3 of the moving of the camp
from Taberah. And yet, at ver. 34, we are told that the
name of Kibroth-hattaavah was given to the place at
which the events recorded in this chapter happened. We
might be disposed, therefore, to infer from this that the
children of Israel must have journeyed from Taberah,
although it is not mentioned ; and this might seem to be
a sound conclusion. A reference, however, to chap. xxxiii.
of this book, in which we find a very complete list of the
stations of the Israelites in the wilderness, throws much
doubt on this conclusion ; for at ver. 16 you will see that
there is no mention of Taberah whatever. It says that
" they removed from the desert of Sinai, and pitched at
Kibroth-hattaavah." As the conclusion from chap. xi., if
taken alone, will be that Taberah and Kibroth-hattaavah
are *two* distinct stations, so the conclusion from this verse,
if taken alone, would be that they indicated *one* place
only, which would be called Taberah if reference were
made to the first sin committed there, Kibroth-hattaavah
if reference were made to the second—both names of
humiliation. But then it so happens that there is a remarkable passage in Deut. ix., in which both these names

are mentioned by Moses, and, what is very singular, another name intervenes between them. It is ver. 22, "And at Taberah, and at Massah, and at Kibroth-hattaavah, ye provoked the Lord to wrath." It is evident, however, here that Moses leaves chronology, and places it altogether out of sight. It is a classification of *sins*, and not a list of stations. At all three places, if they *were* three, and not two only, the sin was of the *same* kind. At Taberah it was least sinful, because it was *complaint* only. At Massah it was murmuring for something that was really necessary,—for water. At Kibroth-hattaavah it was murmuring, as we shall see more at length, for something *unnecessary*,—for *flesh*. Inasmuch, then, as this is a graduated scale of sins, and not a description of localities, it does not throw any material light on the difficulty. It is evidently a point on which different minds will come to different conclusions. On the whole, however, it seems to us most probable, since the moving of the camp is not mentioned in chap. xi., and Taberah is not mentioned in chap. xxxiii., that the two names designate, not two distinct stations, but one.

In considering the events of this chapter, we may notice the origin, the nature, and the consequences of Israel's sin.

Let us begin with its origin. When Israel was brought out of Egypt by the power of God, "a mixed multitude," (we are told, chap. xii. 30,) "went up with them." It may be that they had heard of the promise that God had given to Israel, and wished to share it with them. At all events, they had seen the awful judgments on Egypt, and had learnt that "God was with his people of a truth," and so they cast in their lot with Israel, and journeyed with them through the wilderness. We hear nothing of

this "mixed multitude" for a long time. Had they, on
the one hand, been a snare to Israel, or, on the other, been
faithful to God when the Israelites murmured, it would
probably have been mentioned. We may conclude, therefore, that they shared in all Israel's sins and judgments.
But at Kibroth-hattaavah they became a snare and a
temptation to Israel. "The mixed multitude," we read,
"fell a lusting," and the unhallowed desire for the good
things of Egypt and the spirit of murmuring rapidly
spread throughout the camp of Israel. "They wept and
said, Who shall give us flesh to eat?" This *sin*, then,
unlike those preceding, originated in the "mixed multitude."

Now, if Israel, brethren, according to its calling, be
regarded as a type of the *new* man, then this "mixed
multitude," a remnant of Egypt, and influenced still by
its spirit, will be a type of the old man in the believer.
But we may take another view of Israel, and say that it
is typical of those who walk, not after the flesh, but after
the Spirit—the true members of Christ's body, the living
branches of the true vine ; and then, corresponding with
this, the " mixed multitude " will be a type of those who
accompany the true Israel now, without being partakers
of the Divine nature, and walking in the Spirit—the dead
branches in the vine. History shews that the Church on
earth has ever been made up of these two elements ; and
prophetic parables shew that such will be its constitution
until Jesus comes.

The Word of God everywhere encourages the living
members of Christ's body, by patience, and gentleness,
and unwearied zeal, to win those who have only a name
to live. But it forbids them to take into their own hands
the awful work of separation between the wheat and the

tares, a work which the Searcher of hearts reserves to Himself alone. So that it need cause us no surprise, as it did the Donatists of old, and still does to some, that there is, and always will be, a "mixed multitude" associated with the true Israel. But though, brethren, we are absolutely forbidden to cast out the element from the Church, this passage of Scripture may well impress us with the danger arising from it, and shew how watchful we ought to be. Even if the Church were made up of true Christians only, there would be much evil in it, for the simple reason, that there is so much sin in every heart. But being made up, as it is, not of them only, but also of a " mixed multitude," of many who walk altogether in the flesh, there is *still more* danger, a still greater demand for watchfulness. Many temptations may come to you even from those who are really Christ's, and who are engaged, through grace, in crucifying the affections and lusts of the flesh ; but others will come to you, as they did to Israel of old, from the " mixed multitude ; " and what dangers in particular ? Party spirit, we cannot fail to see, is one ; but, oh, there is a greater and more subtle danger still,— *worldliness*, brethren, conformity to the course of this world ; and with it, forgetfulness of the high and holy calling wherewith we are called, and the adoption of a low standard of holiness, instead of that elevated one which is set before us in our Lord, and so beautifully reflected in His first disciples. We have all a root of worldliness in our own hearts, and this it is that makes us so slow to perceive what we ought to be. This it is which predisposes us to adopt the low and worldly standard around us, instead of striving to be like Jesus. Our only safety is to set the perfect example of our Lord

Jesus Christ before us; to ask ourselves again and again throughout the day, "How would Christ act if He were in my place?" to crucify through the Spirit the root of worldliness within, and to watch all the avenues by which it can enter the heart from without. Only in this way, brethren, can our own standard be elevated; only in this way can we help to elevate the standard of others, instead of being dragged down ourselves; only in this way avoid Israel's sin, that of being carried away by the worldly spirit which originated in the "mixed multitude" which sojourned with them.

And now let us look more closely at the nature of Israel's sin on this occasion. It was murmuring, perhaps you will say; and so it was,—murmuring in a most aggravated form. But this is not a full description of it. We are told in ver. 4 that the mixed multitude *fell a lusting*, or, as it is in the margin, "lusted a lust;" and Israel did the same, as the discontented question shews, "Who shall give us flesh to eat?" And we find this selfsame description of the sin in other passages of Scripture: so Ps. lxxviii. 18, "And they tempted God in their heart by asking *meat* for their lust;" and Ps. cvi. 14, "But *lusted exceedingly* in the wilderness, and tempted God in the desert." And it is evidently in allusion to this that St Paul says, 1 Cor. x. 6, "Now these things were our examples, to the intent we should not lust after evil things, as they also lusted."

It is clear, then, from these passages, that their sin was not murmuring only, sinful as that is, but *uncontrolled desire*. And for what was that desire? It was for meat. They had grown so weary of the bread of heaven which God so mercifully provided; and they wanted something in addition—something, too, as we have already observed,

which was not absolutely necessary to their existence.
When they murmured for water at Massah, they murmured for something *needful.* Their sin *then* was in
murmuring, instead of *praying.* But here they lusted
for something *unnecessary,* and this was an aggravation
of their sin. And thus the Psalmist, evidently comparing
this sin with the murmuring at Massah, says, Ps. lxxviii.
17, "they sinned *yet more* against Him." Whereas, too,
at Massah no punishment followed their murmuring;
on this occasion, as we shall see, a severe judgment came
upon them for their lust.

And we may trace in this history the generative of
their sin,—the process by which it was developed. They
allowed, you will observe, their memories to recall, and
their imaginations to dwell upon the *abundance* of
Egypt. "We *remember,*" they say, "the fish which we did
eat in Egypt freely; the cucumbers, and the melons, and
the leeks, and the onions, and the garlick." We *remember*
—yes, indeed, and too well; but there was much that
they had *forgotten.* They had forgotten the bitter bondage in Egypt, and their own cries for deliverance. Such
was their view of the *past.* What do they say of the
present? "Our soul is dried away; there is nothing at
all, beside this manna, before our eyes." Where, then,
was the pillar of fire and cloud, the symbol of God's presence? Where the promises which God had given to
Israel? And that manna, too, which they contemptuously
call "*this* manna," was it not an extraordinary miracle?
and a very precious gift? Coming down from heaven
with the dew, it had long sustained Israel's natural life.
All this was overlooked. We see, then, with what an
unequal eye they looked upon the past and the present.
Their imaginations reproduced the *bright* part of the past

without its dark shadows ; and discontent, nourished by this retrospect, discoloured all their present mercies. But what is this, brethren, but the usual history of discontent? If you have been thwarted in your purposes, disappointed in your expectations, and severely tried in your affections, have you not often found your memory recalling the past, and your imagination reproducing it, not *perfectly*, but only in *parts*, remembering its blessings, but overlooking its drawbacks? And then, when you have looked around you, your heart has reckoned up its trials, but overlooked the *new* mercies bestowed upon you. Much, it may be, you *have* been tried. The *past* seems to comprehend all your life. But does not manna, which once you knew not, fall upon your camp now? Is not Christ more precious now? Once, perhaps, you thought of Him occasionally, as one gift among many. Now He is *the* gift, the chiefest among ten thousand, and altogether lovely, your all in all. Oh to have this gift always before our eyes, and to feel that this alone is more than worth everything besides !

But let us now pass on to the consequences of Israel's sin. These were manifold ; but we may trace its effects on *Moses* and on *Israel*. Moses, we read, ver. 10, was displeased. He was also greatly *discouraged*. The responsibility of leading such a people must have always weighed heavily on his heart ; but now it seemed almost to overwhelm him. He carried, however, his burden to the Lord, and in this shewed his *faith*. Although with deep love to Israel, there were some signs in his prayer of impatience and unbelief. " Wherefore," he says, ver. 11–15, " hast thou afflicted thy servant? and wherefore have I not found favour in thy sight, that thou layest the burden of all this people upon me? Have I conceived all this people? have I begotten them, that thou shouldest say unto me, Carry them in thy bosom, as a nursing father beareth the sucking child, unto the land which thou swarest unto their fathers? Whence should I have flesh to give unto all this people? for they weep unto me, saying, Give us flesh, that we may eat. I am not able to bear all this people alone, because it is too heavy for me. And if thou deal thus with me, kill me, I pray thee, out of hand, if I have found favour in thy sight; and let me not see my wretchedness." God made gentle allowance for His afflicted servant. He uttered no rebuke, but graciously removed the twofold difficulty which was pressing so heavily upon the spirit of Moses. The first difficulty was the oppressive burden of the people, the second was the provision of flesh. How did God relieve His servant of the first? The 16th verse gives the answer. Seventy men of the elders of Israel were to be chosen, and brought into the tabernacle of the congregation, that there they might receive the Spirit of God, and be qualified to bear the burden of the people with Moses. To bear this burden was, then, a work of the Spirit. Indeed, those who are aright conscious of deep responsibility know that it is the Spirit of God that teaches them to feel it; and they also know that unless the same Spirit enabled them to bring the burden to God, that they would be overwhelmed by it. But there is one thing in this passage, dear brethren, which can scarcely fail to strike you, and that is, that the Spirit, which was given to the seventy elders, did not come straight from God, but was taken from Moses. "I will take," said God, "of the Spirit which is upon thee, and will put it on them." Why was this? It might be to shew that the measure of the Spirit already bestowed on Moses was sufficient for the carrying of this burden. God had not called him to this work without giving him a sufficient supply of grace. It might be also to make those elders feel that it was not independently of Moses, but through him, that they were called to this work, thus to keep up the unity in the history, and *unity* in Israel. But whatever, brethren, be the true reason, it cannot fail to remind us of *Him* who is a Mediator of a better covenant, established on better promises. Jesus is able to do what Moses could not do,— bear the burden of His people, and carry them in His bosom, as a nursing father beareth his sucking child, up to the promised inheritance; and when God gives the Spirit to any soul, He takes of the Spirit which is in Jesus, the one Mediator of His people, the one head of His Church, in whom is all the fulness of grace, the Spirit without measure. Do you feel your need of the Spirit of God? Not only are there beautiful promises to encourage you, promises that cannot fail, but there is also this most blessed fact, that the Spirit of God is already laid up for you in Jesus. Wait, then, on God in earnest prayer, and the Father will take of "the Spirit which is in Him, and will put it, not only *upon*, but *in* you."

But it pleased God also to satisfy Israel's desire, and fulfil Moses's prayer for flesh. He did so, as on a former occasion, by sending them a great abundance of quails. We read, ver. 31, "And there went forth a wind from the Lord, and brought quails from the sea, and let them fall by the camp, as it were a day's journey on this side, and as it were a day's journey on the other side, round about the camp, and as it were two cubits high upon the face of the earth." And this supply was sufficient, not for a day, or two days, or five days, or twenty days, but for a whole month. Thus God answered the doubtful

questionings of Moses, (ver. 22,) " Shall the flocks and
the herds be slain for them, to suffice them? or shall all
the fish of the sea be gathered together for them, to suffice them?" and proved once more that His "own hand
had not waxed short." But though He granted Israel's
unhallowed *desire*, He turned the very gift into a plague.
For, (ver. 33,) " While the flesh was yet between their
teeth, ere it was chewed, the wrath of the Lord was kindled
against the people, and the Lord smote the people with
a very great plague; " or, as the Psalmist says, Ps. cvi. 15,
" He gave them their request; but sent leanness withal
into their soul."

In what a solemn and impressive manner, brethren,
does this teach us the danger of unhallowed and uncontrolled *desires!* We have often thought what a beautiful
prayer that is, Ps. xx. 4, " Grant thee according to thine
own heart, and fulfil all thy counsel," *when* offered for
one whose heart is *subdued,* and whose desires are concentrated on the fulfilment of God's promises. But would
it not be an awful prayer for one whose heart is full of
unhallowed desires? who longs, like Israel of old, only for
earthly things? Oh, we should take heed, brethren, what
we desire, and for what we pray! You may ask for some
earthly *gift,*—it may be worldly prosperity, it may be
wealth, or it may be for some other gift—some far higher,
but still *earthly* gift,—and because you are very intent upon
it, God may give it you; He may grant you *all* that you
desire, and then the fulfilment of that desire may become
a most terrible snare to you. The gift, whatsoever it be,
may become your idol, may let down your affections to
earth; and thus, whilst your prayers have been granted,
God has sent *leanness* withal into your soul. O brethren, it is *mercy*, it is exalted *mercy*, that God does *not*

grant all our desires—that He so often sets aside some desires, and greatly disappoints others. We are prone to fret at this, but it is a part of a merciful plan, whereby He would bring us to *rest* in *Himself,* and in *Himself* only—it is because He would not " send leanness into our souls." When, then, beloved brethren, some of our most fervent desires are not granted, when some of our highest anticipations become shrouded in darkness, when our affections are keenly wounded, oh, then let us think within ourselves, Is it not to teach me the meaning of those deep words, " Delight thyself in the Lord ; and he will give thee the desires of thine heart ? " (Ps. xxxvii. 4.) Oh, then, through grace, I will turn away from earth, with all its treasures, and from the creature, whatever its attractions be. I will turn to Jesus. In Him I cannot be disappointed. His love is altogether pure, altogether satisfying. I cannot commune with Him too frequently, cleave to Him too steadfastly. In Him every desire of my heart shall be fulfilled ; and then there is, there can be, no *leanness* of soul. Oh no ; but peace that passeth all understanding—songs even in the night, joy unspeakable, and full of glory !

MOSES, AN EXAMPLE OF MEEKNESS

Numbers 12:3

"Now the man Moses was very meek, above all the men which were upon the face of the earth."

WE are often struck with the trials of Job and David, and realize vividly the painful circumstances in which they were placed. But Moses also was deeply tried, though in a very different way. Job was tried in his person; David was tried in his family; Moses was tried in consequence of his office. Job was tried in his patience; David in his faith; Moses in his temper. All triumphed, though not without some failures: Job, when he exclaimed, "The Lord gave, and the Lord hath taken away, blessed be the name of the Lord;" David, when he said, "Although my house be not so with God; yet he hath made with me an everlasting covenant, ordered in all things, and sure: for this is all my salvation and all my desire, although he make it not to grow;" and Moses, when, under repeated provocations, he was very meek. The part of the history at which we have now arrived, informs us of the circumstances of one of these provocations—one certainly of the most trying that he had to bear.

"Miriam and Aaron," we read, ver. 1, "spake against Moses." It is not altogether evident what was the *root* of this opposition. If we judge from the language of the 1st verse, it may have been a private spite on the part of

Miriam towards the wife of Moses; if from the 2d verse, it may have been *envy* of the power and authority of Moses. For in ver. 1 it says, that they spoke against Moses "because of the Ethiopian woman whom he had married." It is supposed by some commentators that by this name they intended Zipporah, the daughter of the priest of Midian. It is clear from 1 Chron. iv. 40, that some Ethiopian tribes, the descendants of Ham, had settled in the Arabian desert; and in 2 Chron. xxi. 16, Arabians are spoken of as being near the Ethiopians,— "Moreover, the Lord stirred up against Jehoram the spirit of the Philistines, and of the Arabians, that were near the Ethiopians;" and in Hab. iii. 7 we find Cushan in Ethiopia, and Midian mentioned together,—" I saw the tents of Cushan in affliction: and the curtains of the land of Midian did tremble." Thus Aaron and Miriam might have availed themselves of this connexion between Midian and the children of Ethiopia, to throw contempt upon the Midianite, as if she were a descendant of Ham. The only difficulty in this view are the words that are added, " For he had married an Ethiopian woman." Others, in consequence, suppose that Zipporah must have died ere this, and that Moses must have married one of the descendants of Ham. It does not appear that this would have been contrary to the law, which seems to have forbidden marriages with the Canaanites only ; and could it be proved that not Zipporah, but a real descendant of Ham is here intended, we must hold that such an alliance, on the part of the great lawgiver, to have been prophetic of that blessed time when there should no longer be a separation between Israel and the heathen—when the middle wall of partition should be broken down—when "neither circumcision should avail anything, nor uncircumcision, but a

new creature," (Gal. vi. 15,)—when there should be
neither Jew nor Greek, neither bond nor free, neither
male nor female, but all should be one in Christ Jesus ;
and that beautiful promise should be fully accomplished,
Ps. lxviii. 31, "Ethiopia shall soon stretch out her hands
unto God." But however this point be settled, whether
the wife of Moses at this time was a Midianite or Ethiopian, it is clear that there must have been a strong feeling
in Israel against such a union. And Miriam and Aaron
very unkindly and uncharitably took advantage of the
feeling to weaken Moses's authority and influence, just at
the very time that Moses needed support and sympathy,
and just after he had shewn such an enlarged and noble
spirit, as we see from the words addressed to Joshua,
chap. xi. 29, "Enviest thou for my sake? would God
that all the Lord's people were prophets, and that the
Lord would put his Spirit upon them!" They spake
against him, and, jealousy mixing itself up with private
dislike on the part of Miriam, they said, " Hath the Lord
indeed spoken only by Moses? Hath he not also spoken
by us?" It may seem to some as if we had already laid
too much blame on Miriam. It may be asked what
proof there is that this unkind opposition to Moses originated with her. There are three simple and cogent arguments which, taken together, form an overwhelming proof.
And, first, you will remark that in ver. 1 her name is
put *before* Aaron's, though the latter was high priest ;
whereas in ver. 4 Moses's name is put first, and Miriam's
last ; and if we compare the verses together, we can
scarcely fail to see that the reason of its position in ver. 1
cannot have been any other than that she was the first to
speak against her brother. This is confirmed by another
argument drawn from the Hebrew of the word " spake "

in the same verse, which is in the feminine, and not the masculine gender, and, therefore, applies to Miriam more than to Aaron ; and the last and most convincing argument is, that Miriam, and not Aaron, was smitten with leprosy. And with this view of the history, the characters of the sister and brother quite agree. Miriam was evidently firm and rapid : she was quick in her suggestions ; fearless and decided in her course of action ; more inclined to lead than to be led. We may see an instance of her quickness and decision in her proposal to Pharaoh's daughter, when Moses was a little infant, Exod. ii. 7, "Shall I go and call to thee a nurse of the Hebrew women, that she may nurse the child for thee?" When the host of Pharaoh sank like lead in the mighty waters of the Red Sea, Miriam took a leading part in the song of thanksgiving. Exod. xv. 20, 21, "And Miriam the prophetess, the sister of Aaron, took a timbrel in her hand ; and all the women went out after her with timbrels and with dances. And Miriam answered them, Sing ye to the Lord, for he hath triumphed gloriously ; the horse and his rider hath he thrown into the sea." It is not without cause and meaning, too, that her death is specially mentioned. Num. xx. 1, "Miriam died there, and was buried there." We shall not, therefore, be wrong in supposing that she was *the* woman of influence in Israel, and on every other occasion but this her influence was well exerted. Aaron's character was very different. He was weak and vacillating ; easily led in any direction, whether to good or to evil. One proof of this is sufficient. When Moses went up into the mount, he yielded, even without protest, to the sinful and idolatrous tendencies of Israel, made the golden calf, and used the awful language, "These be thy gods, O Israel." Though

Aaron, as a man, and as Israel's high priest, ought to have stood firm, and strengthened Moses's hands, yet it is no great wonder, when we remember his vacillating character, that he was carried away by Miriam's greater decision.

How did Moses bear this opposition? The words of our text evidently give the answer—"Now the man Moses was very meek, above all the men which were upon the face of the earth." It may seem to some remarkable, that it is just on this occasion that " his meekness" should be spoken of; for his temper was tried over and over again by the frequent murmurings of the Israelites. The reason probably is, that this was the greatest trial of temper that he had to bear, because it came not from an ignorant people, but from near relatives, and from those who, of all others, ought to have strengthened his hands. We often find, brethren, that those who are able to exercise considerable self-control when provoked by strangers, or in the presence of strangers, very easily get out of temper with relatives and servants. They can bear much provocation from some with calmness, but with others the least thing is enough to call forth feelings and expressions of impatience. This, brethren, ought not to be ; but we can know little of the world, and of our own heart, if we have not perceived that so it is. And if this must be confessed to be a fact, why is it that there is this inequality in the power of self-control? It is, and must be, brethren, because the presence of man operates more powerfully than the presence of God. Realize, brethren, the presence of God—realize that the state of your heart towards God is the great thing, and you will be as meek and patient under the provocations of a fretful relative, or a careless servant, as you would under those of a stranger of rank. It was this, without doubt, that enabled Moses to bear so much. He had been with God in the mount. It was in communion with Him that his heart was strengthened to endurance, and bowed down in a spirit of meekness. His shining face reflected the glory of God, but it also reflected the holiness which communion with God produced. Thus Moses triumphed on this occasion of trial. He won the noblest triumph, because he triumphed over the evil of his own heart. He made no angry reply, set up no eager defence of his own conduct, but, like our blessed Redeemer, "committed himself to Him that judgeth righteously." "Moses was very meek."

How beautiful a grace is meekness! It may be somewhat difficult to define it; but whenever we see it, we cannot fail to know it, and to feel its gentle and winning power. It is a grace that implies so very much in the heart. It is the beautiful result of many other graces; whilst its place in the beatitudes shews that it is the root on which others grow. Meekness is quite consistent with power and authority; for Moses had great power and authority in Israel, and yet, altogether unspoilt by it, he was the meekest of men. But we may look to another example, far greater than Moses, — to Him who said, "All power is given to me in heaven and on earth;" and yet added, "I am meek and lowly in heart." It is in such lofty places that meekness is the most beautiful, because it then can, and does, stoop very low. But though this grace is evidently consistent with any power and authority, however exalted, it is altogether inconsistent with the *love* of power and with the *love* of authority. The man who loves power will shew but little patience towards those who limit it. Such conduct as that of Miriam's and Moses's would produce in such a one ungoverned wrath. Meekness can only grow upon the ruins of selfishness in all its forms, whether it be selfishness towards God—that is, unbelief,—or whether it be selfishness towards man, either in its form of pride, love of our own way, love of ease, love of money. Jesus, for His Father's glory, and for our salvation, emptied Himself of His glory; and where shall we find meekness but in the soul that is emptied, and continually empties ˙tself?

But we may trace another feature in meekness from the example of Moses, and learn that this grace is not the attribute of a weak and vacillating character, but the ornament of a firm and comprehensive spirit. Indeed, we seldom find real meekness in weak and vacillating characters; for such yield when they ought *not* to yield, and then, rebuked by conscience for yielding, they become angry. Meekness will more often be found in the firm and resolute character, when it is sanctified by the Spirit of God, and obstinacy is purged out. Moses was a beautiful example of extraordinary strength of character. His *one* will was stronger than the united wills of all Israel. And yet amongst them all there was not one to be found so meek as he; and the reason was, because his will rested on the will of God. It was an unselfish will, and therefore it was that its uncommon power did not exclude meekness. It is clear, then, brethren, that we ought to cultivate firmness of character and meekness of spirit at the same time. We should aim never to be turned from the path of duty through fear of man; but if we should meet with opposition in that path, we should try, through the grace of God, to bear it with meekness. How firm was Jesus! Nothing would turn Him aside from the work which He had engaged to execute; and yet when the Holy One was brought to the bar of the ungodly and unrighteous, whom He came to redeem, how meek He was! Silent under reproaches—silent when His conduct was misunderstood and attacked. "He was oppressed, and he was afflicted, yet he opened not his mouth: he is brought as a lamb to the slaughter, and as a sheep before her shearers is dumb, so he openeth not his mouth."

We all, brethren, need this grace in every relationship of life. As parents, for meekness should be the border and fringe of every act of authority; as mistresses, for in the carelessness and want of conscientiousness of servants your spirit may be tried nearly every day; as Christians, for St Peter exhorts us (1 Pet. iii. 15) to "be ready always to give an answer to every man that asketh you a reason of the hope that is in you with *meekness* and fear;" as teachers, for St Paul says, (2 Tim. ii. 24, 25,) "The servant of the Lord must not strive; but be gentle unto all men, apt to teach, patient, in meekness instructing those that oppose themselves; if God peradventure will give them repentance to the acknowledging of the truth." In these days of collision between system and system, and of sad confusion of views of Divine truth, we specially seem to need the spirit of meekness. For it is not rude attacks upon error, but truth spoken in meekness and love, that avails and has most power. Meekness, brethren, should be the handmaid of zeal. When these two are found united, there you see a reflection of Jesus—those labours will be blessed.

Brethren, all of us must feel, if we have only made the experiment, how difficult of attainment is this grace; and yet there is great encouragement to seek it. We have examples set before us in Scripture that we may see how

beautiful it is.   How beautiful it was in Moses, who was
"very meek!" how far more beautiful in Jesus, whose
meekness and gentleness never failed! We have promises
also to encourage us in the difficult pursuit.   The blood
of Jesus, and the agency of the Spirit of God, co-operate
for its production.   Thus it appears in the cluster of
graces described as the "fruit of the Spirit."   It is the
last but *one*, perhaps to shew us the height at which it
grows.   There is a beautiful promise of guidance to the
meek, Ps. xxv. 9,—" The meek will he guide in judgment:
and the meek will he teach his way ; " and in Ps. cxlix. 4
is a larger promise still,—"He will beautify the meek with
salvation."   And then we cannot forget the beatitude
uttered by the lips of Him whose meekness never failed,
—"Blessed are the meek, for they shall inherit the earth!"

But this part of Moses's history is almost as encouraging to us to exercise meekness as any promise could be.
Had Moses defended himself, there might have been a
long altercation, and the discontented Israelites might
have set themselves in array against their leader ; but he
was silent, and one who could speak effectually spoke for
him.   " The Lord *spake suddenly* unto Moses and unto
Aaron, and unto Miriam."   And then separating the two
last from the first, He himself answered the two questions : " Hath the Lord spoken only by Moses ? "   "Hath
he not spoken also by us ? " by shewing the distinctive
privileges to which the Lord had called Moses.   These
were twofold.   For, first, if any prophet were raised up
in Israel, and spoke the word of God, he had *authority*
only in so far as, and at the time, that he spoke that
word.   He had no lasting and constant authority—no
authority of government.   But Moses had this; for he
was intrusted with the house of God.   " My servant

Moses," we read, ver. 7, "is not so, who is faithful in all
my house." And if any ask what we are to understand
by the expression "house" here, a reference to Heb. iii.
5, 6, where Moses and Christ are contrasted, makes it
clear ; for in the last of the two verses it is explained,—
"Whose house," says the apostle, "are we, if we hold
fast the confidence and the rejoicing of the hope firm
unto the end." Faithful Christians, then, are Christ's
house. What, then, was that which Moses ruled as a
servant, and not as a son ? Evidently, brethren, not a
material house ; not the tabernacle, as some commentators have supposed, but Israel itself. Whereas, then, the
prophets *spoke* to Israel, Moses not only did so, but had
a *constant* and *permanent* authority in the house of God.

And, secondly, there was a wide difference in the manner in which God spoke to the other prophets, and the
way in which He spoke to Moses. He spoke to them
in a "vision and in a dream;" not, that is, *directly*, but
indirectly, not when they were conscious, but in an unconscious state. But with Moses God spake mouth to
mouth even, apparently, and not in dark speeches. God
admitted *him* into near and conscious communion with
Himself. The two questions, then, were answered. Moses,
who was very meek and silent under reproaches, was
lifted up to the lofty elevation to which the grace of God
had called him. Miriam and Aaron, who had exalted
themselves, were abased. But this was not all. "The
anger of the Lord was kindled against them;" and Miriam,
who had misled her brother, "became leprous, white as
snow." Aaron, easily misled, was as easily led to repentance. "Lay not," he says, "the sin upon us, wherein we
have done foolishly, and wherein we have sinned." And
Moses, full of forgiving love, as of meekness, interceded

for her,—"Heal her now, O God, I beseech thee." And
his prayer was heard. She was healed, but yet was shut
out of the camp for seven days, and the journeyings of
Israel were arrested.

What a lesson to Israel and to us, brethren! No words
could shew more forcibly that pride, selfishness, and self-
seeking *must*, and *will*, be brought to shame. Nothing
can prove more convincingly that the power of God's
presence is with the meek. Even now they often inherit
what the selfish, the ambitious, and the grasping desire
in vain to possess. They seek not their own, and therefore God gives them what they do *not* seek. They pray
with Solomon for a wise and understanding heart, and
God grants them the desire of their hearts, and gives
them besides, which they do not seek, honour from man,
as well as from Himself, and the *earth*—perhaps that
earth wherein shall dwell righteousness—as their inheritance.

THE EVIL REPORT

Numbers 13:32

" And they brought up an evil report of the land which they had
searched unto the children of Israel, saying, The land, through
which we have gone to search it, is a land that eateth up the
inhabitants thereof; and all the people that we saw in it are men
of a great stature."

WE have remarked, brethren, on a former occasion, that
the history of the Israelites from Sinai to the confines of
the Land of Promise is little else than the history of increasing rebellion,—the awful progress of unbelief. It
commenced with a complaining spirit at Taberah. It
grew into open and unrestrained murmuring at Kibroth-
hattaavah. It there spread to those in whom we should
least of all have expected to find it, and which proves
strikingly the power of corruption in Israel,—to Miriam
and Aaron. And here, in the portion of Scripture which
we have now to contemplate, it rises to its greatest height ;
and we see a nation, rescued from cruel bondage, daily
fed by bread from heaven, — guided by symbols of
God's presence, brought into covenant with Himself, instructed in His will,—we see this nation renouncing,
deliberately renouncing, God's gracious promise, and
thereby doubting His love,—limiting His power, and *pro-
claiming* that His faithfulness had failed. It is a dark
picture, brethren ; but, after all, it is a picture of our own
hearts,—of what we should do and be, unless the Spirit

of God teaches and restrains us. There is no grace which
we should not lose, if we *could* lose it,—no blessing which
we should not pervert, if left to ourselves,—no perdition
into which we should not fall, did not the grace of God
rescue us from it, and the faithfulness of God uphold us
in the way into which He has brought us.

We may consider the mission, the search, and the
report of the twelve spies.

We begin with the mission. This we find spoken of in
the 1st and 2d verses of this chapter,—"And the Lord
spake unto Moses, saying, Send thou men, that they may
search the land of Canaan, which I give unto the children
of Israel: of every tribe of their fathers shall ye send a
man, every one a ruler among them." Now, we are
tempted to ask, Why should twelve men be sent into
Canaan to spy out the land? The Israelites knew already
what kind of land it was, for God had already more than
once described it as a land flowing with milk and honey.
So Exod. iii. 8, "And I am come down to deliver them
out of the hand of the Egyptians, and to bring them up
out of that land unto a good land and a large, unto a land
flowing with milk and honey." Was not this promise
sufficient? What more could Israel want before they
entered altogether on its full enjoyment? There is a
passage of Scripture which throws some light on this, for
it shews that if God told Moses to send the spies, it was
because the Israelites desired it. You will find the passage, Deut. i. 20–24, "And I said unto you, Ye are come
unto the mountain of the Amorites, which the Lord our
God doth give unto us. Behold, the Lord thy God hath
set the land before thee: go up and possess it, as the
Lord God of thy fathers hath said unto thee; fear not,
neither be discouraged. And ye came near unto me every

one of you, and said, We will send men before us, and
they shall search us out the land, and bring us word again
by what way we must go up, and into what cities we shall
come. And the saying pleased me well : and I took twelve
men of you, one of a tribe : and they turned, and went
up into the mountain." From a comparison of this passage with that in Numbers, we can scarcely fail to draw
the conclusion that the command of God to Moses was an
act of condescension on God's part. It was the fulfilment
of Israel's desire. But was that desire right or wrong?
Did it cast any doubt on God's promise? If so, it must
have been wrong; and its fulfilment was only another
illustration of the principle on which God acted when He
gave His people flesh to eat, but, when giving it, sent leanness withal into their souls ; only another solemn lesson
as to the responsibility of uncontrolled desires, and the
very disastrous consequences which may follow their fulfilment. But if you refer again to the passage quoted from
Deuteronomy, you will perceive that no doubt seems to be
cast by that desire upon the fertility of the land. What
they desired to know was, " by what way they should go
up," and into " what cities they should come." But, then,
some will say, Had they not the pillar of cloud to guide
them? Yes, they had. But so also had Moses when he
said to Hobab, (chap. x. 31,) " Leave us not, I pray
thee ; forasmuch as thou knowest how we are to encamp
in the wilderness, and thou mayest be unto us instead of
eyes." As, then, Moses's desire did not necessarily shew
a spirit of unbelief, so also may Israel's desire have been
free from it ; and God may have granted it, not in judgment, but to shew His willingness that the truth of His
promises should be tested and confirmed in the experience
of His people. And this willingness on God's part still

continues. We know, brethren, that it is one thing to
rest all our weight on God's bare promise, simply because
the mouth of Jehovah has spoken it; another thing to
believe it because it has been confirmed in manifold ways
in our experience. We know that the first is the highest
act of faith, and that it brings glory to God; but we also
know that it is the will of God that His people should
not always rest upon His bare promises, but experience,
even in this world, their truth and meaning. There are
times when God seems to say to them, "Go, search out
the land." Make trial of my promise, and see how true
and precious it is.

Moses acted at once on God's command. Twelve men
were selected,—out of every tribe a man. It is needless to
pause and make any remarks on the order of the names.
One thing, however, we ought not to pass over, for it
shews that the mission of these spies was an *act* of *faith*
on the part of Moses; we mean the change in the name
of that one who was the head of the tribe of Ephraim,—
Oshea, the son of Nun. On this occasion, Moses called
him, (as we are told, ver. 16,) "Jehoshua." The first
name means, "help a salvation;" the second, "Jehovah is
help," or salvation. Joshua had already proved his faithfulness to God. He was intrusted by Moses with the
command of the force that fought with Amalek, and prevailed. It was this victory, probably, as well as his name
and character, that marked him out especially to become,
by a change in his name, an encouragement to Israel.

Thus Moses would remind these heads of the twelve
tribes that He who gave them victory over the Amalekites
at Rephidim would fulfil His promise, and be their help
and salvation against the tribes of Canaan. It must have
been a solemn moment when these spies were dismissed

to search out the land, on the very confines of which
Israel now stood. Their journeyings, painful and fatigu-
ing, now seemed to be brought to a close. Some persons
even at this time began to question the promise, and to
doubt whether the land would, after all, be so very good.
But we see where Moses's hope was. He looked with
simple faith and undaunted hope to Jehovah. To his
mind, whatever there was to others, there was no uncertainty as to the result. And hence, when he commissioned the spies to "go up into the mountain : and see the
land, what it is ; and the people that dwelleth therein,
whether they be strong or weak, few or many ; and what
the land is that they dwell in, whether it be good or bad ;
and what cities they be that they dwell in, whether in
tents, or in strongholds ; and what the land is, whether it
be fat or lean, whether there be wood therein or not;"
he could add, " and be ye of good courage." Yes, brethren, whatever our circumstances be, and whatever our
difficulties, whether within or without, whether very pressing or very long-continued, yet, if we trust with simple
faith and unfaltering hope in Jehovah-Jesus, we need not,
and shall not faint—we may be of good courage. God's
promise secures us success and victory. " In the Lord
Jehovah is everlasting strength."

Such, brethren, was the mission of the twelve spies,
and such the hope of Moses with regard to it. Now, let
us follow the spies in their *search* of the land. They
started, we are told, from the wilderness of Sin, which
seems to be that part of the wilderness of Paran in which
Kadesh was situated, and from thence they went to the ex-
treme north, to Rehob, near Sidon, and therefore through
the whole length of the land. Nothing was wanting in
their diligence in searching the land. But two other inter-

esting facts were mentioned. They were of a very different kind. The one was discouraging, the other was full of encouragement. The first was the *discovery* of Hebron, a very ancient city, for it was built before Zoan, a place well known to the Israelites in Egypt. *There* they found three families descended from Anak, who shared the city between them, and these, we learn from ver. 33, were, like their ancestor, of gigantic stature. " And there," it says, " we saw the giants, the sons of Anak, which come of the giants, and we were in our own sight as grasshoppers, and so we were in their sight." This discovery produced the greatest depression of spirit, which was not removed by the other fact, the discovery of the great fertility of the land, especially of the valley of Eshcol, where they found one cluster of grapes of such enormous size, that they bare it between two upon a staff. This, with some pomegranates and figs, they brought back with them to the congregation of Israel, as a proof of the fruitfulness of the land, as an earnest of what they would have when the promise was fully accomplished.

We can scarcely fail to see, brethren, that there is a typical meaning in this; but before we enter upon it, there is one conclusion we may draw from some other words, which is not altogether without interest. We are told, ver. 20, that the "time was the time of first-ripe grapes." Now, a modern traveller of great accuracy and research has informed us that the grapes ripen in the mountains of Judah about July or August. So that it was probably in one of these months that the spies returned from their search; and if so, we may conclude that the Israelites had been about *four* months on their journey from Sinai to Kadesh, on the confines of the Land of Promise; and in all, *eight* months had elapsed since they had left Egypt,—not one-fortieth part of the time which it took up before they actually entered into the Promised Land. Now, we all know, brethren, that that land was typical of a rest which still remains for the people of God. Of what, then, can those fruits which the spies brought to Israel be typical, but of that *earnest* which God now gives His people of the inheritance to come? There are many beautiful passages in which it is clearly explained what this earnest is. Turn, for instance, to Eph. i. 13, 14, "In whom also after that ye believed, ye were sealed with that holy Spirit of promise, which is the *earnest* of our inheritance until the redemption of the purchased possession, unto the praise of his glory." We may refer also to 2 Cor. i. 21, 22, "Now he which stablisheth us with you in Christ, and hath anointed us, is God; who hath also sealed us, and given the earnest of the Spirit in our hearts." And once more, 2 Cor. v. 5, "Now he that wrought us for the selfsame thing is God, who hath also given unto us the earnest of the Spirit." It has pleased God, then, not only to give a promise of glory—a bare promise—but to put His Spirit in the hearts of His people to be an *earnest* and foretaste of the glory to come. The apostle just simply states it as a fact, a great fact in God's kingdom, that God gives the Spirit, not only to do a work in the hearts of His people, but also to be an earnest of things to come. He does not explain to us in what particular way the Spirit is so; but you will remark that it is not some one thing that the Spirit works which is thus spoken of, but the Spirit himself, and doubtless all the fruits and effects of His indwelling in the heart of the Christian. Just as the fruits of Canaan, the grapes of Eshcol, the pomegranates and figs, were an earnest to them of the richness and fertility

of the Promised Land, so is the Spirit, along with the
fruits that He produces, an earnest of the perfect holiness
and the unsearchable glory of that land whither God is
now conducting His people.   We cannot but fear, brethren, that this view of the Spirit of God is very frequently
overlooked.   There are many who seem to have run well
and long also, and yet they are in constant doubt as to
their standing before God and their final salvation.
Many reasons may be assigned for this.   With some it
is that they do not see the freeness and fulness of salvation as offered to us in Christ Jesus.   They do
not see that to be in Christ, one with Him, is eternal
life.   They are conscious of their own sinfulness, un-
worthiness, and poverty, but do not realise that in
Jesus all things are theirs.   If they had clearer views
of the security and glory of the Christian standing in
Christ, of the perfect righteousness wherewith He is
clothed, of the unrestricted title to heaven which it gives
Him, if there were more simple recumbency of the soul
on the all-sufficiency of Jesus, then the indwelling of the
Spirit would become clearer, His effects more marked,
and His presence would be an *earnest* of the glory to be
revealed.   With others it is, that they do not *search* the
land.   But you may ask, How can this be done?   The
spies could enter the Land of Promise, walk through its
whole length, and see and gather some of its fruits; but
our inheritance is *unseen.*   Yes, brethren, and yet, *unseen*
though it be, there is a way in which this land may be
searched.   We may carefully study the promises that
speak of it, and the descriptions that set it forth.   Its
realities may become and remain ever present to our
minds, and may fill us with joyful anticipations, and,
compared with that " far more exceeding and eternal

weight of glory," things which to the world appear very important, may seem to us altogether vanity; and affliction, which otherwise would be very heavy, may become light. Oh, let us, then, brethren, *search* the land, and walk in the light of the glorious promises! But look at it in another way. Heaven is a *place;* but it is not so much as a *place* that the Christian desires it, as to *be with Christ.* When we ask you, then, dear brethren, to *search* the land, it is not only to realize what heaven is as a place, but to get deeper and deeper into the *fulness* of Christ. This manner of *search is* indeed, and always must be, a work of faith; and yet it is more tangible than the other. For Jesus is a living Person, whose perfect picture is presented to us in the Gospels, and whose fulness is unfolded to us in the Epistles. The way, then, to search into the fulness of Jesus is to *search* the Scriptures, in a patient, trustful, expectant, and reverential spirit; and if we *so* search, what fruits shall we gather, what earnests of glory shall we, even now in this dark world, behold and enjoy!

But it is more than time that we speak of the *report* of the land which ten out of the twelve spies gave. It was an *evil* report. They could not deny that the land was fruitful. "We came," they say, ver. 27, "unto the land whither thou sentest us, and surely it floweth with milk and honey." In this point, they could not do otherwise than confirm God's promise. Our text tells us the *evil* part of their report. "The land," they say, "through which we have gone to search it, is a land that eateth up the inhabitants thereof; and all the people that we saw in it are men of a great stature." It is difficult to understand exactly what is meant by the words, "eateth up the inhabitants thereof." It cannot be that it was unfruitful;

probably it was an allusion to the frequent wars amongst the inhabitants of Canaan. But this, and the gigantic stature of the Anakims, had really nothing whatever to do with the children of Israel; and so Caleb felt, as we see from his noble testimony, ver. 30, — " And Caleb *stilled* the people before Moses, and said, Let us go up at once, and possess it; for we are well able to overcome it." How different do the very same difficulties appear to the trustful and unbelieving heart! Caleb, altogether undismayed by difficulties, because he trusted in God, said, "We are well able to overcome it." The unbelieving spies said, " We are not able to go up against the people; for they are stronger than we."

We must reserve for another occasion the paralysing effect of the evil report upon the people of Israel. It only remains for us to inquire, whether there be not some danger of Christians acting like the unbelieving spies, and bringing up a bad report of the land.

For it cannot escape us, that the world judges of Christianity much more from the spirit and lives of Christians than the Word of God itself. This is, of course, quite wrong; but still it is a fact. And it follows from this, that the spirit and life of each Christian, consciously or unconsciously to himself, is constantly giving in some report of the things unseen which he himself professes to believe; and the world is quick enough to discern whether, and in how far, that report is good or evil. If, brethren, there is no fixed Christian principle in our hearts—if we are vacillating in our walk, religious, if we can use the word, by fits and starts—or if, though we are really in earnest, we are gloomy and desponding in our spirit, and complaining in our language—then is it not evident that we give an evil report of the land, for we give a false impression of the promises and of the nature of the Christian life? But if, brethren, we walk with Jesus—if we act on principle—if we live as pilgrims and strangers on earth—if we are self-denying in our lives, charitable in our thoughts of others—and if, through simple dependence on Jesus, we maintain a spirit of Christian cheerfulness, of patience and resignation in tribulation, of joyful hope, as the apostle says, " rejoicing in hope"—then, brethren, like Caleb, we may still many an objection, remove many a prejudice, and it may be, almost impossible as it may seem, through grace, win many a heart to Jesus ; for then we shall give a good report of the land— the testimony of faith to the truth and preciousness of God's promise. And such calm testimony glorifies God, and may lead others to glorify Him in the day of visitation.

THE BREACH OF PROMISE

Numbers 14:34

"And ye shall know my breach of promise."

YOU will remember, dear brethren, that we considered the mission of the twelve spies, their search of the land, and the evil report which ten out of the twelve gave of it. We saw that in more than one important sense Christians are called to search out the land. First, by realizing the meaning of the beautiful promises of an inheritance to come, and still more by penetrating deeper and deeper into the fulness of Christ. We saw also that God graciously gives His people an earnest and pledge of the glory to be revealed, even His own Spirit. And, lastly, we endeavoured to point out the danger that Christians are in of doing *unconsciously* that which the ten spies consciously did,—namely, of giving an evil report of the land. For such a report is practically given by inconsistency of life, or by despondency and discontentedness of mind. But there was one point, and that a far-reaching one, which we were obliged to leave unnoticed, and that is, "the *consequences* of this evil report of the ten spies." And we shall perhaps get the clearest view of this subject if we notice its direct effects upon Israel; then, its indirect effects upon the position of Caleb and Joshua; thirdly, on that of Moses; and lastly, if we may use the expression with reverence, on "the mind and purpose of God."

If you will refer to Deut. i. 28, you will find an expression which well describes its general effect upon their minds. They say, "Our brethren have *discouraged* our hearts." And the 1st verse of Num. xiv. opens with manifest signs of this discouragement,—"And all the congregation lifted up their voice, and cried; and the people wept that night." Now, we are very prone, brethren, to speak gently of discouragement, and to think that this at least is something which we cannot well help. We are very ready to say, "Is there not a cause?" Well, *this* was just what Israel thought. But in their case we cannot fail to see that it was the result of unbelief. There *were*, indeed, difficulties in their path. It *was* a trial of their faith to hear that there were giants in the land. But their sin was just this, that they looked *exclusively* at *these difficulties*, and ignored the great promise of God, ignored the faithfulness which made the promise sure, and the power which could fulfil it, had the difficulties been tenfold greater. This was *unbelief;* and so Jehovah complains of them, ver. 11, "How long will it be ere they *believe* me?" Brethren, we ought never to believe any report which is contrary to the Word of God and its precious promises, whether that report comes from *without*, or is suggested by our own *evil* hearts. God has *said* it. This ought to be enough for us, "It is *written*." This is the great weapon which we should use in our conflict with Satan and the world. "Do as thou hast said;" this should be the utterance of our hearts in prayer. So to walk, brethren, is to walk by *faith*. But if the evil reports of the world be allowed to sink into our hearts, we yield to unbelief; and what *can* and *must* follow but discouragement? But you will notice that in Israel's case discouragement led to *murmuring*, ver. 2,—"And all the

children of Israel murmured against Moses and against
Aaron : and the whole congregation said unto them,
Would God that we had died in the land of Egypt! or
would God we had died in the wilderness !" And this
murmuring, of which we have so often spoken, issued in
more fearful rebellion. The proposal was made to set
aside God's choice, to set aside Moses, and to choose another captain, under whose guidance they might return to
Egypt. In *this*, unbelief rose to its greatest height, for
it was nothing else than a public and national rejection
of God's promise. We see in it the awful spectacle of a
nation setting to its seal that the faithfulness, truth, and
power of Jehovah had altogether failed.

But even this, brethren, was not the last and greatest
of Israel's sins. This was but the foreshadow of a still
darker time, when there was again a national rejection
of God's promise, a still more awful setting aside of
God's choice, even of Him who from all eternity was and
is the "Word of God,"—who was predicted in hundreds
of prophecies,—who offered one atonement for the sins of
the world. Never could unbelief rise higher than when
Israel denied the Holy One and the Just, and desired a
murderer to be granted to them,—when, in all the blind-
ness and infatuation of unbelief, it exclaimed, "His blood
be on us, and on our children." It were all too easy,
alas ! to point out in the page of history similar national
rejections of the Saviour,—such as when France heaped
honours on the remains of the miserable Voltaire, and
thereby, as well as by other fearful acts, proclaimed the
rejection of Christ; but it is more important to notice
that this same process goes on secretly and silently in
many hearts. There may, perhaps, be no open avowal,
no manifest renunciation of God's promises, and yet there

may be a preference given to some one else, or something else, instead of Christ. The soul may choose some other guide—may rest in something else as a Saviour—may seek satisfaction somewhere else than in the person and atonement of Jesus. And then, is not Israel's national history being repeated again in that individual soul? Brethren, our only safety lies in clinging with simple faith to Christ; and let no difficulties without, no sense of guilt or conflict within, make you question His unchanging love, His steadfast faithfulness, His invincible power. Whoever changes, "He is the same yesterday, to-day, and for ever." Whatever fails, His promise is ever sure. "For ever, O Lord, thy word is *settled* in heaven."

But the evil report of the ten spies affected indirectly the position of Joshua and Caleb. From the very beginning they had given a good report of the land; and now, in the midst of Israel's rebellion, they fearlessly and faithfully renewed their testimony, and expressed their confidence in the faithfulness and power of God. "The land," they say, ver. 7–9, "which we passed through to search it, is an exceeding good land. If the Lord delight in us, then he will bring us into this land, and give it us; a land which floweth with milk and honey. Only rebel not ye against the Lord, neither fear ye the people of the land; for they are bread for us: their defence is departed from them, and the Lord is with us: fear them not." Thus Israel's unbelief was the means of bringing out with greater relief the faithfulness and holy courage of these two witnesses. It was in God's strength that they bore this noble testimony, and God crowned it with an encouraging promise, as we read, ver. 24, "But my servant Caleb, because he had another spirit with him, and hath

followed me fully, him will I bring into the land where-
unto he went; and his seed shall possess it." We see thus
what it is to follow the Lord *fully*. It is to follow Him
with a *single* eye—to follow Him with all our hearts—
to follow Him to the end. But, *more*, it is to follow Him
in spite of all difficulties, and in the face of strong opposition, if such there be. Brethren, the providence of God
has cast our lot in a time when those who desire to live
to God meet with many encouragements. We have not,
as many before us have had, to endure the "spoiling of
our goods." We are not threatened with a "trial of cruel
mockings and scourgings, of bonds and imprisonment."
We are not called "to wander about in sheepskins and
goatskins, being destitute, afflicted, tormented." But we
know not yet whether we may not be. Other days
may come, and, we believe, *will* come upon the Church
of God,—days of sifting temptation. Some there are,
brethren, who think that the gospel will spread more and
more, and gradually leaven every nation, and that thus
the millennium will dawn upon the world ere Christ comes.
But the Word of God seems to us to speak very differently
of the last days. It does, indeed, say that the gospel shall
be preached among all nations; but mark, it is as "a
witness." It does promise that the "earth shall be covered
with the knowledge of the Lord, as the waters cover the
sea;" but this will be subsequently to Christ's coming, "in
that new earth wherein shall dwell righteousness;" for
St Paul tells us, (2 Tim. iii. 1, 2,) that in the last days
perilous times shall come,—not bright and millennial, but
perilous times shall come,—not days in which all shall
love God, but when men shall be lovers of their own
selves. The prophet Daniel lays it down as the characteristic of the last days, (chap. xii. 10,) that "Many shall

be purified, and made white, and tried; but the wicked shall do wickedly." Observe, the two elements of holiness and wickedness shall co-exist: both shall be developed. The living members of Christ's body will stand forth in more complete separation from the world than they do now. Like Caleb and Joshua, they will stand alone, witnessing for God in the midst of an evil generation, having nothing to support them but the faithfulness and truth of God. But the wicked shall do wickedly, sink deeper and deeper into unbelief and sin, and shew more and more what spirit they are of. Caleb and Joshua are a picture of what the Church will be, the rest of the people a picture of what the world will be, in those solemn days which immediately precede the coming of Jesus. Brethren, if these things are so, ought we not to have our loins girded and our lamps burning? Ought we to be halting between two opinions now, undecided on what ground we shall stand? Ought we not to be *careful*, very careful, to use the words of St Paul, (1 Cor. ii. 5,) that "our faith should not stand in the wisdom of man, but in the power of God?" for this faith alone is saving—this faith alone will endure unto the end. But let us pass on to *Moses*.

The unbelief of Israel drove him (and *we* often need, brethren, to be *driven* there) to the throne of grace. His intercessory prayer, which begins at ver. 13, is most beautiful. Time will not allow us to enter fully into it; we will, therefore, only notice the *basis* on which it rests; and you will find that basis to be the great truth, that God is glorified in the display of His attributes—that is, of Himself. We ought never to forget that God's great purpose is *self-manifestation*. This runs as a golden thread throughout Scripture, sometimes along the surface, oftener deep underneath. This, brethren, gives an answer

to many questions, which admit of no answer from any
other point of view. Why, for instance, was evil permitted to enter the world? and why is it permitted to
deface it? We answer, that it is for the more complete
manifestation of the attributes of God. His love, for
instance, is manifested towards the unfallen angels; but
if we wish to see it in all its beauty and fulness, we look
at it as displayed in the cross of Christ—we look at it as
rescuing some blasphemer, persecutor, and injurious person, or some woman that is a sinner, from the path of
destruction. The attribute which Moses brings forward
here is the *power* of God, as ver. 15, 16 shew,—"Now
if thou shalt kill all this people as *one* man, then the
nations which have heard the fame of thee will speak,
saying, Because the Lord was *not able* to bring this
people into the land which he sware unto them, therefore
he hath slain them in the wilderness." Now, you will
not fail to notice, that even if all Israel had perished in
the wilderness, this would not have demonstrated any
want of *power* on the part of Jehovah. It might have
been said to objectors of those days, " God's attribute of
power has nothing to do with this question; turn your
attention to His righteousness and holiness." Moses
must have seen clearly enough, that there could be no
real, but only an *apparent*, limitation of God's power;
yet he urges this argument in his prayer, and He who
invites man to plead with Him acknowledged its force.
And from this, brethren, we think that we may safely draw
this practical conclusion,—that whilst, on the one hand, we
ought not to be in bondage to the *opinions* of the world,
on the other, we ought to avoid that kind of conduct which
may, and must, *seem* to limit any of God's attributes.

It may not really do so. It may only *seem* to do ; yet concern for the glory of God, and that love which forbears to put a stumbling-block in another's way, should lead us to practise self-denial and circumspection. But we have still to rise to the highest and most difficult part of our subject,—the effect of Israel's unbelief on the mind and purpose of God. He said, ver. 12, " I will smite them with the pestilence, and disinherit them." But then Moses prayed. His prayer prevailed, and, ver. 20, God says, " I have pardoned according to thy word ;" and then He added the remarkable words, " But as truly as I live, all the earth shall be filled with my glory." It was a dark moment, brethren, when these words were spoken. All the heathen were in utter darkness, and the one chosen nation had just renounced their Redeemer. There were no signs of a millennium then. Yet this was the time which God chose to announce the great truth, that this earth, fallen as it is, shall be filled with His glory,—this the time that He chose to place His own light and glory in contrast with all the surrounding darkness. And if you turn to the prophet Hab. ii. 14, you will find this beautiful promise repeated at another time of darkness, almost as great as that which we are considering, when people and priests were thoroughly corrupted. " For the earth," it says, " shall be filled with the knowledge of the glory of the Lord, as the waters cover the sea." May we not conclude from this, that this is one great truth which ought to comfort the hearts of God's people, when the earth is corrupt and filled with ignorance and violence ? Ought we not to rejoice in the assurance, that this earth, which has been the platform on which redemption has been accomplished,

will also be that one on which the glory of God will be
displayed? It *was* displayed in our great *Redeemer*. It
will be displayed in the *redeemed*.

But our text speaks of another most remarkable effect
of Israel's unbelief. "Ye shall know," says God, "my
breach of promise;" or, as it is in the margin, the "alter-
ing of my purpose." Now, what was the breach of promise? The 28th and following verses give the clearest
explanation of it, "Say unto them, As truly as I live,
saith the Lord, as ye have spoken in mine ears, so will I
do to you: your carcases shall fall in this wilderness;
and all that were numbered of you, according to your
whole number, from twenty years old and upward, which
have murmured against me, doubtless ye shall not come
into the land, concerning which I sware to make you
dwell therein, save Caleb the son of Jephunneh, and
Joshua the son of Nun. But your little ones, which ye
said should be a prey, them will I bring in, and they
shall know the land which ye have despised." We see,
then, brethren, from these words, in how far there was an
alteration of purpose on God's part. There was no change
in the *promise* itself. There it stood unaltered and un-
repeated; but there was a *delay* in the time of its fulfilment, and there was a change in the persons to whom it
should be fulfilled. The unbelief of Israel did not, and
could not, set aside God's promise altogether; but it *did*
hinder its fulfilment to themselves. In one sense, the promise of God was *absolute*. In another sense, it was *conditional*. We see the selfsame thing in the Jews now.
There are beautiful promises which were given to them,
which have not yet been fulfilled. Why not? Because
of their unbelief. St Paul says, Rom. xi. 19, 20, " Thou
wilt say then, The branches were broken off, that I might

be graffed in. Well; *because* of *unbelief* they were broken off, and thou standest by faith. Be not highminded, but fear." What then? Have those promises failed? No; by no means. What does the apostle say, ver. 29? "For the gifts and calling of God are without repentance." The promises given to Israel are only in *apparent abeyance.* They still belong to Israel, and will in due time be fulfilled to them,—at *that* time when, through grace, they shall "turn to the Lord, and the veil be taken away from their hearts." And thus St Paul concludes his argument in Rom. xi. with these words, ver. 32, "For God hath concluded them all in unbelief, that he might have mercy upon all," in his exclamation, "O the depth of the riches both of the wisdom and knowledge of God! how unsearchable are his judgments, and his ways past finding out!"

But this, brethren, is a deep subject, and it would take long to trace it throughout Scripture, and elucidate it. We must, therefore, leave it to you, brethren, as a subject for thought and scriptural research. Such thought and research will, we think, leave two great truths on your minds. The first, that "God is faithful;" the second, "the great danger and sin of unbelief."

THE PLAGUE STAYED

Numbers 16:48

"And he stood between the dead and the living; and the plague was stayed."

WE resume our subject, brethren, at an event of great importance, viz., the rebellion of Korah, and its consequences. May the Spirit of God mercifully influence our hearts, that this and the succeeding subjects may help us forward on the way of life!

Korah, with the others, Dathan, Abiram, and On, were the chiefs in this rebellion. We cannot, however, doubt but that Korah himself was the originator of it. We are told in ver. 1 that he was the son of Izhar. Now, if you will refer to Exod. vi. 18, you will find that Izhar was the brother of Amram, the father of Moses and Aaron. Korah was therefore related to these servants of God, and this must, of course, have made the opposition on his part more painful and unexpected. The other three were of the tribe of Reuben. The last one mentioned is not spoken of again, and therefore it is quite possible that the earnest words of Moses may have led him to separate himself from the cause and operations of Dathan and Abiram. It is very important, I think, in order to get a clear insight into the spirit of these men, that we should carefully notice the fact, that they *did* belong to different tribes. Korah, let us remember, was of the tribe of Levi; the rest were Reubenites. Now, if we look at the history, we shall find proof that although they were all united in their opposition to Moses, they were not all influenced by exactly the same spirit. What, then, was Korah's motive in instigating this rebellion? Moses, who, no doubt, was a good discerner of spirits, gives us an insight into his heart, and the hearts of those Levites who were associated with him, in ver. 8–11,—"And Moses said unto Korah, Hear, I pray you, ye sons of Levi : seemeth it but a small thing unto you, that the God of Israel hath separated you from the congregation of Israel, to bring you near to himself to do the service of the tabernacle of the Lord, and to stand before the congregation to minister unto them ? And he hath brought thee near to him, and all thy brethren the sons of Levi with thee : and seek ye the priesthood also ? For which cause both thou and all thy company are gathered together against the Lord." It was ambition, then, that swayed the heart of Korah,— he wanted a higher office than the one which he already had ; and because the positive appointment of God placed a barrier around him, his mind fretted against these obstacles, and against those who were appointed to carry out the will of God.

The spirit of the Reubenites was not the same. Indeed, it could scarcely be the same. None of that tribe *could* be occupied in the service of the sanctuary. The priesthood was not sufficiently *near* them to kindle their ambition ; hence Moses does not address them in the same language. *Their* spirit seems to have been one of *haughty independence,* and impatience of *all* rule and authority,— a spirit of defiance. When Moses sent for them, they said, "We will not come up." They charged him, ver. 13, "with making himself a prince over them," and with having altogether failed in his mission to bring them into

the Land of Promise. " Thou hast *not* brought us," ·they
say, ver. 14, " into a land that floweth with milk and
honey." Thus, brethren, they, as we have so often seen
before, altogether overlooked the hand of God. On the
one hand, they would not recognise the government of
God ; on the other, they would not recognise the power
of unbelief in depriving them of promised blessings.
And what do we see in both these cases, but the natural
heart of man ?

It was an unhallowed alliance, the alliance of different
evil principles against the truth and the God of truth.
And, oh, brethren, how often we see this in history ! how
often around us now ! We may see now, and we shall see
it, we believe, still more shortly, infidelity and supersti-
tion, unlike as they are to each other, in alliance against
the truth as it is in Jesus, laying down their weapons
for a while that they may unite their forces against that
which neither understand, neither love. And what do we
learn from this, but the *unity* of evil ? There is one principle underlying all the different forms of evil. One infidel,
for example, may refute another infidel's arguments to set
up a system of his own. But the two are alike in spirit ;
one influence sways them both.

And now, brethren, that we are speaking of the nature
of Korah's sin, it may not be amiss to notice an application of this history, which does not commend itself to
our mind, and which will not, we believe, commend itself
to many minds here. We mean, brethren, the comparison
which is sometimes made between the opposition of those
who differ from the Church to which we belong, and this
insurrection of Korah against the constituted rulers of the
Jewish people.

Now we, dear brethren, are most heartily attached to

that Church in which the providence of God has graciously placed us. We feel that the clear and scriptural statements of our Articles, and the calm and solemn spirit of our prayers, have been most helpful to us. We think it no narrow-mindedness, as many do, to act upon our own principles; but, on the contrary, that it must be an injury to the cause of truth and to ourselves to ignore them. We quite expect that some here may differ from us in these views; but if so, we believe that we shall not love each other less. But such, brethren, are our feelings— such the ground on which we stand. We rest on nothing but Jesus and His finished work as our hope of glory; but, in seeking to do His work, we believe that we can glorify Him most in walking as consistent members of the Church of England. All will think us right in resting, not on church principles or the Church, but on *Christ*, and *Christ* alone, for salvation. But all will not think us right in our view that principles should not be sacrificed for the sake of co-operation. Brethren, we have not yet felt that ground tremble under our feet. But, with all this, it is contrary to all charity and Christian forbearance to pass such a sweeping condemnation as that comparison, which is to be met with in books of theology, and often heard in conversation, implies. Nor is there any justice in the comparison; for it assumes that our Church is virtually identical with the Jewish Church, and that our spiritual rulers are just what Moses and Aaron were. Nothing can be more erroneous. There is no passage in Scripture which lays down the doctrine that Episcopacy, though scriptural, is essential to the being of a church. We have no book of Leviticus in the New Testament— no minute rules as to all the details of church-government. There is a unity between the new dispensation and the

old. But this is not its ground. In this the two dispensations differ. The Old Testament laid the greatest
stress on external things,—on forms, ceremonies, and suc-
cessions. The New lays stress on principles and the spirit.
None, then, now can rightly claim the authority which
Moses had and exercised. This is the first point in which
the comparison fails.

It fails in another. Korah, we have seen, was an ambitious man. The Reubenites overlooked God's hand altogether. They were under the power of unbelief. But
blind indeed we must be, if we have not seen in some
of those who differ from our views, a most conscientious
spirit, the gift of humility and real trust in God. It is
only those who are swayed by ambition, and who would
level everything above them, that they may *themselves*
rise, who *can* be compared with " Korah and his company."

Korah's spirit of rebellion spread rapidly, as several
expressions shew. We read, ver. 2, of " two hundred
and fifty princes of the assembly, famous in the congregation, men of renown," joining his unhallowed cause,
and when they took it up, it is not wonderful that it
spread still further; and so we read, ver. 19, of Korah
" gathering *all* the congregation against Moses." But
Moses bore this trial with his usual meekness. He put
forth no claims for higher authority. He uttered no de-
nunciations, but committed himself, as Jesus did afterwards, to " Him that judgeth righteously." He left it to
God to decide who were His, as we read, ver. 5, " Even
to-morrow the Lord will shew who are his, and who is
holy; and will cause him to come near unto him : even
him whom he hath chosen will he cause to come near
unto him;" and, in order that he might be proved, he

told the men who claimed the priesthood to take their censers, and put fire in them, and lay incense thereon, and Aaron also to bring his censer. They did so, and the "glory of the Lord appeared," and would have consumed the whole congregation, had not Moses again interceded for them. But Dathan and Abiram were not present. They murmured in their tents, and refused to come up. Moses, therefore, went to them with some of the elders of Israel; and warning the congregation of their sin and danger, and exhorting them to "touch nothing of theirs," he predicted that the earth would swallow them up. The judgment soon followed; and a fire came out from the Lord, and consumed the two hundred and fifty men that offered incense.

You remember, brethren, the words of the apostle, "The Lord knoweth them that are his." Yes, some may fall away, but God knows who are *His*. The world knows them not; often they do not know themselves; but God *knows* them, and will graciously keep them unto the day of redemption. But there are *times* when God does *shew* who are His. There is a judgment going on in the world even now. We imply this when we speak of the day of judgment as the *final* judgment. That judgment will not be something altogether new, but a perfect consummation—a full manifestation of the sons of God. Meanwhile, as we said just now, there is sometimes even now a manifestation of His own people. This was frequently effected under the Old Testament, as on the occasion which we are considering, by *miracle;* under the New, by large gifts of grace, as in the case of the persecuted Stephen, when his face shone as the face of an angel. Oh, does not this, brethren, suggest solemn thoughts? Are we of that blessed company which the

Lord now knows to be His? Is it our most earnest desire to *be* His, and to *walk* as His in this sinful world? A day will come in which all secrets will be revealed—the thoughts of all hearts will be made manifest. It will be the day in which God will finally shew who are His. And where shall we, brethren, be?

We should have supposed that the two solemn judgments, the cleaving earth and the consuming fire, would have effectually hushed Israel's murmurings. We should have said, "Now they will acknowledge their sin, and will prostrate themselves before God." But no, brethren. So alienated is the natural heart of man from God, so contrary in its whole state to the will of God, that it does not seem that any miracle, any judgment, can subdue it. There is *one* thing only that can bring it into unison with God's will, can make it respond to God's voice, can still the rising murmur, and teach it to say, "Not my will, but thine be done," and that is the grace of God—the love of God shed abroad in the heart through the Holy Ghost. We see how ineffectual the most solemn judgments may be, and *are*, without this; for we are told, ver. 41, that on the very morrow *all*—observe, not *some*—but all the congregation of the children of Israel murmured against Moses and against Aaron, saying, "Ye have killed the Lord's people." So that, after all, they *would* not see God's hand in these miraculous judgments—*would* not yet see who were on the Lord's side, "*Ye* have killed the *people of the Lord.*" Another judgment was needed. Another plague was sent. Again *wrath* went forth from a God of love. As soon as Moses perceived this, he told Aaron to take his censer, and put fire thereon from off the altar, and put on incense, and go quickly into the congregation, and make an atonement

for them.   Aaron, only just before rejected as priest by
the verdict of the rebellious people, did so.   And the
result is given in the words of our text, the most striking
and beautiful in the whole chapter,—" He stood between
the dead and the living ; and the plague was stayed."   We
need scarcely observe what a beautiful example of meekness and long-suffering these two men shewed on this
occasion.   Moses had had a long succession of trials, and
we can scarcely help wondering that his patience did not
give way.   But he seemed quite to disregard himself, and
no sooner did suffering befall his people than he hastened
to the throne of grace, and provided an atonement for
them.   To Aaron this must have been a special trial ; but
there was very much to solemnise his spirit.   It was not
long since that he was found amongst the murmurers, and
now it was specially his high priesthood against which
this opposition had raised itself.   His sin had again found
him out.   But he bore the trial in silence.   He forgave,
even as he had been forgiven.   He made a speedy atonement as high priest, and the plague was stayed.

But in the high-priestly act of Aaron we cannot fail
to discern a striking type of a better priesthood and a
never-dying Priest.   How different was Aaron's appointed
censer from the usurped censers of those ambitious men !
They brought death.   His stays it.   The efficacy was
complete, the atonement was accepted, and the raging
plague was stayed.   And just so, when a universal
plague was raging fearfully, the plague of sin, and that
condemnation which ever rests on unacknowledged sin,
did another Priest come forth to make a more perfect
atonement.   Jesus left the bosom of His Father.   He
seized His golden and consecrated censer, filled with much
incense, and stepped in between the living and the dead .

But in the act there was infinitely more love and mercy than in the atonement of Aaron. Moses and Aaron forgave much; but He, *how much* more! Their act of mercy displayed their long-suffering, but cost them nothing; but His, brethren, cost Him his life! He arrested the plague by gathering it all into His own person. He bore our sins, their awful weight and terrible punishment, in His own body, His own sinless person, and by *suffering* arrested the plague. None but Jesus could bear such a weight. No atonement but His could be so efficacious. No censer but His could hold the precious incense which could satisfy the righteousness of an offended God. No human efforts can arrest the plague of sin. There is no merit in all the good works of plague-smitten men to turn aside the anger of God. Each one of them, as far as his own strength is concerned, falls helplessly before the plague. He cannot redeem himself, still less redeem his brother, or make satisfaction for him. But Christ has arrested the plague of sin once for all; and His all-sufficient atonement applied to the heart by the Spirit arrests it there also. Are there some here conscious of this desolating plague within them? Do you feel deep in your own spirit the condemnation of a righteous God? Are you struggling with the plague, longing to escape, yet only finding its power increased? You must cease from any prescription of your own—you must put no confidence in any skill and might of yours—you must look away from the ravages of the plague within you, to Him who "stands between the living and the dead." The look of faith is accompanied by a new power. Life then reigns where death reigned before. You are written amongst the living—the plague is stayed. True it is that the believer still has a conflict to undergo, a warfare to wage, but in Jesus he is free from all condemnation; for it is written, "There is no condemnation to them that are in Christ Jesus," (Rom. viii. 1.) In Christ the power of sin is broken, for it is written again, (Rom. vi. 14,) "For sin shall not have dominion over you: for ye are not under the law, but under grace." In Christ Jesus there is a life which must triumph over all death. For "in all these things," says St Paul, "we are more than conquerors through him that loved us." Oh, let us rest more on Jesus,—on His finished work, His perfect atonement, His continued intercession, His living person. Let us realise His perfect love, His unchanging faithfulness, His invincible power. Let us wait on Him in conflict and in suffering, in work and in rest; and then, brethren, we shall know more what His fulness is, and what the meaning of the words "The plague is stayed."

THE SMITTEN ROCK AT KADESH

Numbers 20:11

" And Moses lifted up his hand, and with his rod he smote the rock
    twice : and the water came out abundantly, and the congregation
    drank, and their beasts also."

IF we compare, brethren, this chapter, and especially ver.
23 to the end, with chapters xxxiii., xxxvii., xxxviii., we
cannot fail to come to the interesting conclusion, that what
is here recorded must have taken place in the fortieth
year of Israel's journeyings, for we learn from the last
passage, that Aaron died in the first day of the fifth
month of the fortieth year after the children of Israel
were come out of the land of Egypt. And the 1st verse
of our chapter informs us that it was in the *first month*,
that the children of Israel came into the wilderness of
Zin. We must evidently, therefore, understand the first
month to be that of the fortieth year. And if so, brethren,
then there are thirty-seven years of which we have scarcely
a vestige of account, for thirty-seven years had elapsed
since the national rejection of Jehovah, or the return of
the spies from the Promised Land. It has been assumed
by infidels that the Bible professes to give a complete
history of the time of which it treats, and then it has been
charged with failing in the fulfilment of this plan. Nothing, brethren, is more false than that assumption ;
nothing shews greater ignorance. Shew me (we may say
to such a one) where the Bible professes this object ;

and we shall get no answer. The Bible is *not* a history of the world. It is *not* even a complete history of the Jews. It constantly omits what an uninspired historian would have inserted, and inserts what such a one would have omitted. The golden thread which runs throughout it, and which the sceptic does not discern, is *redemption.* In the Old Testament it is redemption prefigured in promise, in prophecy, and in type ; in the New Testament it is redemption fulfilled. The great promise of the Old Testament is this, (Jer. xxiii. 5, 6,)—" Behold, the days come, saith the Lord, that I will raise unto David a righteous Branch, and a King shall reign and prosper, and shall execute judgment and justice in the earth. In his days Judah shall be saved, and Israel shall dwell safely : and this is his name whereby he shall be called, The Lord our Righteousness." The great and most precious words of the New Testament are, " It is finished." The great purpose of the Bible, brethren, is not to give a complete history, but to reveal a perfect and all-sufficient Saviour. Take this thread of gold into your hand, and how radiant does every page become ! But if you read the Bible without Christ, all is dark, unconnected, and confused. Oh that we may read it more and more in Thy light, thou Sun of righteousness !

The circumstances which we have to consider this morning took place at Kadesh. You will remember that this was the very place where the people, in the unbelief of their hearts, set to their seal that the great promise of Jehovah had failed. So that after thirty-seven years of weary journeyings in a barren wilderness, of murmurings and chastisement, they came back again to the *selfsame* place. Oh, here, brethren, you see the history of the backsliding and inconsistent Christian. The path of some is beautiful, because it is *onward*, ever *onward*. It is a "reaching forth" after Jesus, not only for justification, but for holiness. It is a "pressing after the mark" of conformity to His holy image. It shines more and more unto the perfect day. It is like the flight of the eagle, upward and soaring. But the path of the inconsistent and wavering Christian is in a weary circle. Sometimes he advances, and then again recedes, and so years pass away, and there he is still at Kadesh, still without peace, without holy liberty of spirit, without joy, it may be, like Israel, "murmuring." Such a walk, brethren, brings no glory to God, and is always accompanied by great darkness and perplexity. To be happy Christians, we must be *decided*—we must give up the world through the power of Christ's cross—we must walk with Jesus. There is a fragrance and a freshness in such a life. It has many foretastes of heaven.

The first thing that happened at Kadesh was the death of Miriam. She, though the sister of Moses and Aaron, and a prophetess, was not allowed to enter into the Land of Promise. We know the reason. She had taken part in Israel's rebellion against Moses, and, in him, against God. She had murmured, and, therefore, the sentence of death passed upon Israel must be fulfilled in *her* likewise. She died in Kadesh, and was buried there. It must have been a solemn and afflicting time for Aaron. His sister had fallen. Could *he* hope to see the Land of Promise? His memory must have recalled the golden calf, and his sinful rebellion against his brother. The chamber of death throws a new light upon past sins.

But it still remained to be seen whether Moses himself would lead the people with whom, and for whom, he had suffered so much, into Canaan. As yet he had continued faithful, firm as a rock, when all wavered—meek, when repeatedly provoked. Alas! brethren, the verses that follow give us the account of his fall. Like Miriam and Aaron, he also must die in the wilderness.

Israel's fall was the cause of his fall; so often does one sin provoke another.

The faith of the Israelites was again tried by want of water, as at Rephidim; and, as usual, "they gathered themselves together against Moses and against Aaron." There was no originality in their complaints on this occasion; they were the same as before. They wished again that they had never left Egypt, or that they had perished with their gainsaying brethren by the judgments of God. This fresh trial drove Moses and Aaron into the presence of God. "Moses and Aaron," we are told, "went from the presence of the assembly unto the door of the tabernacle of the congregation, and they fell upon their faces : and the glory of the Lord appeared unto them." Again, too, as at Rephidim, God promised to bring forth water out of the rock. The only difference in the command being, that at Rephidim Moses was enjoined to *smite* the rock; on this occasion, he was commanded to *speak* to it. "Speak ye," we read, ver. 8, "unto the rock before their eyes." But he did not adhere closely to God's command. Addressing the Israelites with the words of severe rebuke, "Hear now, ye rebels; must we fetch you water out of this rock?" he smote the rock, not once only, but twice, and the water came out abundantly. This was Moses's sin. The sentence is recorded, (ver. 12,) "Therefore ye shall not bring this congregation into the land which I have given them."

It has been the opinion of some Jewish commentators, and, like many of their opinions, is a very strange one, that this material rock was miraculously made to follow the Israelites in the wilderness. They hold it to be the selfsame rock that was smitten at Rephidim, and here at Kadesh, more than thirty-seven years afterwards. St Paul teaches us the real truth, (1 Cor. x. 4,) "And did all drink the same spiritual drink: for they drank of that spiritual Rock which followed them: and that Rock was Christ." It was *Jesus*, then, that followed them. He was present in the *material* rock at Rephidim and Kadesh, and it was *His presence* that made the dry and hard rock pour forth refreshing streams. And, thanks be to God, brethren, Jesus is still the Rock, still follows His people through this wilderness. Now, if we realise the position of Israel in the wilderness, we shall understand that nothing could seem more *improbable* than that water should come out of a *hard* rock. Even in countries where water abounds, we look elsewhere for living springs; much more should we do so in the East, where rocks are exposed to the incessant action of a burning sun. But God's thoughts, brethren, are not as our thoughts. Just that which to us seems most improbable, is often the very thing which He accomplishes, to make His power known. To the world it still seems a most improbable thing that there should be life and salvation in Christ Jesus. They cannot see how living streams of water can flow from a crucified Redeemer, and how salvation can be a gift altogether free. If they look for righteousness, it is in their own doings that they look for it. If they want a title to heaven, they think that they have found it in their own *moral* lives. No foundation seems to them so weak as Jesus—no foundation so strong as themselves. And even when the heart is awakened, when it begins to feel its sinfulness and deep need, it does not even then go straight to Christ the spiritual Rock. It looks for living water everywhere else *first*, until, at last, driven from everything else, disappointed everywhere, wearied with conflicts, it looks away from self to Jesus, and then the *waters*, the living waters, such as this world cannot supply, flow with freshness, and in great abundance. O brethren, let us not take the world's report of Christ. Do not listen to *your own* thoughts, often so full of unbelief. Say not within yourselves, " There is nothing there in that Rock." Listen to God's thoughts, and to the blessed invitation of Jesus, " If any man thirst, let him come unto me, and drink." Have you tried to quench your thirst at other cisterns, but found them all broken, unable to hold the waters of life ? Oh, come to this Rock in a weary land, " and drink, yea, drink abundantly." Drink, brethren, not like the camel, largely but seldom— drink every day, for Jesus is ever near you. He follows you wherever you go, stays with you wherever you stay.

Again : We are apt to settle it in our minds how and in what way God will communicate to us the water of life. There is, it may be, some particular place in which some particular ordinances through which you look for a blessing. We say in our hearts, " Now surely Jesus will meet me." But it pleases God often to overturn all this. He often separates us from the place that we love, from the persons whose society and communion we value, and from the ordinances in which our souls delight. We look around us, and there is no verdure—no stream of refreshing water ; nothing appears but a hard and dry *rock*. We turn away from it desponding and hopeless. Brethren, we ought not to do so. We ought to turn to it. The presence of Christ *can,* and often *does,* change the dry rock into a fountain—the very wilderness into a fruitful garden. We ought not to limit Christ. We should look for Him *everywhere* and in everything. He who supplied Israel with water from a hard rock when they were murmuring in unbelief, can surely supply us everywhere with living water. "If thou knewest the gift of God, and who it is that saith to thee, Give me to drink ; thou wouldest have asked of him, and he would have given thee living water."

Once more : Water is never so sweet as in the wilderness. We do not know what it is, unless we have been exposed to a burning sun, or have over-exerted ourselves in scaling some lofty mountain. It is so, brethren, with grace. It is not when our path is smooth, and we are encompassed with blessings on every side, that we value the grace of God most. It is when some thorn in the flesh presses us sore—when we feel the weariness of the world—when earthly cisterns are dried up,—oh, then to realise that we have a smitten Rock, One that follows in the wilderness, One whose streams can never fail, is indeed an unspeakable blessing ! It is God's purpose, brethren, that grace should be valued. If we regard the blood of Jesus and the gift of the Spirit as common things, we dishonour God, and grieve His Spirit. It is *His* will that we should prize the gift of Jesus above every gift— that we should count *Him* as the pearl of great price— that we should catch every breath of the Spirit in our sails. And this is one reason why God so often leads His children into the wilderness—why He suffers them to hunger and to thirst—why He brings them into darkness, and not into light. Oh, let us value, brethren, the mercy that has provided a *smitten* Rock for us, and *such a Rock !*

We have spoken, brethren, of the rock. Let us now turn to Moses, and consider the nature of the sin by which he forfeited the privilege of leading Israel into the Promised Land. We are not left to guess what it was, for we are told distinctly that it was *unbelief.* God says, ver. 12, "Because ye believed me not." We cannot hesitate, then, to say that the root of his sin was *unbelief.* And is not this, brethren, the root of *all* sin? What but this was the cause of all Israel's idolatry and murmurings? Unbelief always has been, and always is, the great and *deadly* sin of the world. We cannot hold the Church of Rome's false distinction between mortal and venial sins in the way she holds it. But this, brethren, we hold, and *must* hold, that *the deadly* sin is unbelief; for Jesus says, "If ye believe not that I am he, ye shall die in your sins." And unbelief is not only the *world's* great sin; it throws its dark vail over the Church's beauty. If we trace, brethren, our own inconsistencies, our too uneven walk, our want of perseverance in prayer, our want of love to God's Word, the sins of our tongues, our defects in charities, and our sloth,—if we trace all these to their root, we shall find that root to be unbelief.

But the inquiry is not done when we say, as we must say, that unbelief was the root of Moses's sin. We may proceed to ask, How did it shew itself? and, Were any others included in this great parent sin?

First, then, we may answer, that it shewed itself in a departure from minute obedience; for you will notice that on this occasion God told him to *speak* to the rock; whereas Moses, instead of *speaking*, smote it. We need not, and ought not, to ask why at Rephidim God told Israel's leader to *smite* the rock; at Kadesh, to speak to it. There are many "whys" which are interdicted, and this is one of them. It is enough for us to know that God saw fit to make this difference, and Moses ought to have acted according

to His word.　We may see from this that it is not enough
for us to pay a sort of general obedience to God's Word;
we must study the mind of God, and obey in little things.
The world, brethren, exercises far more power over us in
this matter than we are aware of.　It is to be feared that
there are but few of us who do not *interleave* our Bibles,
and fill them up with the world's *comments*, notes, and
qualifications of God's Word; and the consequence is, that
we often depart from God in *little* things—which yet are
not, brethren, and cannot be, *little*, because they have
reference to Him who is great.　If God tells us to smite,
we should smite.　If He tells us to *speak*, we should
speak.　Brethren, it seems enough for us to *speak* to our
Rock.　We need not smite it.　Jesus has been smitten,—
smitten and bruised by His Father for our sins.　Speak,
brethren, in faith—speak in prayer, "Lord, save me, I
perish," and the Rock will pour forth its living and abundant streams into your soul.

　　Secondly, we may notice that he *spoke* angrily to his
people, though he did not speak, as bidden, to the rock.
"Hear now, ye rebels."　Moses, the meekest of men, failed
in meekness.　After all his great victories, after standing upright in many a storm and keen temptation during *forty* years,—no slight time to bear without faltering
such great and repeated provocations,—this noble believer
failed in just that grace for which he was most remarkable—he failed in meekness; and, as the Psalmist says,
"spake unadvisedly with his lips."　What a lesson, brethren!　It teaches us that we may have made much progress
in the knowledge of God, that we may have weathered
many a storm, have gained many victories, and if we
have done so, we may be thankful and give glory to God,
but we must never trust in any of these; a besetting sin,

which has been kept under even more than forty years,
may break forth again—a grace, which has been more
than forty years in constant exercise, may fail. What,
then, brethren, are the strongest? Nothing in themselves. Our only security is to rest fully and firmly on
Christ Jesus. Our wisdom is to remember the words,
"Thou standest by faith; be not high-minded, but fear."

But once more: Moses seemed almost to forget on this
occasion that he was but an instrument in God's hands.
He took too much upon himself and Aaron. Mark his
language,—"Must *we* fetch you water out of this rock?"
Whereas he ought to have said, "God will bring water
for you out of this rock." This would have given glory
to God. It may have been with reference to these words
of Moses that God says, "Because ye believed me not, to
sanctify me in the eyes of the children of Israel." God
is a jealous God, and will not give the glory to another.
Whenever we take to ourselves, or attribute to others,
that success which God only can give, we rob Him of
His glory, and grieve His Spirit. Our sinful hearts,
brethren, wish to be *something*. They wish to have some
share, even if it be but a little, in the glory that belongs
to God, instead of desiring to be nothing, and that Jesus
may be all. It is the most difficult thing of all to be low
before God, and to cease from ourselves altogether. It
is the top-stone in the work of grace. All the tendencies
of the human heart, and of the present age, are quite the
other way. There is a strong tendency in the world to
deify men, and in the Church to overestimate human
instrumentality. A withering blight has been cast over
many a congregation in consequence of the exaltation of
man, instead of looking upward for the teaching of God.

It was a painful and trying sentence that was passed

upon the man of God, and one which he felt very deeply. But this subject we must reserve, if the Lord will, to some future occasion, when we shall have to consider its execution and also its full meaning. Meanwhile, brethren, may we know Christ to be our smitten Rock! May streams of Divine grace water our souls day by day, and make us fruitful in everything which is to the praise and glory of God! May we live upon Jesus! for this is the only way to be kept from idolatry, worldliness, and sin— the only way to put and to keep the world, ourselves, and others, in their right places,—the world behind our backs, ourselves in the dust, and others in honour indeed ; but such honour only as God giveth unto His saints—not that which belongs to Him, and to Him alone.

THE SERPENT OF BRASS

Numbers 21:8

" And the Lord said unto Moses, Make thee a fiery serpent, and set it upon a pole : and it shall come to pass, that every one that is bitten, when he looketh upon it, shall live."

THE solemn sentence, recorded Numbers xiv. 34, was now nearly executed. " After the number of the days in which ye searched the land, even forty days, each day for a year, shall ye bear your iniquities, even forty years; and ye shall know my breach of promise." For the Israelites, you will remember, were now in the fortieth year of their wilderness journeyings.

Again they were on the very confines of the Promised Land, into which they were not meet to enter before. If we study the history of the last year of their journeyings, we cannot fail to notice a marked difference between it and the history of many of the preceding years. In the wilderness the chief trials of their faith arose from the want of food and water. But *now*, at the close of their pilgrimage, as at its commencement, they met with many enemies. At the beginning Egypt struggled hard to retain its prey ; and now a host of enemies seek to bar up Israel's entrance into the Land of Promise. Edom was one of these,—Edom, a people related to Israel, as the words of Moses—chap. xx. 14, " Thus saith thy brother Israel "—remind us. Moses asked permission to pass through their country. We read, (ver. 17,) " Let

us pass, I pray thee, through thy country : we will not
pass through the fields, or through the vineyards, neither
will we drink of the water of the wells : we will go by
the king's highway, we will not turn to the right hand
nor to the left, until we have passed thy borders." But
Edom would not suffer it. " Thou shalt not pass by me,
lest I come out against thee with the sword." And they
put their threat into execution ; ver. 20, " Edom came
out against him with much people, and with a strong
hand ;" and Israel was obliged to turn away from him
This was not the only discouragement. Arad, king of
one of the tribes of Canaan, displayed the same spirit.
He either remembered or had heard how, thirty-seven
years before, Israel had sent spies to search out the land,
and he resolved, if he could, to hinder their purpose.
" He fought against Israel," (chap. xxi. 1,) and with some
success, for he " took some of them prisoners." But on
this occasion the Israelites shewed more faith in God
than usual. They were not dismayed by their defeat,
but " vowed a vow unto the Lord, and said, If thou wilt
indeed deliver this people into my hand, then I will utterly
destroy their cities." This vow was acceptable to God,
for it was but the carrying out of God's purpose, (Gen.
xv. 16,) "But in the fourth generation they shall come
hither again : for the iniquity of the Amorites is not yet
full." In the strength of God Israel triumphed, and
called the name of the place " Hormah," which, according
to some, means " banishment," in which case it can only
refer to Israel's being banished thirty-seven years before
from the Land of Promise. According to the original
reading, it means " utter destruction," and in that case
refers, of course, to the destruction of Arad. Now, in
the varied character of its wanderings, Israel is evidently

a type of the Christian's life and experience; and if so, brethren, then we may gather from it, what is also in many cases confirmed by experience, that it is at the *beginning* and *end* of the Christian's life that the most severe conflicts take place. For at the *beginning* our three enemies, like Egypt of old, are reluctant to give up their captive, even though God himself in mercy and love breaks off his chains, and leads him out with a strong though gentle hand. Satan loses no opportunity to instil into the awakening and anxious heart thoughts of despondency and fears, which deeply harass it. The world spreads out its wiles to allure it back again, and the flesh, the corrupt nature within, pleads for its usual indulgence. Those, brethren, who have felt it, know how severe the struggle is. One moment the brightness of hope gleams in upon the troubled heart, and then it sinks again into darkness. And we need not remind you, brethren, that when the net is thoroughly broken, and we escape out of the snare of the fowler, our enemies still pursue us. They do not leave us altogether. But still, perhaps, their attacks are not quite *so severe*, until Canaan comes into view, and the wilderness is almost crossed. We read of Jesus, our great Head, (Luke iv. 13,) that "when the devil had ended all the temptation, he departed from *Him for a season.*" And so it is with those who are one with Jesus. There are seasons of special conflict, and times when the enemy *departs for a season.* We do not mean, brethren, that in that interval the Christian faith is *not* tried. Israel's faith was tried every step of the way during forty years; and our faith must be tried likewise, to teach us, too, that man doth not live by bread alone, but on Christ, the bread of life. We simply mean that when first the *soul* begins to long for God, and for holiness in Him, then *first* Satan hurls his fiery darts at it; and again, when the Christian is safely brought to his dying bed, and the land of promise comes full in view, he often returns to the charge with violence. He puts forth all his power to harass, if he cannot separate him from Jesus altogether. But then, brethren, happily the believer has a stronger faith with which to meet the tempter in his last assaults. He has proved his armour. He knows in whom he has believed. He looks through the dark cloud, or if he cannot, he knows that behind and above it his Saviour stands at the right hand of God. He is made more than conqueror through Him that loved us, in his *last* as in his *first* conflicts.

Having gained this victory, the Israelites journeyed onwards "from Mount Hor by the way of the Red Sea, to compass the land of Edom." The journey was wearisome, and "the soul of the people was much discouraged because of the way." It is a strong expression, brethren, "the *soul* of the people." The *soul* is the centre of our being. It shews, then, how completely and thoroughly discouraged they were. The faith which enabled them to triumph over Arad quite failed now. Though Canaan was not far off, though God was present with them, still they were much discouraged. This, perhaps, may be regarded as a proof that though many of the condemned generation must, like Miriam and Aaron, have already died, still some remained. It is quite probable that they set an example of discouragement and murmuring to the younger men of Israel. Brethren, there is great danger of *discouragement* in the Christian life. When difficulties throng our path, and one disappointment follows close upon another, we are prone to think that we have reason to be discouraged, and even to *yield* to discouragement. We are disposed to give up in despondency. Whence, brethren, does this feeling come? It is not of God; for if we realise the glory of that inheritance which He has prepared for His people, the certainty and preciousness of His unfailing promises, oh, then we should never faint—discouragement would never issue in murmuring—its distressing feelings would soon be overcome, and give way to those of thankfulness and praise. No, brethren, discouragement comes from the remaining *corruption* of our hearts, from indwelling sin; and it ought therefore to be resisted. When the cloud begins to creep over our spirits, we should set forth under the bright beams of the Sun of righteousness, and there we shall find comfort, endurance, and strength.

But you will remember that St Paul, speaking of the particular sin of Israel, calls it "tempting Christ," 1 Cor. x. 9,—"Neither let us tempt Christ, as some of them also tempted, and were destroyed of serpents." We should have thought, brethren, that he would have called it "tempting God." Why does he call it "tempting Christ?" The reason seems to be this,—The Son of God, as the Divine *Word*, was working amongst men before the fulness of time came, and He took our nature upon Him. It was not the Father *himself*, but the Father in and through the Son, who led the children of Israel through the wilderness. For it is He who (Josh. xv. 5) is called the "Captain of the Lord's host," and (Isa. lxiii. 9) "The Angel of his presence." Even before the incarnation, "in all their affliction He was afflicted." And so St Paul calls the sufferings which Moses willingly endured, "the reproach of Christ"—not the reproach of God, but of Christ. It was *Christ*, then, whom the Israelites *tempted* by their discouragement and murmurings, for He led

them, He carried them through the wilderness. And it is
Christ whom we tempt, brethren, when we yield to discouragement, when we murmur. For He has made atonement for our sins. He has sprinkled us, if we are His,
in His own blood. He guides us, if we follow Him, with
His own counsel. Oh, let us beware of committing Israel's
sin, and "tempting Christ."

Chastisement, as usual, followed this sin. The Lord
sent fiery serpents among the people, and they bit the
people, and much people of Israel died. They are called
fiery serpents to shew their *activity;* for it appears that
the people could not get away from them, and still more
because their bite was deadly. It caused not only incon-
venience and pain, but death. What an illustration,
brethren, is this of that deadly disorder which we may
trace in ourselves—that disease which is occasioned by
the bite of that old serpent, the devil, the disease of sin !
It is *universal,* for the Scripture says, " All have sinned,
and come short of the glory of God." It is *deadly,* for
St Paul says, "The wages of sin is death." It deserves
the wrath of God, for St John says concerning all who do
not believe in Christ, "The wrath of God abideth on him."
It was the consciousness of this disease that made Job
exclaim, " Behold I am vile ;" that led Israel to pronounce
a woe upon himself, " Woe is me ! for I am undone ;" that
led St Paul to cry out, " O wretched man that I am ! who
shall deliver me from the body of this death ?" Have you,
dear brethren, uttered such a cry ? Have you traced in
your own hearts the dreadful effects of this disease ? Have
you felt it corrupting all your motives ? shedding its death
like stupor over your soul ? alienating your heart from
God ? Have you realised, too, the *danger* of your soul ?
the certainty that the work of God must rest now, and will

for ever rest, upon unforgiven sin, and on those who are
impenitent and unbelieving? No state, beloved brethren,
can be so perilous as a state of indifference. The Israelites knew full well when they were bitten, and it was this
that led them to cry to the Lord for help. If they ceased
to feel it, it would be a sign that mortification had taken
place, and that death was very near. And so, beloved, we
may be sure, that where there is indifference, no consciousness of sin, no real repentance, no cry, " O wretched man !"
there *death* is very near. Is this your state? Is your
heart cold or lukewarm? Oh, then, speak not peace to
yourself—say not all will be well. The case is urgent,
your soul is in danger! Arise, and call upon God. Pray
for that Spirit whose first work it is to convince of sin.
Moses's prayer in behalf of the bitten Israelites was heard
and answered, but not by the removal of the fiery serpents,
but by a command given to Israel's leader to make a
" fiery serpent, and to set it upon a pole," with a promise
added, " And it shall come to pass, that every one that is
bitten, when he looketh upon it, shall live." The serpent
called, ver. 8, a "fiery" serpent, is also called, ver. 9, a serpent of *brass*. The reason why it was made of *brass*,
probably was to shew that the *cure*, which it would be
the means of effecting, would be a *lasting* cure—not a
mere temporary alleviation of pain, but a complete *cure*.

We all know, brethren, of whom this serpent was a
type. It was a type of Jesus lifted up upon the cross.
Our Saviour himself says, John iii. 14, "And as Moses
lifted up the serpent in the wilderness, even so must the
Son of man be lifted up, that whosoever believeth in him
should not perish, but have eternal life." In both cases,
brethren, we must say that this method of cure was one
which shews that "God's thoughts are not as our thoughts,

or his ways as our ways." Strange it must ever seem
to the world, that a serpent of brass should be the means
of healing those bitten by serpents; and that the man
Christ Jesus, lifted up on the cross, should give salvation
to dying men. But in this wonderful arrangement we
may discern a great principle. You have doubtless heard
it put forth as a principle in the physical world, that " like
cures like." In the spiritual world this is undoubtedly
true. We cannot fail to see this principle in the type of
which we are speaking, and no less clearly in its great antitype. Augustine says, in his own striking and beautiful
way, " The serpent is lifted up, that the bite of the serpents
might not avail ; death is lifted up, that death might
not triumph ;" and this last clause, you will perceive, refers
as fully to the work of Jesus. We see in Him life conquering death, but we also see death conquering death.
It is because Jesus has died, that every believer in Him
lives, and lives for ever. Without His death there could
not be any triumph over death. This great principle dis-
tinguishes God's way of salvation. God displays death
in its full power, and so overcomes it ; but you will not
find this principle in any of man's schemes for saving
himself. Again, brethren, we may notice that the serpent
was *lifted up* upon a pole, was placed in a situation in
which *all* might see it; for, as we shall see presently,
something more was required besides the lifting up
of the serpent in order that the bitten Israelites
might be healed. They must *look* upon it. Thus,
brethren, was Jesus *lifted* up, lifted up upon the cross,
that dying sinners, conscious of their sins, might look
to Him and live. " I," said Jesus, " if I be lifted up,
will draw all men unto me." But we must pause
a little upon the importance of the command that

they should *look* upon it. "Every one," it says, ver. 8, "that is bitten, when he looketh upon it, shall live." "If," we read, ver. 9, "a serpent had bitten any man, when he *beheld* the serpent of brass, he lived." A *look*, then, brethren, was necessary; without it, the serpent of brass was of no practical use to a bitten Israelite. A look was sufficient, it was all that was necessary. It did not effect a *part* of the cure merely, and leave something else still to be done. It was health. It is easy to see how many objections might occur to the Israelites as to the mode of cure. Some might question the possibility of any cure being effected by a serpent of brass. Others might ask how simply *looking* upon it could avail anything. Meanwhile, brethren, if some doubted and refused to look, and consequently perished, others believed in the wisdom, power, and truth of God. They *looked*, and were "healed." Need we remind you, brethren, of the many passages of Scripture which shew the *power* of *one* look to Jesus? Prophecy proclaims it, for we read, Isa. xlv. 22, "Look unto me, and be ye saved, all the ends of the earth." Apostles set it forth, for St Paul said to the anxious jailer, "Believe in the Lord Jesus, and thou shalt be saved;" and to the Hebrews, (chap. xii. 2,) "Looking unto Jesus." And we are taught the same lesson by the beautiful history of the woman who *touched* the hem of Christ's garment; one touch was sufficient. She was healed. Brethren, this is a point which perplexes many. They see that there is salvation in Christ, but how and in what way that salvation is to become theirs, they do not, and cannot see. Some hope that by a constant attendance on ordinances— others by a long course of self-denial and self-discipline, they may somehow, in the end, be made partakers of Christ. But such thoughts keep the soul in bondage, and are the result of a self-righteous spirit. What we have to do to obtain the forgiveness of sin, is simply to believe the record which God gave of His Son. It is to *look* to Jesus. One look is life and salvation. It is not half a cure. It is life. It is forgiveness, victory over sin, the world, and the devil, and meetness for glory. It is not, brethren, that there is any merit or virtue in the *look* itself. All the merit and all the virtue is in Christ. Such great results follow a *look* upon our crucified Redeemer, simply because it is the appointed means whereby Christ becomes ours. Or does it seem to you, brethren, that this way of salvation is too easy and simple to be true? Its simplicity can be no objection, because all God's works are beautifully *simple;* and with regard to its being *easy*, we would ask you, brethren, "Have you tried it?" Those who have tried it will tell you that they have found nothing so difficult. It is easier to go through the longest course of self-denial or bodily chastisement, because, in the midst of all this, "self" may retain its throne, and self-righteousness may hold its sway. But a look at Jesus implies a renunciation of self-righteousness, and, therefore, it is itself, and ever must be itself, the result of a work of grace in the heart. We assert, then, brethren—we assert, with the utmost distinctness— that it is to no easy thing that we exhort you, when we bid you *look* to Jesus. We know that your hearts and our own are naturally inclined to look anywhere else in preference; but God will enable you to *look*, if you ask Him for His grace. It will give *strength* to the palsied hand, that it may lay hold of this great salvation. Look, brethren, to Jesus. Do not say, "I will wait until I grow better;" for that will never be. Christ himself is the root of all holiness, and, consequently, in us faith, which alone can receive Him, is its root. Look to Jesus, and you will have the full and free forgiveness of all your sins. Look to Jesus, and His strength will become yours. Look to Jesus, and then you will have even now that life which is the beginning of glory. We can well wish for you below, brethren, and for ourselves, no better and greater thing than this, that we may live and die with our eyes fixed upon Jesus.

ISRAEL'S SECOND SONG

Numbers 21:17, 18

" Then Israel sang this song, Spring up, O well; sing ye unto it: the princes digged the well, the nobles of the people digged it, by the direction of the lawgiver, with their staves."

WE observed, brethren, last Wednesday, that the last year of Israel's wanderings differs in some features from that of the preceding years, and we pointed out one feature in particular,—their frequent battles and victories on the confines of the Land of Promise. We also noticed, that on many occasions they shewed more faith at this period of their history, and we thought it probable that this might arise in part from the fact, that the old generation, the one that set not their heart aright, had now nearly passed away. There is some confirmation of this supposition in the verses which precede our text. We are told the names of some of the stations at which they pitched their tents:—according to ver. 10, in Oboth; according to ver. 11, at Ije-abarim; and then, in ver. 12, we read of the valley of "Zared." But if you refer to Deut. ii. 14, you will find that this was the very place at which the last of the condemned generation died. Moses says, "And the space in which we came from Kadesh-barnea, until we were come over the brook Zered, was thirty and eight years; until all the generation of the men of war were wasted out from among the host, as the Lord sware unto them." And then, in ver. 25 of the same chapter, we are told of another fact, which is of very great interest in connexion with this year, and *that fact* is, that God put a "spirit of fear" into the hearts of Israel's enemies. "This day," said God, "will I begin to put the dread of thee and the fear of thee upon the nations that are under the whole heaven, who shall hear report of thee, and shall tremble, and be in anguish because of thee." In which verse, brethren, we ought specially to notice the words, "This day will I begin," as if it were something new, the commencement of a new period in their history; and hence, too, it is that special mention of this time is made in a book that was called "The Book of the Wars of the Lord," in which, as ver. 14 of our chapter shews, the "Red Sea" and the "brooks of Arnon" are mentioned together,—"What he did in the Red Sea, and in the brooks of Arnon."

The words of our text might seem to some to be very unimportant. But if we look at them carefully, we shall see that they are very instructive, both on account of the light which they throw on this period of Israel's history, and also as typical of the Christian life. There are three points which claim our notice,—Israel's thankfulness, Israel's faith, and Israel's labour.

Israel's thankfulness, for they " sang this song." The circumstances under which they sang it are quite evident. There was again, as there had been so often before, a want of water, but this time they did not *murmur*. We read of no *complaints* made concerning God's ways—no threats uttered against Moses; on the contrary, when God gave them the promise, ver. 16, "Gather the people together, and I will give them water," they broke forth in a joyful song. It was long now, brethren, since Israel had sung a song of thanksgiving. For thirty-nine years we have no record of praise. This song, short and peaceful as it is, reminds us of the more exalted one which Israel sang when Pharaoh and his host were drowned in the Red Sea. Does not this new feeling of thankfulness—this absence of murmuring during trial—this resumption of praise, hushed during so many years, clearly shew us that Israel's state of mind was now a better one, and that in the new generation there was more faith?

And all this, brethren, seems to throw light upon the Christian's course. When the young Christian is enabled by faith to cast himself on his Redeemer, and finds in Him the forgiveness of all his sins, and a supply for all his need, his heart is often filled with joy, and he thinks that he can easily endure all things. But then there generally follows a season of conflict and trial. The sensible joy of acceptance with God is withdrawn, and a process of training begins, the object of which is to teach him to walk by faith and not by sight. Many hidden evils of his heart are gradually brought out,—self-confidence, unbelief, and impatience. But all this discipline, so painful to us, is sent not to destroy us, but to prove us, that we may know our own hearts and God. "Thou shalt remember," says the Lord, (Deut. viii. 2,) "all the way which the Lord thy God led thee these forty years in the wilderness, to humble thee, and to prove thee, to know what was in thine heart, whether thou wouldest keep his commandments, or no." The painful part of the Christian's life and experience is the laying deep and wide God's foundation in the soul, that a firm and beautiful superstructure may be reared upon it by degrees,—stone laid upon stone, grace added to grace. And then, brethren, you often find towards the close of the Christian's pilgrimage, more enlargement of heart, more steadfast faith

in God, more calmness and peace, and what we should
specially notice here, a more *thankful* spirit. The spirit
of discontent and murmuring, if it was once indulged, has
been overcome, and the song of praise often ascends to
God for daily mercies, for creation, preservation, and all
the blessings of this life, but above all for redemption,—
for the means of grace and the hope of glory. "Israel
sang this song." It may be that we are speaking now to
some who are in heaviness through manifold temptations.
You may have some hidden sorrow, known only to yourself, which weighs your heart down. You are tempted
to ponder all the circumstances of your path, to weigh
all its difficulties, until you think that none are tried as
you are ; and sometimes the *hard* thought of God will
enter your mind, and you are disposed to murmur, because
this thing and that are not changed. Oh, when that
murmur begins to rise, still it with the thought, "It is
the Lord—it is His hand which appoints my path,"—still
it with the recollection of the words, "Be still, and know
that I am God." There are reasons even now in the
midst of your sorrow for *thankfulness* to God. Are the
tenderest cords of your heart rent asunder by bereavement ? Perhaps the departed one was taken from evil to
come—*taken* to be with Christ Jesus. To be with Jesus,
oh, is there no mercy in this ? Or is it some affliction
more hard to bear than even bereavement ? Still God
would teach you some lesson, some deep lesson by it.
And is it no mercy to have such a Teacher ? But perhaps you feel impatient because you seem to be learning
nothing, and your heart appears to you to grow worse
and worse. And yet in all this God may be preparing
you to sing a *new* song—may be attuning your heart to
thankfulness. He begins by shewing you that all the

strings of your harp are broken; but His own hand is
mending them, that your thankfulness may be calm, holy,
and continuous—your song may rise high, and re-echo
the praises of Heaven. "Israel sang this song."

Brethren, Israel was far too long in learning it. Sad it
is to see them surrounded daily by such miracles of love,
yet so unthankful. It is difficult to *praise*—difficult
to attain to a spirit of *thankful cheerfulness.* Yet, brethren, we should not rest without it. We should pray,
earnestly pray, that we may not be as long as Israel in
attaining to it. There is much in the short but beautiful
exhortation of St Paul, (Col. iii. 15,) "Be ye thankful;"
and in the verses that follow,—"Let the word of Christ
dwell in you richly in all wisdom; teaching and admonish-
ing one another in psalms and hymns and spiritual songs,
singing with grace in your hearts to the Lord. And whatsoever ye do in word or deed, do all in the name of the
Lord Jesus, giving thanks to God and the Father by him."
"Israel sang this song."

But we may notice also "Israel's faith." There is a
kind of thankfulness, brethren, which arises from good
natural spirits and a strong constitution of body, and we
would not underrate these blessings; but this thankfulness
will fail, when its cause fails. Let health fail, the spirit
sinks, and probably repining will follow. But true thankfulness has a higher source—God himself—and it is
therefore always connected with "faith." So it was in
Israel's case. God had promised them water in the wilderness,—"I will give them water." They believed the promise. We do not find them asking on this occasion those
questions which they had so often asked before,—questions which our sinful hearts are so prone to ask,—"Can
God give us water? Can He provide a table in the

wilderness?" Oh no. Their song was the utterance of faith,
—"Spring up, O well." Was not this faith, brethren? It
is the characteristic of faith to look at the promise of God,
and not at difficulties. When God promised a son to
Abraham in his old age, he staggered not at the promise
on account of the difficulties which appeared to bar its
fulfilment, but was fully persuaded that what God had
promised, He was able also to perform. When God told
him to offer up his beloved son, he obeyed without hesita-
tion, although the act seemed to blot out at one stroke
all the promises, the repeated promises, of a " seed which
should be as the sea-shore for multitude." He knew that
God could fulfil the promise in His own way, and at His
own time, as St Paul says of him, (Heb. xi. 19), " Account-
ing that God was able to raise him up, even from the
dead." This, brethren, was *faith*. And it was in the same
spirit of faith that Israel, when no water was to be seen
in the parched wilderness, but simply *because* God had
promised, sang this song, " Spring up, O well." Brethren,
there is a *well*, which God has opened for His people in
the wilderness. Jesus is the gushing *Well*, as well as the
smitten Rock; and the Holy Spirit, which Christ has without measure, is the living water ; and so abundant and life-
giving is this water, that every one who drinks the waters
of this well, is himself made a little well in the wilderness.
Jesus says, (John iv. 14), " But whosoever drinketh of the
water that I shall give him shall never thirst ; but the
water that I shall give him shall be in him a well of
water springing up into eternal life." There is a well in
this wilderness, though unseen. It may be that there is
some one here who has tried one earthly cistern after
another, and you have found them all fail. You know that
you are not yet satisfied. The waters which you have

tasted, are not the waters of life. You have thirsted again, and still thirst. If you could get rid of that uneasy craving, you must cast away all the broken cisterns, which the world tries, and come to a fountain, unseen, but full of living waters—to Jesus Christ, full of grace ; and then, in entire dependence on His word, you must say in faith, "Spring up, O well," and it *will* spring up, and its waters be the waters of life to your soul. Or, perhaps, you have tasted of this well, you have gone to it often, and been refreshed. But now it seems far away. You may have been careless in your walk, and grieved the Spirit of God ; or God may have led you into darkness, and not into light, to discipline your soul—to teach you to trust Him in the dark ; and now, instead of trusting, you are faint and desponding, writing bitter things against yourself, and, what is worse, beginning to think that God has forgotten you. Oh no ! What saith the Lord, (Isa. xlix. 15, 16,) " Can a woman forget her sucking child, that she should not have compassion on the son of her womb ? yea, they may forget, yet will I not forget thee. Behold, I have graven thee on the palms of my hands ; thy walls are continually before me." Remember the invitation, Rev. xxii. 17, "The Spirit and the bride say, Come. And let him that heareth say, Come. And whosoever will, let him take the water of life freely." Can that invitation fail ? Oh no. Act upon it with unquestioning faith. *Believe* what you cannot see and do not feel, and in the words of Israel of old say, " Spring up, O well." But once more : Perhaps it is not for your own soul alone that you want water. You drink yourself and are refreshed. But there is *another* soul, dear to you as your own, who cares not for the living well. You have often prayed, but as yet there is no answer. Your tears and sighs seem to have been disregarded. Will the Lord absent Himself for ever? Will He cast out your prayer? You sometimes think so, and feel very desponding and weary. But no. The very man who said, (Lam. iii. 8,) "He shutteth out my prayer," adds afterwards, (ver. 26,) "It is good that a man should both hope and quietly wait for the salvation of the Lord." Try, then, difficult as it is, to "wait quietly" on God—to wait in the confidence of faith and in the patience of hope. Continue to urge prayer in behalf of the beloved though wandering soul. "Spring up, O well."

But we have still to look at this subject in another point of view, as shewing Israel's, and as illustrative of the Christian's *labour*.

It is evident that they not only spoke the words of faith, "Spring up, O well," but actually *dug* it. All Israel's energy was thrown into this work—all classes joined in it. "The princes," our text says, "digged the well, the nobles of the people digged it, by the direction of the lawgiver, with their staves." Now, you will notice at once, brethren, that this also is another distinctive feature in the closing scene of Israel's wilderness life. When God gave them water before, they had nothing to do themselves. They saw the rock smitten for them, and the water gush out. They were altogether passive. But on this occasion the promise of God called out all their active powers, and they *dug* the well, whilst they uttered the prayer, "Spring up, O well." And thus, brethren, it is with the state of the Christian's mind. He is both passive and active. He *looks* and he *works*. There is a Rock, brethren, which is *smitten* for us—smitten by the hand of God, by the rod of His power. It is the Lord

Jesus Christ, and what you have to do is to *behold* Him,
—to stand still and see His great salvation, to look at the
living streams gushing from forth the smitten Rock ; and
more than *look*, to " drink, yea, drink abundantly." One
look is salvation—one *taste* is life. But this is not all.
God calls us to be *active*, as well as *passive*,—to *dig* the
well, as well as sing the song, " Spring up, O well." You
may ask, In what way ? We answer, *first*, that you must
diligently apply your mind to the *study* of God's Holy
Word. You must dig into that well, from whence all the
streams of truth flow. We should not, brethren, be satisfied with the slight acquaintance with it which so many
shew. It is not enough to gather from it the *little* which
you may learn from sermons. Not enough just to know
the way of salvation. We should *search* the Word of God.
It, like any other book, and more than any other book,
has its surface truths, and those which lie deeper. Its
most precious truths, just as in science and in nature, are
only found by diligent search, by deep digging below the
surface. You will generally, if not invariably, find that
those Christians whose minds are the most occupied by
the study of God's Word, the careful and patient digging
into it, are the happiest and most fruitful Christians.
Their hearts are most enlarged. Their views are more
comprehensive. You will not find them trusting in, and
perplexed about, their own feelings. They are searching
into the mind and will of God, and drinking of the living
water which springs up as they dig. Many, brethren, of
the defects which we feel within us, and most of the evils
which we see around us in the Church, arise from our own
very *partial* knowledge of the Word of God. Numbers
are never rooted in Christ, because they are never established in *His* truth. They do not live upon what they

know, because they do not *dig* for more. Others are harassed and perplexed by false doctrines, simply because their principles have not been thoroughly fixed. Brethren, if there ever was a time in which it was needful to *study*, not simply to *read*, but to *study* God's Word, it is the present—with all kinds of errors, old and new, so rife around us—with most solemn events thickening along our path—with the coming of Christ approaching, and, it may be, already at our doors. And how needful it is to be clear in our views, established in our walk, and more and more filled by the Spirit of God! And in digging this well, brethren, you will find it most useful and interesting to compare passages of Scripture together. If one is difficult, another will often elucidate it. Besides, even in the case of the most simple truths, two or three passages conveying the same doctrine will carry a much deeper conviction than one. And, *secondly*, this *searching* of *Scripture* should be accompanied by *earnest prayer* for guidance and Divine teaching. We should pray, not by fits and starts, but with steady perseverance—not with formality, but by trying to penetrate with our staff deeper and deeper, until we reach the well, and the water springs up.

We do not wonder that, after this, Israel gained many victories, for their faith was strengthened. Sihon, king of the Amorites, was smitten, and his cities were taken. Og, the king of Bashan, was delivered into their hands. And so, brethren, when the Christian " draws water with joy out of the wells of salvation," he is strengthened for his daily conflicts—he is made more than conqueror through Him that loved us. And even when he feels most the power of those who oppose him, he can enter into the triumphant words of the great apostle, (Rom. viii.

38, 39), "For I am persuaded that neither death, nor life, nor angels, nor principalities, nor powers, nor things present, nor things to come, nor height, nor depth, nor any other creature, shall be able to separate us from the love of God, which is in Christ Jesus our Lord."

THE CHARACTER OF BALAAM

Numbers 22:12

" And God said unto Balaam, Thou shalt not go with them ; thou
shalt not curse the people : for they are blessed."

WE purpose, brethren, to resume the subject, which we
have left incomplete,—"Israel's history as typical of the
Christian life." Hitherto we have attempted to keep
closely to our subject, and to select only those passages
which evidently bore directly upon it ; but this part of
Israel's history is so remarkable, and the account which is
given of their enemies is so complete and full of instruction, that we shall endeavour to draw instruction from
them as well as from Israel, and to elicit lessons from
their destruction, as well as from Israel's salvation. It is
striking to observe how much Israel had to suffer in the
early part of its history from nations to which it was intimately related. The very first foe which it encountered
after leaving Egypt was, you remember, Amalek, the
descendant of Edom ; and now that they were on the
confines of the Land of Promise, two peoples unite their
forces in the hope of destroying them,—Moab, the descendant of Lot, and Midian, the offspring of Abraham by
Keturah. Their relationship to Israel ought to have led
them to welcome the chosen and suffering nation into the
Land of Promise. It seemed to have the opposite effect,
and to call forth a deeper animosity. When Balak saw
what Israel had done to the Amorites, he was afraid, and

summoned the elders of Midian to his counsel, and there probably together they formed a *scheme*, whereby they hoped to rob Israel of his power, and lay him prostrate before them.

This bitter experience of Israel has its counterpart in the trials of some of the followers of Jesus. There is *one* cross which Christ lays upon all His people. If you refuse to take *that* up, you cannot be a Christian at all. Like Israel, every Christian must leave Egypt, must give up a worldly and sinful life, and pass through this world as a pilgrim and stranger; but there is *another* cross, which is laid upon some of His people only, and especially upon those who are children of Abraham according to the flesh, when they embrace the Saviour, to whose day the father of the faithful looked forward, we mean the cross of which Christ spoke when He said, " A man's foes shall be they of his own household." Opposition is always hard to bear, but most of all from those who are nearest to us, and whose love we value more than all. We can ill afford to give up any love, and least of all can we do without a parent's, a brother's, or sister's love ; and yet, brethren, when it comes to be a choice between Christ's love and theirs, we must never halt. Dutiful and loving we should ever be. Gentleness and patience will often soften down opposition, will touch the heart which has long excluded the Saviour ; but we must never, brethren, forget the solemn words, (Matt. x. 37,) " He that loveth father or mother more than me is not worthy of me : and he that loveth son or daughter more than me is not worthy of me." A heavy cross it must be to bear. If called to bear it, God will give grace ; if not, how deeply should we sympathise with those who are called to follow Christ at the sacrifice of everything that is dearest to them !

We have spoken of Balak's *scheme* for overcoming Israel. We are all familiar with it. There was a man living near the Euphrates who was remarkable at that time for his power of divination. The king of Moab imagined that if this man could be prevailed upon to curse Israel, they would be forsaken by their God, and would fall an easy prey to their enemies. The man whom he thus consulted, Balaam, was a remarkable character, one which has puzzled many people. Let us look at it, especially in so far as it is set before us in the chapter from which our text is taken.

The name Balaam is made up of two Hebrew words, which signify "consumer of the people." In what sense these words are to be taken, the 6th verse clearly shews, where Balak says, "Come now therefore, I pray thee, curse me this people; for they are too mighty for me : peradventure I shall prevail, that we may smite them, and that I may drive them out of the land : for I wot that he whom thou blessest is blessed, and he whom thou cursest is cursed." According to these last words, Balaam was regarded as possessed of a power to bless and to curse, but which of the two predominated is very evident from his name, for he was regarded as the "*consumer* of the people." His dominion over the minds of the people was founded in dread. How different, brethren, from Jesus ! In Him there is no curse,—all is blessing. Balaam was held to be the consumer of the people ; Jesus is their Saviour. He wins by the greatness of His love, and gives peace.

When this name was given to the son of Beor we are not told, whether at his birth, or in consequence of his supposed power ; but one thing seems to be certain, and that is, that his father was an enchanter before him, for "Beor" means nearly the same as Balaam. It signifies *destruc-*

tion, a name without doubt given to him because a power of destruction was held to reside in his *curses*.

This meaning of the word " Balaam," is confirmed by a remarkable passage in the Book of Revelation, (chap. ii. 6,) " But this thou hast, that thou hatest the deeds of the Nicolaitanes, which I also hate." Some have taken this passage *historically*, and supposed the Nicolaitanes to be the followers of Nicolas the deacon, who is said to have fallen into heresy. We believe that it ought to be taken *symbolically*, and that St John means by " Nicolaitanes," the very same heretics whom he describes (Rev. ii. 14) as " holding the doctrine of Balaam, who taught Balac to cast a stumbling-block before the children of Israel, to eat things sacrificed unto idols, and to commit fornication." For the Greek word " Nicolaus " means " conqueror of the people," just as the Hebrew word " Balaam," means " consumer of the people." It was the characteristic of Baalam and of the Nicolaitanes, that they led souls into sin, and brought down the wrath of God upon His people. Two very opposite views have been taken of the character of Balaam. Some have thought that he was altogether a false prophet—a man wholly given to idolatry, without any fear of Jehovah whatsoever ; others, again, have held him to be a true prophet, and even a righteous man at first, but one who, in consequence of the power of a besetting sin, fell from Jehovah. The truth seems to lie between these two views. He was not altogether a false prophet, as the beautiful prophecies concerning Israel distinctly shew. He was not altogether ignorant of Jehovah, even previous to these events, as his words to the elders of Midian prove, (chap. xxii. 8,) " Lodge here this night, and I will bring you word again, as the Lord shall speak to me." There is difference of opinion as to how he had gained this knowledge of Jehovah. Some think by immediate inspiration of God, and others that it had come to him through the Israelites. It is quite clear that on this occasion he was *inspired* by Jehovah to prophesy concerning Israel, but we cannot suppose him to have been *so* previous to these occurrences. We are, therefore, disposed to adopt the view, that the account of the wonderful dealings of God with Israel had penetrated to the banks of the Euphrates, and had awakened the curiosity of Balaam, and that from that time he had inquired of Jehovah in cases of difficulty. There is nothing improbable in this. Many passages of Scripture shew us what a deep impression God's miraculous dealings with Israel produced on the surrounding nations. Take, for example, the instance of Jethro. We read, (Exod. xviii. 1,) "When Jethro, the priest of Midian, Moses' father-in-law, heard of all that God had done for Moses, and for Israel his people, he came to Moses;" and (ver. 11) he says, " Now I know that the Lord is greater than all the gods : for in the thing wherein they dealt proudly he was above them." But the words of Rahab are still more striking, (Josh. ii. 9–11,)—" And she said unto the men, I know that the Lord hath given you the land, and that your terror is fallen upon us, and that all the inhabitants of the land faint because of you. For we have heard how the Lord dried up the water of the Red Sea for you, when ye came out of Egypt ; and what ye did unto the two kings of the Amorites, that were on the other side Jordan, Sihon and Og, whom ye utterly destroyed. And as soon as we had heard these things, our hearts did melt, neither did there remain any more courage in any man, because of you : for the Lord your God, he is God in heaven above, and in earth beneath." Balaam then had doubtless heard

of Jehovah, and, like Simon Magus, had been much
attracted by what he had heard.   He was not altogether
without good emotions, as his remarkable wish shews,
" Let me die the death of the righteous, and let my end
be like his!"   But his heart, like Simon Magus's, was *never*
renewed.   His last sin demonstrated its entire estrangement from God, and even his conduct at first, when carefully examined, shews a want of *sincerity*, notwithstanding
all his professions.   For when Balaam first inquired of
God, whether he should accompany the elders of Midian,
the command was clear and distinct,—" Thou shalt not go
with them ; thou shalt not curse the people : for they are
blessed."   And Balaam seemed satisfied with it, for he
said to the princes of Balak, " Get you into your land : for
the Lord refuseth to give me leave to go with you."   Thus
far nothing could appear to be more *upright* than the
conduct of Balaam, and when Balak sent the second time,
his professions seemed most decided and consistent.   He
replied to all the king of Moab's tempting offers, (ver. 18,)
" If Balak would give me his house full of silver and gold,
I cannot go beyond the word of the Lord my God, to do less
or more."   But then he added, (ver. 19,) " Now therefore,
I pray thee, tarry ye also here this night, that I may know
what the Lord will say to me more."   Now, it is just here,
brethren, that Balaam failed first.   He ought not to have
inquired a *second* time.   God had said, " Thou shalt
not go with them," and this ought to have been sufficient.   When God has once revealed His will, it is
sinful to make further inquiry, as if it were not revealed, or as if circumstances would change it.   This it
was that Balaam secretly wished.   He did not dare to go
without God's permission ; but notwithstanding all his
professions, he could not quietly resign all Balak's offers

of promotion and gold. We take this, then, brethren, to be the great crisis in Balaam's life. We take this *act*, which to many appears so excellent, to be the *first* step in his downward course. It was a solemn moment for Balaam, the turning-point in his history; but he knew it not. It was not only the day of God's power towards Israel, but a day of grace to Balaam; but, alas! he *knew* it not. The precious moment on which so much depended, was lost and perverted; henceforth his downward course was rapid and fearful. He perished in the rejection of grace and mercy. How full of solemn warning is this period of Balaam's history! There is, brethren, there must be, a crisis in our histories as in Balaam's, a time, perhaps a *moment*, on which our eternity depends. There may be nothing evidently solemn in that moment, nothing to mark it out as a great crisis at the *time*. The Spirit of God may strive with you, gently strive. There may be some conviction in your mind, and all may depend on your yielding up your heart to Christ, and acting upon that conviction at *once*. If you WAVER when you ought to act, wait for more light. When you have light enough, if you allow any *second* thought to come in to determine what you shall do—anything selfish or worldly, when you ought to act simply for God, then the Spirit may leave you, your day of grace, like Balaam's, may pass by, or it may be some temptation which is presented to you. We do not mean any awful temptation, one which the world itself would counsel you to resist. It may be some offer which you would be deemed foolish in rejecting, something that the world thinks an advantage; and yet if you *do* give way to the temptation, oh, what unforeseen consequences may follow, step by step, with unerring, irretrievable certainty, alienation of the heart from God, and, finally, the eternal loss of the soul! Let it now be impressed upon your hearts, beloved brethren, what great and eternal consequences may depend upon *one little act.* Remember that God will try you, as he did Balaam. Oh, be faithful to God, faithful in apparently little things, as well as in great. But we must go a step further, and ask, "What was it that gave this bias to Balaam's will, and led him still to inquire, when he ought to have felt, ' God has revealed His will ; it is enough. I will not move from my place ? ' " Scripture gives a complete answer to that question. It was a besetting sin, and we are told what it was. It was the sin of covetousness. Thus St Peter says of him, (2 Pet. iii. 15,) "Who loved the wages of unrighteousness." There are two most solemn lessons which this ought to rivet on our hearts. First, we see the amazing power and awful effects of one besetting sin. We see how it perverts the will, how it keeps the heart from resting on the plain word of God—how it leads it to neglect, yea, not even to know, the day of visitation— and how it hurries the soul onward, blinded and debased, to a point at which at first it would have shuddered. These, brethren, are the effects which besetting sins are still producing at this very day and hour—it may be in some one here present—in some one who least of all expects it; for we are slow to think that any indulged sin can be so ruinous in our own case, and yet, brethren, it is, it must be, ruinous. The history of Balaam proclaims, in the most solemn tones, " Beware of a besetting sin."

The other lesson is the deceitfulness of the human heart. Here we see a man professing to go to God for guidance, declaring most solemnly that he must and would abide by God's decision, and that no amount of reward should ever induce him to say more or less than God commanded him to speak, yet all the time he was longing for Balak's gold—was hoping that God would revoke His own words, and was willing to have cursed Israel, if only God suffered him. Does not all this prove the deceitfulness of the human heart? Its wishes may be quite opposite to its most solemn professions; and at the very moment when it seems to be guided by the will of God, it may be following some device or desire of its own. To what earnest self-inspection, to what a careful scrutiny of our wishes and motives, should this character lead us, lest *our* hearts, too, should be hardened by the deceitfulness of sin—lest a deceived heart should turn *us* also aside—lest, satisfied with a sound and decided profession, we forget that God is the searcher of the heart, and that He deals and will deal with us, not according to what we *profess* to be, but according to what we *are*, according to the real state of our hearts.

The permission which God gave to Balaam to go with the princes of Moab, is certainly difficult and perplexing, especially when taken in connexion with what follows. If God gave him permission to go with them, why was an angel sent to arrest his progress? and why was God angry? We should answer to questions of this kind,—The great crisis of Balaam's life was now past. He had shewn his insincerity. Though he would not outwardly break away from God, he had really chosen evil—his heart was intent upon gold. The permission, therefore, on God's part was really a *punishment*. It was as if God had said to him, "You wish to go with the princes of Moab. Notwithstanding all your professions, your heart is set upon it. Go then; but know this, that your sin shall find you out." And yet mercy was blended with judgment. It was another moment of visitation when

the angel of God stood in his way ; and, to use the words
of St Peter, "He was rebuked for his iniquity : the dumb
ass, speaking with man's voice, forbade the madness of
the prophet." It was a moment of impressive warning
when the angel said to him, "Wherefore hast thou smitten
thine ass these three times ? Behold, I went out to withstand thee, because thy way is perverse before me : and
the ass saw me, and turned from me these three times :
unless she had turned from me, surely now also I had
slain thee, and saved her alive." But even then, brethren,
Balaam's love of money prevailed over every other consideration. He ought to have turned back at once. It
ought to have been clear to him that God was displeased
with him. But what does he say ? "Now, therefore, if it
displease thee, I will get me back again." Here, again,
he disregards present light and warning, whilst he professes to be looking for something more.

There is much, brethren, that is peculiar and miraculous in this story—miraculous in its outward circumstances. But if we penetrate beneath these, if we
look for the *principle* on which God dealt with Balaam on this occasion, we shall find it to be one of the
fundamental principles of His government. God often
chastens people, not by thwarting all their wishes, not by
placing them in a position in which they cannot do what
they will, but by granting them the desires of their hearts,
by giving them their own way. As with Israel of old, He
gives them their desires, "but sends leanness withal into
their souls." But then in mercy He also gives them
checks. At *this* and *that* point He will hedge up their
way with thorns, and present a drawn sword, that they
may be led to feel that their own way is displeasing to
God, and is leading them downwards to the shades of

death. Is there any one here with whom God has been thus dealing? Have you been disregarding God's will, and seeking your own? And has He met you with disappointments? Has your way been sprinkled with thorns? Oh, these are the warnings of love! By these God would lead you to feel, before it is too late, the misery of walking in selfish and self-chosen paths. By these He would lead you to Jesus, and to the fountain opened for sin and for uncleanness, and would bring you to feel and say with Israel of old, "I will go and return to my first husband; for then it was better with me than now." Brethren, let us endeavour to live in more complete dependence on God. Let us delight ourselves in Him, and then it will be unmixed mercy when He grants us the desires of our hearts. Let our constant prayer be, "Lord, what wilt thou have me to do?" and when He shews us by His Word and the guidance of His providence, let us act upon it *at once*. What He calls us to do may involve trial, may require self-denial; still let us not shrink from it. Leaning on Christ, and cherishing every influence of the Holy Spirit, let us go forward, and then "our path will be as the shining light, which shineth more and more unto the perfect day."

BALAAM'S FIRST BLESSING

Numbers 23:10

"Let me die the death of the righteous, and let my last end be like his !"

SOME of you, brethren, will remember that we considered in our last sermon the character of Balaam, as set forth in the preceding chapter, and we saw that it was the first and great crisis in his history, when, instead of simply obeying the command, "Thou shalt not go with them," he made a second inquiry of God. And why did he make it? Not because there was any uncertainty about God's will, but because he wished to get Balak's rewards. God granted his unhallowed wish to a certain extent, and allowed him to go. But whilst he was going, Jehovah gave him another proof that his way was very perverse and sinful before Him. The very beast on which he rode rebuked him at the very time when a large host was regarding him as their deliverer. But even then Balaam did not turn back again, as he ought to have done, but said, (ver. 34), "Now therefore, if it displease thee, I will get me back again." There was much insincerity here. Balaam *really* wished to have his own way at this very time that he outwardly appeared to acknowledge Jehovah. And it is just in this that his character is so full of warning to us. Are there not some now who dare not break away from God altogether, and yet, under shelter of their profession of Him, they withhold their hearts from Him, and are bent upon acting according to their own will? We may trace the same state of mind in the request of Balaam to Balak, (chap. xxiii. 1,)—"Build me here seven altars, and prepare me here seven oxen and seven rams." Balaam thus hoped to propitiate Jehovah, and so to obtain permission to curse Israel. He did not dare to curse Israel without God's permission, but he cherished the hope that God would *relax* his commands. How great was the difference between his *real* state of mind and that which his beautiful words seem to indicate! "God," he could say, "is not a man that he should lie; neither the son of man, that he should repent: hath he said, and shall he not do it? or hath he spoken, and shall he not make it good?" and yet all the time he secretly wished and hoped that God *would* change His mind. After the sacrifice was offered, God met Balaam; and what was the result? The latter returned to the king of Moab with the words, "How shall I curse whom God hath not cursed; or how shall I defy, whom the Lord hath not defied."

Here, then, we see that God interposed on behalf of His people, and turned the curse into a blessing, as it is said, (Deut. xxiii. 5,) "Nevertheless the Lord thy God would not hearken unto Balaam; but the Lord thy God turned the curse into a blessing unto thee, because the Lord loved thee."

But here, brethren, a difficult question meets us. Was there any *reality* whatever in Balaam's curse? Or was it altogether a harmless thing—in fact, *nothing at all?* If there was nothing in it, why should it have been averted? Why should it be said that God "would not hearken unto Balaam?" Why not let it be pronounced? The result would have shewn that there was no power or reality in it. On the other hand, it is difficult to suppose that such power could reside in a curse, especially when spoken by such a man as Balaam.

One thing, brethren, is certain, that *God* himself never did give false prophets power to curse. Could they, then, derive it from any other quarter? Yes, brethren. Why not from Satan? No creature is absolutely independent; all are instruments in the hands of another. If through grace we have been placed in the kingdom of light, then we are instruments in the hands of God. If we are in the kingdom of darkness, we can only be instruments in the hands of Satan; a curse and not a blessing to others. Now, heathenism is one great territory of Satan's power— one chief part of his kingdom of darkness. He reigns supreme there. In that kingdom there is no true worship. Consciously or unconsciously, the heathen worships devils. As St Paul says, (1 Cor. x. 19, 20,) "What shall I say then? that the idol is anything, or that which is offered in sacrifice to idols is anything? But I say, that the things which the Gentiles sacrifice, they sacrifice to devils, and not to God: and I would not that ye should have fellowship with devils." We believe, then, brethren, that within the sphere of his kingdom of darkness, Satan has power to employ false prophets as his instruments—has power to enable them to curse, and to fulfil their curse when pronounced. The conflict here, then, was not merely one between the king of Moab and Israel, but between the kingdom of light in Israel and the kingdom of darkness in Moab and Midian. Balaam's curse would have been the utterance of the power of darkness; but he was obliged, however reluctantly, to confess his impotency before God. It was an act of Divine power when God turned the curse into a blessing. It shewed His watchful care and love towards His people.

And what is it that God is accomplishing now by the gift of His Son and the power of His grace, but turning the curse into a blessing. Oh, there is a wide-spread curse, which has long been resting, and rests still, upon this guilty world, the curse pronounced on man's disobedience; and what makes it so awful is, that it is a *righteous* curse. Wherever, brethren, we look, we see its tokens—man doomed to a life of weary labour, suffering from different kinds of sickness, and at last seized with the irresistible hand of death; so that St Paul says, "The whole creation groaneth and travaileth in pain together until now." But to the children of God this threefold curse is changed by the grace of God into a blessing. Look, brethren, at the lowest element of the curse, that of labour, according to the sentence, "In the sweat of thy face shalt thou eat bread." How wearisome is ceaseless toil in itself! Is it not all too common to see powerful minds give way, and bodies worn out by the pressure of toil; and what is its results? How much of it is altogether vanity; much is occasioned by that which is sinful; much ends in nothing. But to the true Christian, brethren, how different is toil and labour. He consecrates his powers to Him who has redeemed him with His precious blood. He submits to it as God's appointment. He connects all his labour with Christ. He aims at God's glory in it, and so none of it is lost. Often there may be no apparent result; but if done in Jesus and to Jesus, it cannot be lost. There is no vanity in it. "Ye have not chosen me; but I have chosen you, and ordained you, that ye should go and bring forth fruit, and that your fruit should *remain*." The grace that transforms the heart changes the curse of labour into a blessing. The true Christian can bless God for toil. He may be often wearied, sometimes overdone; but still he can bless God for the labour and service which are appointed for him.

Or look at sickness. What is it but the visible reflection of a spiritual disease within? If the image of God had not been obliterated from the soul by sin, there would have been no sickness or sorrow in the world. Sickness is a direct consequence of sin, not of our own individual sin, but of the corruption of man's nature. Considered in itself, it is a part of the curse pronounced upon fallen man. But when the image of God is restored to the soul by the operation of His Spirit and the indwelling of Christ, then the curse is changed into a blessing. Sickness still continues. No miracle is exerted to exempt the Christian from this trial. But its nature is changed; there is no longer any curse in it. How many can bless God for it, painful as it may have been—can bless God for His sanctifying and sustaining power—for the near communion with Jesus which they then enjoyed—for the hallowed impressions made upon their souls; and, most of all, for the manifestations of God's faithfulness and tenderness—of His power and gentleness. It may be that there are some here who have experienced all this, and more than this. You can look back, it may be, to a period of sickness as to one of the happiest seasons of your life—happiest because Christ was with you, teaching you deeper lessons of His love and salvation, and bringing you nearer to Himself. Do you not feel on looking back that whatever there was of the curse in sickness, to *you* it was turned into a blessing. Your sickness, like Lazarus's, was not unto death, but for " the glory of God, that the Son of God might be glorified thereby."

But of all the elements of the curse, the most manifest and the most awful is death—so universal in its reign—

so tremendous in its power—so mysterious in its nature. We can scarcely stand by a dying bed without the question pressing itself upon our thoughts, Oh, why this convulsion? Why this rending asunder of the elements of our being, so long and intimately united? Why this distressing and humiliating close to our life here? One answer can only be given,—It is because of sin. In the language of Scripture, "Death passed upon all men, in that all have sinned." Death was, and still is to the impenitent and unbelieving, the penalty of sin, the reflection and foreshadow of the second death. But to the believer in Christ Jesus there is no second death. The first death is not its shadow. Its sting is drawn. It is but the rending of the vail which separates his soul from the visible presence of his Redeemer. See Stephen dying. Hear him saying, " Behold, I see the heavens opened, and the Son of man standing on the right hand of God." Or listen to St Paul, in anticipation of his own departure, exclaiming,— " I am now ready to be offered, and the time of my departure is at hand. I have fought a good fight, I have finished my course, I have kept the faith : henceforth there is laid up for me a crown of righteousness, which the Lord, the righteous Judge, shall give me at that day ; and not to me only, but unto all them also that love his appearing." There was no dread of death here, no feeling that it was a curse. It was not so ; it was changed into a blessing.

Thus, brethren, does God still do for His people what He did for Israel of old, change this manifold curse into a blessing. But what was the *blessing* which God put into Balaam's mouth? It had reference to two points,— Israel's separation and Israel's multitude. With regard to the first, he says, " Lo, the people shall dwell alone, and shall not be reckoned among the nations." With regard to the second, " Who can count the dust of Jacob, and the number of the fourth part of Israel ? "

We must all be aware how literally and strikingly the first part of this prophecy has been fulfilled, " The people have dwelt alone." Scattered amongst all nations of the earth, sifted, as we read in Amos, among all nations, like as corn is sifted in a sieve, they have everywhere been a distinct nation. Since Israel's dispersion, numbers of other nations have amalgamated, but Israel has never done so. Everywhere it has " dwelt alone," sympathising but little with others, and nowhere meeting with sympathy. And why has it dwelt alone ? Because the gifts and calling of God are without repentance, because all the promises given to Israel must be fulfilled. It must be restored to its own land, now usurped by others ; and when it is restored, the Redeemer shall come to Zion and turn away ungodliness from Jacob.

And there is a sense, brethren, in which Christians also may be said to " dwell alone." When Jesus was upon earth, though He went about doing good—though He associated with publicans and sinners—though he was followed by multitudes—though he lived so completely for others, and not for Himself, yet there was a deep sense in which He " dwelt alone." He was separate from sin, much as he loved sinners. He was alone, for none sympathised with Him. What comfort we feel, if we can find any who can enter into our plans and purposes ; but no one, brethren, could enter into *His*. He " dwelt alone." So it is in measure with true Christians. The world cannot enter into their feelings, and has no conception of their hopes ; and, more than this, many a one dwells alone as concerns other Christians. He is gradually taught to feel that he must dwell with God—must seek the sympathy of Christ. Separate from the world, he must seek closer communion with Him—must desire to walk with Him, and to act for Him, however lonely the way may be.

The second part of Balaam's prophecy has been as manifestly fulfilled,—" Who can count the dust of Jacob, and the number of the fourth part of Israel?" No nation has ever been so thinned by persecutions, and yet it has ever increased. Like the burning bush, which, though on fire, was not consumed, an unseen, and by them too often forgotten, Hand has kept them from becoming extinct—has fulfilled the promise given to Abraham, " As the stars in number, so shall thy seed be."

But when Balaam had thus predicted Israel's future, another point came before his mind. He knew that Israel was the people of God, a people in one point of view *sinful* enough, but in another *righteous*, a people whose transgressions God loved to pass by, and of whom He himself said, (ver. 21,) " He hath not beheld iniquity in Jacob, neither hath he seen perverseness in Israel: the Lord his God is with him." Bishop Butler, to explain the word " righteous," has referred to the striking passage in Micah vi. 5, where we read, " O my people, remember now what Balak king of Moab consulted, and what Balaam the son of Beor answered him from Shittim unto Gilgal, that ye may know the righteousness of the Lord." And then Bishop Butler goes on to say, Balak demanded, " Wherewith shall I come before the Lord, and bow myself before the high God? Shall I come before him with burnt-offering, with calves of a year old? Will the Lord be pleased with thousands of rams, and ten thousands of rivers of oil? Shall I give my first-born for my transgres-

sion, the fruit of my body for the sin of my soul?" And
Balaam answered him, "He hath shewed thee, O man,
what is good: and what doth the Lord require of thee, but
to do justly, and to love mercy, and to walk humbly with thy
God?" And then he adds, "that righteous means 'good,'
and that no words can more strongly exclude dishonesty
and falseness of heart, than doing justice and loving
mercy; and both these, as well as walking humbly with
God, are put in opposition to those ceremonial methods of
recommendation which Balak hoped might have served
his turn." We know not, brethren, what you may think
of this exposition. We confess that we find it very difficult ourselves to conceive that Balak did ask those striking questions—questions which imply an earnestness of
spirit, which Balak's history nowhere shews. But, however this be, we must remind you that all righteousness
is of God, and though it is possible in our earthly relationships to "do justly," and "love mercy," yet no one
can "walk humbly with God," without His grace. All
the righteousness which Israel had, and all the righteousness which can make our dying hour blessed, is and must
be of God in Christ. "The death of the righteous." It
may be, brethren, that you have witnessed it. You may
have seen the beautiful patience with which the sufferings
of the wasted frame have been endured;—you may have
watched the calm and placid eye, which told so forcibly
of a peace within which passeth all understanding, and
already, before it was closed to this world, was all radiant
with the prospect of future glory;—you may have witnessed the thirsting spirit drinking in the Word of God,
and consciously resting on Jesus, an ever-present Saviour,
fearing nothing, because He is faithful and true, and then
passes with each one of His people through the valley of

the shadow of death. Such calmness and peace, brethren, in such an hour, has proved to many a sceptic the *reality* of the grace of God, and has produced deep convictions and emotions in many an ungodly man's heart. Balaam felt deep emotion when he thought of it, even though it was not given to him to witness it. Yes, so deep was his emotion, that he could not help exclaiming, " Let me die the death of the righteous, and let my last end be like his!" Was it so ? Oh no, anything but that. When all his devices to obtain God's permission to curse Israel had utterly failed, the wretched man suggested to Balak to cast a stumbling-block before the children of Israel, and to tempt them to sin. Balak did so, and wrath fell upon Israel. But some chastisement fell upon the tempter. Israel was commanded to slay the Midianites, and Balaam fell amongst them. He died the enemy of God and his people, amongst their enemies. There is something deeply solemn and full of warning in this. It shews us, brethren, that it is not enough for us to have the most beautiful wishes. Your understandings may be so enlightened, that you may have the clearest view of the difference between the true Christian, and the impenitent. Your emotions may be so deep, that you may pray that you may *not* die as you *now* are—that you may die the death of the righteous. And yet your wish may prove utterly vain,—your emotions may fade away, and in the end you may die in your sins. And oh, why so ? Because you wish for the *peace* of the righteous in your dying hour, and for the crown of the righteous in heaven, but not for the holiness of the righteous now. You see what you ought to be, but are content *not* to *be* so. You hope to be very different some day, but withhold your heart from God now, and day after day neglect salvation. It may be that you do not like to look at your sins, that you cannot bear to say, " Search me, O God, and know my heart." Or it may be that there is something which you do not like to give up just yet ; or it may be that your soul is lulled by spiritual sloth, and that you shrink from exertion. Or it may be that the cross of Christ still appears to you as foolishness ; and that you do not like to come by that new and living, and only way to the Father. Oh, whatever it be, brethren, that hinders you, in the strength of Jesus cast it aside. Beware of resting satisfied with *mere* wishes, however good,—or with *resolutions,* however strong they may seem. Christ knocks at the door of your heart, open it at once to Him and welcome Him in. The Spirit of God greatly strives with you, do not resist His influences. Then in Christ you will have the forgiveness of all sins, and a new nature. You will be enabled to walk with Him now, and then the wish will be no idle one, as it was in Balaam's mouth, but will have its fulfilment, " Let me die the death of the righteous, and let my last end be like his !"

BALAAM'S SECOND BLESSING

Numbers 23:21-23

" He hath not beheld iniquity in Jacob, neither hath he seen perverseness in Israel : the Lord his God is with him, and the shout of a
king is among them. God brought them out of Egypt : he hath
as it were the strength of an unicorn. Surely there is no enchantment against Jacob, neither is there any divination against
Israel : according to this time it shall be said of Jacob and of
Israel, What hath God wrought ! "

THESE beautiful words form a chief part of Balaam's
second blessing on Israel. They contain deep and most
important truths.

Balak, we find, was astonished when Balaam pronounced
his *first* blessing on the people, whom he had wished
him to curse. Yet he was not altogether disheartened
at once. The superstitious fancy entered his head that
the failure had entirely arisen in consequence of Balaam
not being *so* placed as to see the utmost part of Israel ;
and he hoped that by taking the prophet to another and
more favourable situation the blessing might still be revoked, and changed into the wished-for curse. Whether
Balaam himself indulged any hope of the same kind we
are not told. But, if so, it was dissipated as soon as
Jehovah again met him. The first words of Balaam to Balak shew the impression which that solemn meeting had
made upon the prophet's mind, (ver. 19,) " God is not a
man, that He should lie ; neither the son of man, that He
should repent : hath He said, and shall He not do it ? or

hath He spoken, and shall He not make it good?" Balak was superstitiously hoping that a change of place would change the mind and purposes of Jehovah. These words taught him that God is at *all* times and in *all* places the same—unchangeable in His nature, and faithful to His word. What a simple but grand truth. How needful to us, whilst we live, that we may live to God; and how supporting when we die. Hence it is that it is so often repeated in Scripture in so many ways, and by so many mouths. Prophets and apostles love to dwell upon it. The Psalmist says, (Ps. cxix. 89,) "For ever, O Lord, thy word is settled in heaven. Thy faithfulness is unto all generations." It is *settled*, not, you will observe, in this changeful earth, but where there is no change, in heaven, and settled *for ever*. In the prophet Malachi we find the truth of the unchangeableness of God connected with His patience and long-suffering in His dealings with His wayward people, (chap. iii. 6,) "For I am the Lord, I change not; therefore ye sons of Jacob are not consumed." So that every victory which the true Christian is enabled to gain on his way, and his abundant entrance into glory at the end, shews the unchangeableness and faithfulness of God. You will remember that it is spoken of again in something of the same kind of connexion, (James i. 17, 18,) "Every good gift and every perfect gift is from above, and cometh down from the Father of lights, with whom is no variableness, neither shadow of turning. Of his own will begat he us with the word of truth, that we should be a kind of first-fruits of his creatures." As there is no variableness in God's nature, so there is no variableness in His gifts. But here, perhaps, some will feel a difficulty—*one* which we cannot state better than by referring to the history of Saul. You will remember that Samuel said to Saul, (1 Sam. xv. 28, 29,) "The Lord hath rent the kingdom of Israel from thee this day, and hath given it to a neighbour of thine, that is better than thou." And then he adds, in words exactly parallel to those of Balaam, " And also the Strength of Israel will not lie nor repent : for He is not a man, that He should repent." Here, then, we see unchangeableness of purpose. But in verse 11 of the same chapter we read that God said, " It repenteth me that I have set up Saul to be king : for he is turned back from following me, and hath not kept my commandments." Here there seemed to be a change of purpose with regard to Saul. How, brethren, are these, and such passages as these, to be reconciled ? We should say by making a simple and important distinction, and it is this :—Some of God's gifts are variable and *conditional*, dependent upon the faithfulness and obedience of man ; others of God's purposes and gifts are absolute and invariable, and not dependent upon the state of man's mind. The grant of the kingdom to Saul was of the former kind. It was *conditional*. The crown could be forfeited by disobedience, and was so. On the contrary, the grant of the kingdom to David and his descendants was not conditional, but absolute, as the beautiful passage in Ps. lxxxix. 28, &c., shews—" My mercy will I keep for him for evermore, and my covenant shall stand fast with him. His seed also will I make to endure for ever, and his throne as the days of heaven. If his children forsake my law, and walk not in my judgments ; if they break my statutes, and keep not my commandments ; then will I visit their transgression with the rod, and their iniquity with stripes. *Nevertheless* my loving-kindness will I *not utterly* take from him, nor suffer my faithfulness to fail,

My covenant will I not break, nor alter the thing that is gone out of my lips. Once have I sworn by my holiness, that I will not lie unto David." No language could express more strongly an *absolute* gift; and hence we find, that deeply and grievously as Solomon sinned, the kingdom was not rent from him as it was from Saul, and given to another.

We have another instance of an absolute gift in the case of Israel. Scattered and desolate as they now are, it might seem as if their gifts had been all conditional, and were *now* all lost; but it is not so, for St Paul, speaking of them, says, (Rom. xi. 28,) "As concerning the gospel, they are enemies for your sakes; but as touching the election, they are beloved for the fathers' sakes;" and then he adds, "For the gifts and calling of God are without repentance,"—that is, God does not change His mind with regard to His gifts. Israel's calling is absolute, and unalienable. How blessed, a thing, brethren, is it to rest upon that unchangeableness in God's character, and the faithfulness of His Word! His grace can alone *make* us *His*—His faithfulness and power alone keep us His. It may sometimes seem long before He fulfils His promises to us, but *they* cannot fail. "Thy testimonies," says David, (Ps. cxix. 138,) "that thou hast commanded, are righteous and *very faithful.*" But Balaam, you will notice, does not stop here, but proceeds to pronounce a distinct blessing upon Israel,—"He hath not beheld iniquity in Jacob, neither hath He seen perverseness in Israel: the Lord his God is with him, and the shout of a king is amongst them."

The foregoing verse, of which we have spoken, shews us what *view* we ought to take of God. These words shew us the view which God takes of His people. The language is very strong and remarkable,—" He hath not beheld iniquity in Jacob, neither hath He seen perverseness in Israel." Indeed, they are so strong, that many cannot fail to find them very perplexing. For does not God search the hearts of His people? Does He not abhor all sin; and if in one more than another, in those whom He has brought near to Himself, more than in those who are afar off? At whatever part of the Bible we look, do we not see that God is a *jealous* God—that He claims the affections of His people—marks the very first wanderings of their hearts, and often sends them chastisements, to bring their wavering affections back to Himself. The history of Israel, which we have been contemplating so long, affords so many proofs of this, that it seems needless to refer to any passages in particular. But if this be so, then how can it be said that " God hath not beheld iniquity in Jacob, neither hath He seen perverseness in Israel?" Take it *historically* of Israel, and we should say, God did not view Israel as it was *in itself*. If so, He would have seen much perverseness in it; but He viewed them as His covenant people. He looked at them in the light of His own forgiving love. He covered Israel's sins, so that He beheld them no more. We refer, then, these expressions, not, you will observe, to *sanctification*—for the old man always remains in us— but to the *forgiveness* of sins. When we speak of having forgiven others, we often see the fault in them still; but the reason is, because our forgiveness is often incomplete. But God's forgiveness is full and perfect. When He forgives, He so forgives, so covers sin, that He does not behold iniquity in His people. They are as fully justified, and free from all charge of sin, as if they had never sinned. Look at some of the beautiful expressions

whereby God shews the fulness of His forgiving love.
Take, for instance, Isa. xliv. 22,—" I have blotted out, as
a thick cloud, thy transgressions, and as a cloud thy
sins." What a word, brethren, "*blotted* out!" Is sin
blotted out? Then it is gone; it is no longer visible.
God does not behold it. Or refer to Micah vii. 19,—
" Thou wilt cast all their sins into the depths of the sea."
Is there any place where a thing is so surely lost, so certain not to be seen again, as the *depths* of the sea? So
it is with forgiven sin. The ocean tide of God's love
flows over it. It lies in the depth below, and can never
more be seen. And, once more, you will remember the
beautiful promise of the new covenant,—" Their sins and
their iniquities will I remember no more." But this historical explanation of the passage would be a very imperfect one. The New Testament casts its light backwards
upon the Old, and enables us to understand expressions
which otherwise would be very obscure. We must remember, then, that Israel of old is a type of a people
who are brought into a better covenant, established upon
better promises. The Church of the new covenant is
chosen in Jesus—made one with Jesus—and justified
from all things, from which it could not be justified by
the law. Christ is her Head, and she is His body. There
is a real and vital union between them, and, consequently,
all that Christ is, and all that Christ has, belongs to His
people. His robe of righteousness covers them, so that they
may sing, in the words of the prophet Isaiah, (chap. lxi. 10,)
—" He hath clothed me with the garments of salvation, He
hath covered me with the robe of righteousness." In Him
they are complete, as St Paul says, "Ye are complete in
Him," (Col. ii. 10.) In Him they are meet for the inheritance of the saints in light, as St Paul declares, (Col. i. 12,

" Giving thanks to the Father, which hath made us meet
to be partakers of the inheritance of the saints in light."
Observe, brethren, He does not say " will make us meet,"
but *hath* made us meet. How, but in Jesus? Now, this
union being so real, so close, so living, and so influential,
God views His people, not as they are in themselves, sinful, weak, destitute, but as they are in their covenant
Head—forgiven, justified, and complete. Their faith
may be very feeble—their progress in holiness small—
their conformity to Christ's image imperfect; conscious
of their own sinfulness, their own shortcomings, their
own waywardness, they may cry with the Church, (Song
of Sol. i. 6,) " Look not upon me, because I am black."
But to the Father's eye they are all comely, because His
robe of righteousness covers them, as we read, (Ezek. xvi.
14,) " And thy renown went forth among the heathen for
thy beauty : for it was perfect through very *comeliness*,
which I *put* upon thee, saith the Lord God." So that he
beholds no iniquity in Jacob, and sees no perverseness in
Israel. Brethren, if we know anything of our own hearts,
we must see, oh, how much iniquity, how much perverseness there ! and deeply, indeed, ought we to be humbled.
But do not look within only—look to Jesus also, and
much more to Him than to ourselves. Contemplate the
unsearchable riches of His grace—the height, depth,
length, and breadth of His love—the sacredness of that
union wherewith His people are joined to Him. We
have often said, but it cannot be repeated too often, that
the more you humbly and reverentially realize these
truths, the more dead we shall be to the world. The
more we shall walk worthy of the high vocation wherewith we are called, the more we shall mortify our members which are upon the earth; and the more prepared

we shall be to make any sacrifice of self, of ease, comfort, and even lawful enjoyment, for the glory of God and the advancement of His kingdom. Something, brethren, we must care for; would we care less for the world, we must know more what Christ is—His glory and beauty make everything else look dim. It is a great thing to know the grace of our Lord Jesus Christ, to realize our oneness with Him, and go deep into the great truth, "He hath not beheld iniquity in Jacob, neither hath he seen perverseness in Israel." But there is another point which Balaam's prophecy brings out, and that is Israel's safety—we read, (ver. 23,) "Surely there is no enchantment against Jacob, neither is there any divination against Israel;" and why this security in the midst of all the devices of the enemy? A beautiful answer is given, (Deut. xxxiii. 27,) "The eternal God is thy refuge, and underneath are the everlasting arms: and he shall thrust out the enemy from before thee, and shall say, Destroy them." You will find another promise of the same kind, (Isa. liv. 17,) "No weapon that is formed against thee shall prosper; and every tongue that shall rise against thee in the judgment thou shalt condemn. This is the heritage of the servants of the Lord; and their righteousness is of me, saith the Lord." Safety, brethren, is not the only, or perhaps the chief, thing that we need, but still it is a great mercy, and, moreover, a wonderful thing, when we consider the powerful enemies with which we are surrounded. They are so powerful, that many a Christian asks the anxious question, "Shall I ever get safe to the end?" Scripture gives a consoling answer to such questions. It says, "Yes, weak and sinful as you are in yourself, God is able to hold you up and to keep you from falling. He who is for you is greater than they who are against you." How greatly St

Paul was strengthened and comforted by this truth. He says, (2 Cor. i. 10,) looking on the past and the present, "who delivered us from so great a death, and doth deliver;" and what does he say of the future? "in whom we trust, that he will yet deliver us." And again, (2 Tim. i. 12,) "For which cause I also suffer these things: nevertheless I am not ashamed; for I know whom I have believed, and am persuaded that he is able to keep that which I have committed to him against that day." But his hope and joy seemed to rise highest of all, when he wrote the triumphant words, (Rom. viii. 35–39,) "Who shall separate us from the love of Christ? shall tribulation, or distress, or persecution, or famine, or nakedness, or peril, or sword? As it is written, For thy sake we are killed all the day long; we are accounted as sheep for the slaughter. Nay, in all these things we are more than conquerors through him that loved us. For I am persuaded, that neither death, nor life, nor angels, nor principalities, nor powers, nor things present, nor things to come, nor height, nor depth, nor any other creature, shall be able to separate us from the love of God, which is in Christ Jesus our Lord." Let us trust, then, wholly in Jesus, and lean all our weight on that chief corner-stone which God hath laid in Zion. Let us daily commit our souls in all our dangers into His keeping, not only in order that His hand *may* hold us, but *because* it holds us, and then we shall be safe. The wiles of Satan will be laid bare to us, the power of Satan will be controlled. Of the *present* we shall be enabled to say with Asaph, "Nevertheless I am continually with thee, for thou hast holden me by my right hand;" and of the future, (Psa. xxvii. 1,) "The Lord is my light, and my salvation; whom shall I fear? the Lord is the strength of my life;

of whom shall I be afraid?" When we look at the *safety* of those who are Christ's, may we not say, as it was said of old, (Deut. xxxiii. 29,) "Happy art thou, O Israel: who is like unto thee, O people saved by the Lord, the shield of thy help, and who is the sword of thy excellency! and thine enemies shall be found liars unto thee, and thou shalt tread upon their high places." So manifest was God's hand in the deliverance of Israel, and in turning the curse into a blessing, that Balaam predicted that, "according to this time it would be said of Jacob and Israel, What hath God wrought!" Balak, doubtless, thought that Israel's escape from Egypt was an act of their own, and one which shewed indeed their own prowess but nothing more. Balaam pointed out the hand of Jehovah in it all; "*God*," he says, (ver. 22,) "brought them out of Egypt." It will be said of them, "What hath *God* wrought!" And this may be said of God's people now. There is, it is true, a kind of religion for which the powers of man are quite sufficient—morality of life and outward services. But true religion is deeper than this; it is the renewal of the heart—its transformation into the image of Christ, walking by faith and not by sight, and looking at things unseen—and all this is *God's* work in the *soul*. No self-discipline, however persevering—no self-control, however watchful, can produce any such change in the deep springs of man's being. All true holiness, all pure self-discipline and self-control, are the product and the results of a change effected by the Spirit of God in the depths of the human heart.

The true Christian cannot but wonder at times at all that God has done for him and in him, when he contemplates the cross of the Redeemer, the mystery of His sufferings, known and unknown; when he looks back on his own past history,—the dangers to his soul from which the providence of God has shielded him, or the grace of God has kept him; when he feels that some sin which once powerfully beset him, and perhaps reigned in his heart, is now brought into subjection,—temper brought under control, pride subdued, a forgiving spirit taking the place of revenge,—still more, when he feels that the world which he once loved is an empty thing, the cross of Christ, which he once despised, is now all his hope and joy,—the Saviour whom he once neglected is now precious to him beyond any other being; when he looks at all this, *may* he not, and ought he not, to say, in deep humility and with warm gratitude, " What hath God wrought ! "

It is given to some to say this of others also. Many who are labouring in God's vineyard are often downcast, and constrained to exclaim with the prophet, " Who hath believed our report, and to whom is the arm of the Lord revealed ? " But there are times when He gives to His faithful servants much encouragement. The providence of God opens a wide door, where they looked for nothing but difficulties. The grace of God touches souls, and leads them to repentance. A desire is kindled in the hearts of some who are deeply fallen, to escape to a city of refuge. Oh, when we see such tokens of God's presence, ought we not to feel, " This is not *man's* work, but *God's* work." God is bringing them out of Egypt. Ought we not to exclaim with thankful joy, " What hath God wrought ! "

BALAAM'S THIRD PROPHECY

Numbers 24:5-9

"How goodly are thy tents, O Jacob! and thy tabernacles, O Israel!
As the valleys are they spread forth, as gardens by the river
side, as the trees of lign-aloes, which the Lord hath planted, and as
cedar-trees beside the waters. He shall pour the water out of his
buckets, and his seed shall be in many waters; and his king shall
be higher than Agag, and his kingdom shall be exalted. God
brought him forth out of Egypt; he hath as it were the strength
of an unicorn : he shall eat up the nations his enemies, and shall
break their bones, and pierce them through with his arrows. He
couched, he lay down as a lion, and as a great lion : who shall stir
him up? Blessed is he that blesseth thee, and cursed is he that
curseth thee."

THIS is the *third* blessing of Balaam upon Israel. There
was something peculiar in the manner in which it was
pronounced, for we are told in ver. 1, that when Balaam
saw that it pleased the Lord to bless Israel, he went not,
as at other times, to seek for enchantments, but he set his
face toward the wilderness. We have noticed before that
Balaam was a reluctant instrument in God's hands in
blessing Israel. He hoped, as well as Balak, that by
means of enchantments or sacrifices, God might be in-
duced to curse Israel. The allusion in the words, "as at
other times," seems to be not merely to his practices on
other occasions amongst the heathen, but to his sanction
on more than one occasion to Balak's sacrifices; as, for
instance, (chap. xxiii. 1–3,) "And Balaam said unto Balak,
Build me here seven altars, and prepare me here seven oxen,

and seven rams. And Balak did as Balaam had spoken ;
and Balak and Balaam offered on every altar a bullock and
a ram. And Balaam said unto Balak, Stand by thy burnt-
offering, and I will go ; peradventure the Lord will come
to meet me : and whatsoever he sheweth me I will tell
thee. And he went to an high place." And so again in
ver. 14, 15. But on this occasion Balaam did not resort
to sacrifices. He was thoroughly aware that God pur-
posed to bless Israel, and that nothing which he could do
would arrest the blessing ; so he set his face toward the
wilderness. What wilderness ? The wilderness of Jordan.
And why did he set his face thitherward ? Because *there*
the people of God were encamped, and God himself was
dwelling among them. When Balaam set his face towards
the wilderness, it shewed that he turned away for the time
from everything else but God. His will entered for a
season, however short, into God's will. And whither,
brethren, are our faces turned ? Are they turned towards
the people of God, a sign that we are longing to partake
of their blessings ? You remember the prediction concerning Israel, (Jer. l. 4, 5,) " In those days, and in that
time, saith the Lord, the children of Israel shall come,
they and the children of Judah together, going and weep-
ing : they shall go, and seek the Lord their God. They
shall ask the way to Zion, with *their faces thitherward,*
saying, Come, and let us join ourselves to the Lord in a
perpetual covenant, that shall not be forgotten." Are our
faces turned towards God ? When Hezekiah received the
solemn message from Jehovah, " Thou shalt die, and not
live," he turned his face to the wall and prayed. He
turned his back upon the world, and sought the face of
God. And so the Psalmist beautifully says, (Ps. xxv. 15,)
" Mine eyes are ever toward the Lord ;" and again, (Ps.

xxxiv. 5,) "They looked unto him, and were lightened, and their faces were not ashamed."

It is, doubtless, in close connexion with this conduct of Balaam that we are told, (ver. 2,) "the Spirit of God came upon him." It came upon him, not for his sanctification—this he sought not, but to enable him to prophesy. It is a solemn thought that the gifts of the Spirit are so separable from its sanctifying grace. Still, brethren, there is much encouragement here for those who are seeking God. If already your face is turned towards the wilderness, you need not be discouraged, though you may be still conscious of much darkness, still feel many difficulties. Wait on, look upward, and the "Spirit of God will come upon you," to do far more for you than it did for Balaam; not only to enlighten you, but to sanctify you, to give you the Spirit of adoption, to comfort you in conflict and in sorrow. But there is still another peculiarity which we ought to notice before we enter upon the blessing itself; and that is, that Balaam speaks here far more than elsewhere about *himself*, about his own mind under the illumination of the Spirit, and all this we must connect with his setting his face towards the wilderness, and the Spirit of God coming upon him. First, it is worthy of remark how often he uses the word *said* in this introduction, "Balaam the son of Beor hath said, and the man whose eyes are open hath *said*, He hath *said* which heard the words of God." It may remind some of you of the last words of David, (2 Sam. xxiii. 1,) "David the son of Jesse, *said*, and the man who was raised up on high, the anointed of the God of Jacob, and the sweet psalmist of Israel, *said*." And why this frequent repetition of the same word in both passages? It is because both Balaam and David were conscious that they did not speak their own words, but God's, as the context clearly shews. So of Balaam it adds, (ver. 4,) "which heard the *words* of God, which saw the vision of the Almighty;" and David says, (2 Sam. xxiii. 2,) "The Spirit of the Lord spake by me, and his word was in my tongue." Both, therefore, felt that they were moved by the Spirit of God, and that they uttered His words, and not their own.

Secondly, brethren, notice the two expressions, "The man whose eyes are open hath said," (ver. 3,) and "having his eyes open," (ver. 4.) If you will look at the margin you will see that the first might be rendered, "the man who had his eyes shut;" and this translation is admitted to be the best, by Hebrew scholars—"the man whose eyes were shut;" how, then, could it be said in ver. 4, "having his eyes open?" The first we take literally of his outward eyes. These were closed because he turned from the world to listen to God—closed that he might not be distracted by visible things. The latter expression we understand of the mind. Though the outward eye was closed, the inward one was opened to see the vision of God.

And what did he see? He saw stretched out beneath him the tabernacles of Israel, and exclaimed, "How goodly are thy tents, O Jacob, and thy tabernacles, O Israel!" Israel was still on its pilgrimage, and forced to dwell in tents, and yet its tents were better than the dwellings of the ungodly. They were *goodly*, because God was there, and because He so abundantly satisfied His people with His goodness. He watched over them. His eye was upon them night and day. He sheltered them from the intended curse of Balaam, and in the day of battle. Their tents were better than bulwarks; and in all this, brethren, Israel was a type of God's people now. They are pilgrims and strangers on earth, having no continuing city here.

They are called to sit loose to the things of this life, and to realize what they are, and whither they are going. How soon may their work be done, their course be finished? It is, brethren, when we feel that we are pilgrims, standing on Jordan's brink, and looking over to the land of promise, that we live as God would have us live, and work as God would have us work. It adds intensity to life, and vigour to work, when the eye is fixed upon heaven, and not on earth; and then how goodly are their tents, better than the palaces of kings. They may be all unsettled, but God's presence is with them—not know where to go, but God is their guide. The pillar of Providence shews where their tent is to be pitched, and the grace of God supplies all their need. In those tents sins are daily forgiven and blotted out in the precious blood of Christ. The Spirit of God is given. God is approached by prayer. The song of thanksgiving ascends, and the acts of daily life are consecrated by their connexion with God. So that in the highest sense God makes, as Job says, (chap. viii. 6,) "the habitation of his people's righteousness prosperous," and, as Solomon says, "He blesseth the habitation of the just," (Prov. iii. 33.)

But a series of beautiful comparisons set forth more fully the "goodliness of Jacob's tents." Balaam compares them first to "valleys" and "gardens by the river side." The idea is much the same in both, for the word translated "valley" often signifies streams, but here a valley watered by a brook. Both, then, lead our minds to the source of Christian fruitfulness—the Spirit of God. In Isa. lxiii. 14, Israel is compared to a beast going down into the valley. "As a beast goeth down into the valley, the Spirit of the Lord caused him to rest;" here to the valley itself, well watered, and stretching far away.

And so again (Isa. lviii. 11) we find the beautiful promise, "And the Lord shall guide thee continually, and
satisfy thy soul in drought, and make fat thy bones : and
thou shalt be like a watered garden, and like a spring of
water, whose waters fail not." What a contrast to the
description of the ungodly in Isa. i. 30, "For ye shall
be as an oak whose leaf fadeth, and as a garden that hath
no water." You will remember many passages of Scripture in which the Spirit of God is compared to water.
Thus Jesus said, (John vii. 37, 38,) "If any man thirst,
let him come unto me, and drink. He that believeth on
me, as the scripture hath said, Out of his belly shall flow
rivers of living water." And then St John adds, "But
this spake he of the Spirit, which they that believe on
him should receive : for the Holy Ghost was not yet
given ; because that Jesus was not yet glorified." And
there is another passage which seems to illustrate the
words in verse 7, "He shall pour water out of his buckets," to shew the abundance of the supply. You will
find, (John iv. 13, 14,) " Jesus answered and said unto her,
Whosoever drinketh of this water shall thirst again : but
whosoever drinketh of the water that I shall give him
shall never thirst ; but the water that I shall give him
shall be in him a well of water springing up into everlasting life ; " not only enough, but an abundant supply,
filling the soul to overflowing. What, then, the water is
to the extensive valley or the parched garden, *that* the
Spirit of God is to the weary soul. It refreshes it and
makes it fruitful. It renews it day by day. It guides it
in difficulty. It strengthens it in weakness. It removes
despondency. It enables it to labour,—when dead, it
quickens it, when lukewarm, it revives it, when troubled,
sustains it. But Balaam proceeds, " as the trees of lign-

aloes, which the Lord hath planted, and as cedar-trees beside the waters." We find a parallel to this, (Ps. civ. 16,) " The trees of the Lord are full of sap ; the cedars of Lebanon, which he hath planted." In both the trees are spoken of as God's *planting*, because His sustaining power upholds all things, and still more perhaps to shew that they are flourishing. The lign-aloes and cedars are beautiful pictures of the people of God, and introduce new thoughts. The tree planted by the rivers of water strikes its roots deep into the soil, and thereby takes up more nourishment, and is able to stand firm when the storm bursts upon it. And this is one very important thing in the Christian's life. To grow upward and bear fruit, he must strike his roots deeper and deeper into Christ. And thus St Paul, you will remember, says in Col. ii. 6, 7, " As ye have received Christ Jesus the Lord, so walk ye in him; *rooted* and built up in him ; and, Eph. iii. 17, " rooted in love." The upward growth will always depend upon the deep-rooting. We should seek, by earnest prayer, and frequent meditation, to get enlarged views of the person and work of Jesus, to get deeper and deeper into Him, that so we may draw a more abundant supply of nourishment from Him. Temptations from without and within are sure to assail us. False doctrine will try our faith. But if we are rooted in Christ, we shall be enabled to stand firm, and nothing will move us away from the hope of the gospel.

But this comparison also leads our minds to *growth* and *fruitfulness*. The words of the Psalmist are familiar to us all, (Ps. i. 3,) " And he shall be like a tree planted by the rivers of water, that bringeth forth his fruit in his season : his leaf also shall not wither ; and whatsoever he doeth shall prosper." Growth is the true Christian's mark, fruitfulness is his ornament, and success in God's works follows his steps. There is a beautiful passage in Hosea xiv. 5, where God promises, "I will be as the dew unto Israel." And what is the result ? *growth.* In verse 5 it says "he shall grow as the lily," and verse 7, "he shall grow as the vine." "Grow in grace," says St Peter; and if we do not *grow* there must be something wrong. There must be want of watchfulness in prayer, want of care in our walk, and so the Spirit of God is grieved. The gentle dew does not descend. The supplies fail.

But the lign-aloes were remarkable for their fragrant smell; the cedars for their majesty and beauty, fit emblems of what the people of God are in His sight. In Jesus they are made accepted, are justified freely; and, their persons being accepted, all their works, which are done in the Spirit of God, are accepted too, and not only accepted, but are full of fragrance. Their testimony to Christ, both by their words and in their lives, is so. Thus St Paul says, (2 Cor. ii. 14–16,) "Now thanks be unto God, which always causeth us to triumph in Christ, and maketh manifest the savour of his knowledge by us in every place. For we are unto God a sweet savour of Christ in them that are saved, and in them that perish. To the one we are a savour of death unto death, and to the other the savour of life unto life." The offering of Christ Jesus was so perfect, so precious, such a sweet-smelling savour to the Father,—as St Paul says, (Ephes. v. 2,) "And walk in love, as Christ also hath loved us, and hath given himself for us, an offering and a sacrifice to God for a sweet-smelling savour,"—that it blends with all the Christian's offerings of love. The offering of himself and the offering of his means to God diffuse their own fragrance through all ; not even a cup of cold water given to a disciple for

Christ's sake is overlooked by our heavenly Father; and deeply and utterly sinful as true Christians feel themselves to be,—their holy things so defiled, their motives often so low,—yet in the sight of God there is a beauty in them, for He sees upon them the robe of the Son's righteousness, He beholds in them the work of His own grace. Whilst they say with the Church, in Song of Sol. i. 5, "I am black;" Jesus says, "but comely," as the lily among thorns, the cedar among the trees of the forest.

And as the Christian is thus made and kept fruitful, so it adds that "his seed shall be in many waters." The idea seems to be taken from a tree whose stately branches hang over a flowing stream. The seed drops into it, and is carried far away from the spot, where it first fell. It brings forth fruit at a distance; and how often has this proved true in the case of Christians. The precious seed which they have sown has not been lost, though it might seem to them to be so. It drops and is lost sight of; but the waters do but bear it away further, and there it springs up, known perhaps only to God. Brethren, let us sow beside *all* waters, even there where to the eye of man there seems to be little promise of fruit. God can make it fructify and bear fruit in His own time. His faithfulness is pledged to make it accomplish His own gracious promise. Never, brethren, should we despond, and never shall we do so, even amongst difficulties and perplexities, if we have faith in God, and believe the promises :—"They that sow in tears shall reap in joy. He that goeth forth and weepeth, bearing precious seed, shall doubtless come again with rejoicing, bringing his sheaves with him," (Ps. cxxvi. 5, 6.) "His seed shall be in many waters." But Balaam proceeds, "His king shall be higher than Agag, and his kingdom shall be exalted." As

yet Israel had had no visible king, but it was a part of
His purpose that in time they should have kings, for He
had promised Abraham, (Gen. xvii. 6,) "Kings shall come
out of thee." It was God's will that there should be a
development of Israel's power and influence, and this was
brought about through the instrumentality of her kings,
"her king was higher than Agag." But this was not the
complete fulfilment of this prophecy. The kingly office
in Israel shadowed forth the government of God, and her
kings were types of Jesus, who though He rules over all
nations, and though He is not acknowledged by Israel, is,
yet in a special sense, "The King of the Jews." He is
Israel's real and everlasting King. His kingdom shall be
established upon the ruins of all the nations which have
opposed His people. But into this, and Israel's victories
we will not now enter, as they form the great subject of
Balaam's next and last prophecy, (ver. 17,) "I shall see
Him, but not now; I shall behold Him, but not nigh ;
there shall come a Star out of Jacob, and a sceptre shall
rise out of Israel, and shall smite the corners of Moab,
and destroy all the children of Sheth." We will now
only notice the last words of the prophecy, "Blessed is he
that blesseth thee, and cursed is he that curseth thee."
These words cannot fail to remind us of part of the first
promise given to Abraham, (Gen. xii. 3,) "And I will bless
them that bless thee, and curse him that curseth thee; and
in thee shall all families of the earth be blessed." True
Christians are *one* with Christ. "He that toucheth thee,"
says God, "toucheth the apple of mine eye." To afflict and
persecute them is to oppose Him whose they are. "Saul,
Saul," said the Saviour, "why persecutest thou me?" Once
He was persecuted in His own person,—now in the members of His body. And so, on the other hand, those who

bless them, because they belong to God, are blessed.   As it is not a matter of indifference, but of highest importance what is the state of our minds towards God, so is it also what is the state of our minds towards His people, and the two go together. If we love not His people, whom we can see, how can we love God, whom we do not see. If we love Him who begat, then should we also love those who are begotten of Him, and bear, however faintly, His image.   Yes, we should love them, sympathise with them, should help them, should bless them, and then also shall we be blessed; for "blessed is he that blesseth thee, and cursed is he that curseth thee."

BALAAM'S FOURTH PROPHECY

Numbers 24:17

" I shall see him, but not now ; I shall behold him, but not nigh : there
shall come a Star out of Jacob, and a Sceptre shall rise out of
Israel, and shall smite the corners of Moab, and destroy all the
children of Sheth.

THESE beautiful words form a part of the fourth and last
prophecy of Balaam. To Balak's great consternation, he
had already "blessed Israel three times." But the Spirit
of God would not let Balaam stop here. " Now," he
says, " behold I go unto my people ; come, therefore, and
I will advertise thee what this people shall do to thy
people in the latter days." You will not fail to notice
that this prophecy differs in many respects from the three
preceding ones, which we have already considered. *They*
referred chiefly to Israel as it then was. This prophecy
referred to Israel's future. *They* spoke of Israel and
Israel only. This speaks of One greater than Israel, of
One, who, to use the words of Simeon, " should be a light
to lighten the Gentiles, and the glory of His people
Israel." Both these characteristics of this prophecy are
expressed in the first clause of our text, " I shall see Him,
but not now." Commentators have differed as to the way
of explaining the pronoun " him," some referring it to
Israel. We need scarcely say that we agree with those
who refer to Him who is Jacob's star and sceptre. False
as his heart was, the seer saw Him in the spirit of pro-

phecy, and felt that a time would come when he would *actually* see Him. But the time when Jacob's Star would arise was not come, it was distant, and so he adds, "but *not now;* I shall behold him, but *not nigh.*" This, brethren, seems to be the simple and obvious meaning of the words. But if you look at them in connexion with Balaam's state of mind, do they not contain a deeper and more awful meaning? Are they not prophetic of *himself,* as well as of Christ?—of his own awful end, as well as of Israel's great destiny? "I shall see Him!" Yes, when He comes again; but does he express hope that he will share in the Redeemer's glory and Israel's blessedness? No, there is no word of hope, no expression of desire, as in the words of Job, "For I know that my Redeemer liveth, and that he shall stand at the latter day upon the earth; and though after my skin worms destroy this body, yet in my flesh shall I see God: whom I shall see for myself, and mine eyes shall behold, and not another; though my reins be consumed within me." "My Redeemer!" says the afflicted saint, with an appropriating faith; "whom I shall see for myself," he adds, in hallowed longing; but all that the "unrighteous" prophet could say was, "I shall behold him, but not nigh." Brethren, in what spirit do we speak and think of that day of which these men speak? All of us, without any exception, will see Christ. It is plainly declared, "Every eye shall see Him." But how shall we see Him? nigh, or afar off? Like Job, or like Balaam? Has it been given us to say with the first, "*My* Redeemer—*mine,* for He died for me—*mine,* for He has embraced me in the arms of His mercy and love, and forgiven me all my sins—*mine,* for He holds my wandering soul in His hands, and will perfect that which concerns me? Or do we feel,—must we feel, that we have no part in His salvation; and that when we see Him, it may be "afar off?" Balaam, moved by the Spirit, sets forth Jesus in this prophecy in a twofold character—as the Giver of light, and as exercising kingly power.

First, as the Giver of light: "There shall come a Star out of Jacob." We all know that the Redeemer is more than once compared in Scripture to the sun. Thus in Mal. iv. 2, it is predicted, "But unto you that fear my name shall the Sun of righteousness arise with healing in its wings;" and in Luke i. 78 is a beautiful expression which leads our minds to the same comparison, "Through the tender mercy of our God; whereby the Day-spring from on high hath visited us." Where you will notice that "day-spring" is rendered in the margin "sun-rising." We must all feel how apt and instructive a comparison this is. Just as the sun is the centre of a system, attracting by the power of gravity other bodies towards itself; just as it is the source of light and warmth, and sheds *both* thousands and thousands of miles to the utmost limits of the system; so, brethren, in the spiritual world does Christ draw wandering souls to Himself—His gentle power softens hard hearts—attracts broken and penitent hearts, and guides His people along the path marked out for them by the providence of God. But He does more than this—He pours the warm, bright beams of His love upon their souls, scattering darkness, removing doubts and fears, and turning the withered desert of their hearts into fruitful gardens. It is not, perhaps, quite so easy to see why Christ is compared to a "star;" for as the stars shine with a borrowed light, they seem more suited to be illustrations of the followers of Jesus, than of the Saviour himself. And so you will remember that

they are used in Rev. i. 20 of ministers : "The seven stars
are the angels of the seven churches ;" and by St Paul,
(Phil. ii. 14,) of all Christians : "Do all things," he says,
"without murmurings and disputings; that ye may be
blameless and harmless, the sons of God, without rebuke, in
the midst of a crooked and perverse nation, among whom
ye shine as lights in the world." Applied to Christ, it may
be to teach us how Jesus shines through all the long night
of the Church's sorrows. The *sun* dissipates darkness ;
where it shines, darkness ceases. It is so with the rule
of sin. Into whatever heart Christ shines, *there* the
power of sin is broken. The star gives light without dissipating darkness. It guides the wanderer's feet. So
Jesus gives light in the night of affliction. He does not
altogether remove it, or exempt His people from suffering.
But they are not left in utter darkness. There is a Star
in the heavens above, so bright, that it can penetrate the
darkest cloud, and gladden with its light the loneliness
of sorrow. As yet, Christ has not risen with His full un-
clouded light—not as He will be when the vision (Rev.
xxi. 23) is fulfilled, "And the city had no need of the
sun, neither of the moon, to shine in it ; for the glory of
God did lighten it, and the Lamb is the light thereof."
Now is the time of the Church's night, yet not altogether dark, far from it—it is a *starlight* night.

But you will remember, brethren, that St John teaches
us something more about this star when he records the
words of the glorified Redeemer, (Rev. xxii. 16,) "I am
the root and the offspring of David, and the bright and
morning Star." And why the morning star? The morning star is the last to disappear. It still continues to
shine when the rays of the sun have overwhelmed every
other light ; and thus it is a beautiful emblem of Christ.

When the present dispensation closes,—when the light of eternity breaks in, and dissipates for ever the Church's night, her watches, her sorrows, and her conflicts,—how many a seeming star will cease to shine,—how many of those things to which the heart has foolishly clung will appear all dark then. But the one bright Star which has guided the believer through all his night on earth, the morning Star, will still shine more bright and beautiful than ever. The flood of light which the presence of God will pour over the dark world will not darken one single ray of that morning Star. Brethren, is Christ Jesus your Star, your morning Star? Is it to His light that you look? And if anything, any earth-born cloud, interrupts His light from your soul, do you look through the cloud, and wait, not impatiently, but earnestly, for its removal? Those false lights, brethren, with which we encompass ourselves, the sparks of our own kindling, will certainly all go out, and great will be the consternation of those who will then be left in darkness. But if you are looking to Jesus, guided by His light, then your path will get brighter and brighter, until it ends in the perfect light of His presence, a height to which no cloud can rise. But there is one thing more that we must notice with regard to this Star. Balaam tells us the point from whence he saw it arise. "There shall come," he says, "a Star *out of Jacob*." This points us to the humanity of Jesus. St Paul says, (Gal. iv. 4, 5,) "But when the fulness of time was come, God sent forth his Son, *made* of a *woman, made* under the *law*, to redeem them that were under the law, that we might receive the adoption of sons." And again, (Heb. ii. 16,) "For verily he took not on him the nature of angels; but he took on him the seed of Abraham." It was not then as the Divine Word, which was with the Father before the world was, but as man, as partaker of our nature, that Jesus is Jacob's *Star*, and a light to lighten the Gentiles. All the beams and brightness of the Godhead came to us through the humanity of Jesus. It was when the Word was made flesh that the Sun of righteousness arose with healing on his wings; then that the prophecy was accomplished, "There shall come a Star out of Jacob."

But let us pass on, brethren, to the second part, the kingly office of our Redeemer: "And a Sceptre shall rise out of Israel." It may be thought, perhaps, in consequence of the words that follow, "and shall smite the corners of Moab, and destroy all the children of Sheth," that this prophecy was fulfilled in the time of David, when the boundaries of Israel were so much enlarged, and their enemies overcome. Some commentators have so understood it. But we ought to remember, that just as the prophets and priests of Israel were types of Jesus as prophet and priest, so were its kings types of Him who was and is a King of kings. Indeed, the great reason why it was necessary that there should be kings in Israel, and not always judges as at first, was to shadow forth the kingly office of Jesus. If, then, we admit that this prophecy bears some allusion to the earthly kings of Israel, we must add that it had its full and true fulfilment in Jesus. Many Old-Testament prophecies predicted the kingly office of Messiah. Jacob on his dying bed declared, (Gen. xlix. 10,) "The sceptre shall not depart from Judah, nor a lawgiver from between his feet, until Shiloh come; and unto him shall the gathering of the people be." The Psalmist says, (Ps. xlv. 6,) "Thy throne, O God, is for ever and ever: the sceptre of thy kingdom is a right sceptre." Isaiah (chap. ix. 6) calls Him the "Prince of Peace;" and then adds, "Of the increase of his government and peace there shall be no end, upon the throne of David, and upon his kingdom, to order it, and to establish it with judgment and with justice from henceforth even for ever." Jeremiah prophesies, (chap. xxiii. 5, 6,) "Behold, the days come, saith the Lord, that I will raise unto David a righteous Branch, and a King shall reign and prosper, and shall execute judgment and justice in the earth. In his days Judah shall be saved, and Israel shall dwell safely; and this is his name whereby he shall be called, THE LORD OUR RIGHTEOUSNESS." Jesus *was* a *King* in the days of His suffering on earth. It was under the direction of God's providence that Pilate, though he meant it not so, wrote the title, " Jesus of Nazareth, the King of the Jews." The sceptre was in His hand; but He did not then put forth His great power and reign. His prophetic and priestly offices were displayed. His kingly office was held for a time in *abeyance*. True it is that Christ does reign. He reigns in the hearts of His willing people, and over a reluctant world. But this is the time of His patience and long-suffering. The hour is not yet come for the full manifestation of His kingly office and power. But the time will come, and it may be soon, when the seventh angel will sound, and there will be great voices in heaven, saying, " The kingdoms of this world are become the kingdoms of the Lord, and of his Christ: and he shall reign for ever and ever;" when a loud voice will be heard in heaven, saying, " Now is come salvation, and strength, and the kingdom of our God, and the power of his Christ." And to every eye the many crowns upon his brow, and the name written on his vesture and his thigh, will be distinctly visible, " King of kings, and Lord of lords."

How solemn, brethren, the thought of that day ! Those

alone can look forward to it with calm joy in whose hearts
Christ now reigns. Does He reign in our hearts, destroying and keeping under our spiritual enemies? We
bend, brethren, at the name of Jesus. Do we really bend
in spirit and in truth before Him, giving Him the supre-
macy in our affections, and allowing no rival to share His
throne? It *is* His throne—His by eternal right. Oh,
that every heart here may acknowledge His merciful sway
as King, by receiving Him as a Saviour! For, as in the
history of His humanity, the exercise of His prophetic
and priestly offices preceded in time *that* of His kingly
power, so it is in the history of each soul. When He
teaches you as Prophet, and sprinkles you with His atoning blood as Priest, then, and not till then, does He reign
in your heart as King. Nothing can bring the rebel
heart of man under His sway but the teaching of His
Spirit, and the sprinkling of His precious blood. But
then the heart bends with joy beneath His golden sceptre,
(ver. 19,) "Out of Jacob shall He come that shall have
dominion." But there is one point more in our text
which we must not leave unnoticed, and that is the consequence of the coming of the Star, and rising of the
sceptre—a power given to Israel to overcome his enemies.
Those enemies are described, not generally, but very
minutely. Moab is mentioned first, because, headed by
Balak, the Moabites were then endeavouring to destroy
Israel. The expression, "Smite the corners (or sides) of
Moab," signifies an entire destruction, perpetrated along
the whole compass of its dominions. The next expression, "The children of Sheth," has puzzled commentators.
Some have taken it as a proper name, to designate one of
Adam's sons; but it is impossible to extract any good
meaning from it if so understood. The Hebrew word

has, however, lately been shewn to be the contracted form
of another word, which signifies "tumult;" and this is
strongly confirmed by a reference to a remarkable prophecy of Jeremiah concerning Moab, in which we can
scarcely fail to observe an allusion to this prophecy of
Balaam. You will find it in Jer. xlviii. 42. He says,
"Moab shall be destroyed from being a people, because
he hath magnified himself against the Lord;" and then
he adds, (ver. 45,) "They that fled stood under the shadow
of Heshbon, because of the force: but a fire shall come
forth out of Heshbon, and a flame from the midst of
Sihon, and shall devour the corner of Moab, and the
crown of the head of the tumultuous ones." The enemies of Israel were called the children of *tumult*, because
they were ever restless; *restless* in themselves, because
they knew not Israel's God, and restless as neighbours,
because they would give Israel no peace. Next to Moab,
Edom is mentioned. You will recollect that the Edom-
ites, as descendants of Esau, were related to the Israelites,
and, in consequence, the latter were commanded to treat
them in a friendly manner. Thus (Deut. ii. 5) we read,
"Meddle not with them; for I will not give you of their
land, no, not so much as a foot-breadth; because I have
given mount Seir unto Esau for a possession." And in
the message which Moses sent to the king of Edom, he
reminds him of Israel's relationship — "Thus saith thy
brother Israel." But Edom would not heed the claims of
this relationship. Edom replied to Moses, "Thou shalt
not pass by me, lest I come out against thee with the
sword." And in Amos, who lived some hundreds of
years afterwards, we learn that the sins of the fathers
were still to be visited on the children of this tribe,
(chap. i. 11, 12,) "Thus saith the Lord, For three trans-

gressions of Edom, and for four, I will not turn away the punishment thereof ; because he did pursue his brother with the sword, and did cast off all pity, and his anger did tear perpetually, and he kept his wrath for ever: but I will send a fire upon Teman, which shall devour the palaces of Bozrah." Then follow predictions of judgments on Amalek, Israel's first enemy, on the Kenites, strong as they seemed to be in their mountain-passes, on Asshur and Eber; and so terrible did these judgments appear to the seer, that he could not help exclaiming, " Alas ! who shall live when God doeth this ? "

But all these, brethren, are but typical of the greater enemies with which we have to contend. The " sons of tumult " encompass us about. Satan, knowing that his time is short, is ever busy. The world, so restless because it knows not Christ, pours in its influences upon us. The old man within us, though crucified, is ever struggling for victory. And under these influences our very relatives and friends may hinder us on our way, just as Edom did Israel. What must we do to overcome? We must fix our eye upon Jacob's Star, the bright morning Star. We must cling to the sceptre of Jesus. Remember, brethren, that the enemies of God's people are already doomed to destruction. Yet a little while, and if you are Christ's, Satan will be bruised under your feet. The world will not attract or frighten you. The old man will not struggle and weary you. It will be a solemn day when these enemies are compelled to give up their conflict for ever, a day of judgment. We may say with Balaam, " Who shall live when God doeth this ? " Who, brethren ? Those who are in Christ, and have overcome by the blood of the Lamb. Those terrible judgments shall not fall on them. They shall *live*, and not only live, but wear a crown of glory. They shall gaze with inexpressible joy upon the *Star* which has given them light during the long night of their pilgrimage; and not only gaze upon it, but possess it, for the promise runs, " I will give him the morning Star." They shall be subjects of Christ's everlasting kingdom, and not only subjects, but shall reign with Him. With such a Star to give us light now,—such a sceptre to cling to, such promises for the future,—ought we not, brethren, to do valiantly? Ought we to be cast down, however strong and busy our enemies may be, and are? Is it not enough to remember that He who is for us is greater than they who are against us? With our eyes fixed upon our morning Star, and our hands laid upon His sceptre, and held there by *His hand*, may we not humbly, yet boldly, say with the apostle, " Nay, in all these things we are more than conquerors through Him that loved us. For I am persuaded, that neither death, nor life, nor angels, nor principalities, nor powers, nor things present, nor things to come, nor height, nor depth, nor any other creature, shall be able to separate us from the love of God, which is in Christ Jesus our Lord."

THE DEATH OF MOSES

Numbers 27:12, 13

"And the Lord said unto Moses, Get thee up into this mount Abarim, and see the land which I have given unto the children of Israel. And when thou hast seen it, thou also shalt be gathered unto thy people, as Aaron thy brother was gathered."

SOME of you, dear brethren, will remember that we have been for some time considering the history of Israel as typical of the Christian life. Our last meditations were on the life of Balaam, a life very full of warning ; but we should have left our course very imperfect had we stopped there. Some of the most interesting events in the history of Israel were those which happened on their entrance into the Land of Promise. It will take but a few lectures, in the cursory way in which we have treated this subject, to follow them there. Our next course, should we be mercifully spared, will be on another and altogether different portion of Scripture. The verses which we have to consider to-day bring before us a solemn and touching event in the life of Moses. Eminent as he was in grace and holiness, he was not allowed to enter with his people into the Land of Promise. This in itself must have been a sore trial. But it was tenfold more so on account of the cause ; it was a judgment. He who was the meekest of men once spoke unadvisedly with his lips. Hurried away by Israel's unbelief, he gave way to it himself, and in the strong language of verse 14, " rebelled against the commandment of the Lord." The sentence was forthwith passed, and it was irrevocable. Prayer could not alter this purpose of Jehovah. It might be said of Moses, as of Esau, different as their characters were, " he found no place for repentance, though he sought it carefully with tears." Very touching was the earnestness with which Moses prayed that the sad sentence might be revoked. He has recorded his own words, (Deut. iii. 23–25,) " And I besought the Lord at that time, saying, O Lord God, thou hast begun to shew thy servant thy greatness, and thy mighty hand : for what God is there in heaven or in earth that can do according to thy works, and according to thy might ? I pray thee, let me go over and see the good land that is beyond Jordan, that goodly mountain, and Lebanon." But the Lord would not hear, but said unto him, " Let it suffice thee ; speak no more unto me of this matter." Prayer offered for anything contrary to God's purpose does not, cannot, avail, though, when it is inspired by His Spirit, and therefore according to His mind, it produces such grand results. If, brethren, you have been earnest in prayer, you may have found in your own experience that some of your prayers, though repeated and continued long, never have been answered. It has seemed as if the heavens over your head were brass, and nothing could enter; whereas the answers to some of your other prayers have been so numerous and so striking as quite to have astonished you, and have brought home to your heart the strong conviction that in those prayers at least you were asking according to God's will.

The reason, then, why Moses could not enter into the Land of Promise is evident. One reason only is mentioned ; but we cannot but think, brethren, that there

was another, and that the fact that Moses could not
bring the children of Israel into the Promised Land teaches
us a very deep lesson.

For we may regard Moses in a twofold point of view—
either as an *individual believer*, or as the *representative*
of the *system of law* which he was commissioned to teach.
Many passages of Scripture place him before us in this
latter point of view. So our Saviour said, (Matt. xxiii. 2,)
"The scribes and Pharisees sit in Moses's seat." Here
he is evidently spoken of in connexion with the *law*.
Again, St Paul, contrasting the two dispensations, the law
and the gospel, (2 Cor. iii.,) one of which he calls (ver. 6)
the *letter*, (ver. 7,) the ministration of death, and, (ver. 9,)
the ministration of condemnation; the other, (ver. 6,) the
"Spirit," (ver. 8), the ministration of the Spirit, and,
(ver. 9,) the ministration of righteousness, brings in *Moses*
more than once, evidently not in his individual, but
representative, capacity. So, (verses 7, 8,) "But if the
ministration of death, written and engraven in stones,
was glorious, so that the children of Israel could not
steadfastly behold the face of Moses for the glory of his
countenance ; which glory was to be done away : how
shall not the ministration of the Spirit be rather glorious?" And again, (ver. 13,) "And not as Moses, which
put a vail over his face, that the children of Israel could
not steadfastly look to the end of that which is abolished."
And, (ver. 15,) "But even unto this day, when Moses is
read, the vail is upon their heart." In all these passages
it is quite clear that Moses represents the law. Now we
have seen that, as a believer, Moses could not enter the
Land of Promise, because on one occasion he "spake
unadvisedly with his lips." But look at him as the
representative of the *law,* and what lesson does his ina-

bility to enter the Land of Promise rivet on our hearts? This truth, this important truth, brethren, that the law *cannot bring us into* the *land of promise.* There was a point to which Moses could bring Israel, and then he must lie down and die, and his work must be given into other hands, into the hands of Joshua, whose very name shews that he was an eminent type of Christ. There is a point, too, up to which the law may bring us. Where is it? It is to a knowledge of sin. "By the law," says St Paul, "is the knowledge of sin." "I had not known sin," he says, (Rom. vii. 7,) "but by the law: for I had not known lust, except the law had said, Thou shalt not covet." One great purpose for which the law is given is just to teach us what we are—utterly sinful, utterly lost in ourselves. It requires perfect obedience; and, behold, in many things we offend. It makes no provision for transgression, proclaims no forgiveness. It can give no peace. The voice is terrible to the guilty. Whenever it fulfils its true purpose in the soul it empties it of self-righteousness, lays it prostrate in the dust, and makes it take the lowest place. It teaches it to feel its deep need of a Saviour, and hands it over, with all its wants, all its sins, and all its misery, to Jesus, who alone can bring it into the prepared and promised rest. Thus St Paul says, (Gal. ii. 19,) "I through the law am dead to the law, that I might live unto God." And again, (chap. iii. 24,) "Wherefore the law was our schoolmaster to bring us unto Christ, that we might be justified by faith."

Dear brethren, what, (let us earnestly ask) are you? Under Moses or Christ? What is your hope of glory? Is it that you have not sinned so much as others? that your life is very exemplary? that you leave no duty willingly unperformed, or service unattended? Do you

think that somehow or other Christ must be yours, if
your life is so excellent?　Are these your thoughts?
Then we must faithfully tell you, that you are still under
Moses, still clinging to a broken law; and we must
remind you that the law can never bring you to heaven.
It is Christ only who can save you, and bring you into
the land of promise—Christ only who can reconcile you
to God, and we can never come to Christ without utterly
renouncing our own righteousness, and our own works,
as entitling us to God's favour.　This, then, is the great
lesson which the death of Moses, in his representative
character, whilst he was still in the wilderness, rivets on
our hearts.　It points us to Jesus as the only Saviour
from sin and death—the only One who can bring us to
the rest above.

But Moses, though not permitted to lead the Israelites
into the Land of Promise, was allowed to see the land from
the top of mount Nebo, one of the mountains of Abarim.
"Get thee up," said God, "into the mount Abarim,
and see the land which I have given unto the children of
Israel."　This must have been a great consolation; for of
all the Israelites not one could have longed as Moses did
for the fulfilment of God's promise.　The prospect of the
promised rest sustained him during many a weary hour
in the trials of the wilderness.　Doubtless he could have
said with the Psalmist, "I had fainted, unless I had
believed to see the goodness of the Lord in the land of
the living."　In this we may see the goodness and
severity of God.　In Moses's death, severity—a mysterious
severity.　In his summons to Pisgah's top, to behold the
land which was the type of one whither Moses's spirit was
going, God's goodness.　God did not grant Moses all his
desire, for this was not consistent with His righteousness

and purpose; but He did grant as much of that desire as was right, and comforted the spirit of His servant before he departed hence.

And does not God, brethren, deal with His people now as He dealt with Moses? Yes, He does. They too must die before they cross Jordan. It has been given to *two* only, and will be given to only a few to be translated to heaven without dying. Most of God's people have, like Jesus, to pass through death; but before they die, how often does a gentle, merciful voice speak to their hearts and say, " Get thee up into the mount, and see the land which I have given to my people," He gives them glimpses of heaven, sweet foretastes of the inheritance above; shews them in some measure the greatness of the price by which it was purchased, the freeness with which it is given, the infinite blessedness of its rest. What a moment must that have been to Moses, when from Pisgah's top he beheld the land. What moments are those, how rich in blessing, when the Spirit of God raises our souls to the contemplation of things to come—when we are enabled to leave for a while our cares and anxieties—our schemes and labours—our studies and pursuits, and soar away unto things unseen yet most real, and expatiate on the glory and vastness, the riches and eternity, of the promised inheritance. There to be free from all sin, to be beyond the reach of all conflict, to be far away from all disappointment—above all, to be with Jesus—to see Him as He is, face to face, and by beholding to be like Him, catching the rays of His spotless holiness, and reflecting them as we cannot reflect them now.

Dear brethren, let us listen to the voice of God, for through carelessness and unbelief we often fail to catch its sound. Are you careful about something, weighed down by some secret anxiety, or distracted by many little cares? Do they haunt you whilst you read the Bible, and break in upon you in seasons of prayer, occupy your mind the first thing in the morning, and leave it the last thing at night? It is not God's will that you should be so burdened. There is another world beside this troublous one, and God wishes you even now by faith and hope to know something of its joy—to look not at the things which are seen; for the things which are seen are temporal, but the things which are not seen are eternal. Yes, God says to you, "Get thee up into the mount, and see the land." How different does the world look when we come down again from the mount. Those all-engrossing cares which distract our hearts so much, how comparatively small they appear after we have stood upon the mount and looked at the things already prepared for those who love God. Oh, brethren, that we were often upon the mount looking at the land!

Or, again, perhaps you are in bondage from the fear of death. It appears so very awful to die, that you cannot help shrinking from it. Brethren, it is very solemn to die—but why do you fear it? Is it from the consciousness that there is still something between you and God, something unsettled? If so, get all settled; go at once to the fountain opened for sin and all uncleanness, and never leave it until your conscience is purged from dead works to serve the living God,—and you know that you stand in Christ, justified from all things, as clear from all charge of sin, as your great Surety. Or is it that, although pardoned, you have not been careful to *walk* with God,—and so a kind of strangeness has sprung up between you and Him. If so, endeavour to break through that sloth, or whatever else it is, that hinders a close walk with Him.

But there may be another cause. You may not think frequently enough about your departure—may not habitually look for it—or you may think too much about the last conflict, the pain of separation of the soul from the body, and not enough of the inheritance beyond. What, then, is the cure for this fear? It is to have faith in Jesus, to leave all the circumstances of your departure in your Father's hands, to feel sure that He can and will support you in that hour. And then it is to look beyond the stream of Jordan, the mere passage, to the eternity of joy in the presence of God, to act upon the merciful invitation and command, "Get thee up into the mount, and see the land." But we must notice, brethren, the spirit in which Moses received the intimation of his departure. It is often a time of great struggle, even in the hearts of Christians, when they are first told they must soon die. It is so difficult to realize our own death, that though we often think of it and talk of it, when it actually comes it is like something new and unforeseen. We have seen what a trial it must have been to Moses to die in the wilderness, and how earnestly he prayed that he might be allowed to enter the Land of Promise. But when he saw what the purpose of Jehovah was, he quietly *submitted,* and said nothing more about himself. He uses an expression in ver. 16, which seems to throw some light upon his state of mind—" God of the spirits of all flesh." He uses that expression with reference to Israel, and appeals to Him to whom all spirits belong, to care and provide for His people. But the expression might also have reference to his own spirit, and shew his conviction that God had a *right* to his spirit, and had a right to separate his spirit from his body whensoever he thought good. It helps much, brethren, to a submissive spirit to realize the

sovereignty of God,—His right to act according to His
own will. It helps us to feel and say, " Let Him do as
seemeth him good." The Psalmist felt it, when he said,
" I was dumb, and opened not my mouth, because Thou
didst it." May we, dear brethren, depend so simply upon
the blood of Christ, live so near to God, and be so weaned
from this world, that we may receive our message in *submission,* if not with joy.

But there is another feature in the spirit of Moses which
is very beautiful ; and that is his *calmness,* his *unselfish
calmness.* He calmly thinks not about his own bright
future, but Israel's, and wishes to make arrangements for
their welfare. How beautiful is the prayer, " Let the
Lord, the God of the spirits of all flesh, set a man over
the congregation, which may go out before them, and
which may go in before them, and which may lead them
out, and which may bring them in, that the congregation
of the Lord be not as sheep which have no shepherd."
This prayer was answered in a twofold way. The immediate answer was the appointment of Joshua, (ver. 18,)
"And the Lord said unto Moses, Take thee Joshua the
son of Nun, a man in whom is the Spirit, and lay thine
hand upon him, and set him before Eleazar the priest,
and before all the congregation, and give him a charge in
their sight," and yet Joshua was not to Israel all that
Moses had been. It was only some of Moses's honour that
was put upon him, and in spiritual matters Eleazar the
priest was to " ask counsel for him after the judgment of
Urim before the Lord." But that prayer had its complete
fulfilment in the gift of Jesus, and His investiture in the
Shepherd's office. Jesus goes out before His people—He
goes in before them—He leads them out and brings them

in—He is their Shepherd for ever.   God's Israel now can
never more be as sheep which have no shepherd.

In his unselfish calmness then, brethren, Moses is a
beautiful example to us.   He thought of the advancement
of God's kingdom, when his departure was near at hand—
left everything, as far as might be, in perfect order—and
he set about all this with great calmness.   A deathbed,
brethren, should be a calm place.   All the bustle of the
world should be excluded from it ; and yet, brethren, our
thoughts at that hour need not be occupied with ourselves
alone.   The dying parent may think of her children ; and
whilst leaving them in God's hands, and to God's care,
she should calmly arrange as far as may be, for their
future.   The dying minister should think of his beloved
flock ; and commending them into the hands of Jesus,
should deeply care that the truth as it is in Jesus should
continue amongst them.   All this should be done in dependence on God, and so quite calmly, without anxiety or
excitement.

Before we conclude, brethren, there is one more expression to which we would call your attention ; the expression " shall be gathered unto thy people."   It may,
perhaps, be understood by some as applying to the body,
but we take it to refer to the soul, and as one proof amongst
others from the Old Testament, of the existence of the
soul after death.   It is an expression which is very touching to many hearts ; for many there are, whose chief
treasures, those whom they loved best on earth, have been
gathered to heaven.   But what we would have you notice,
brethren, is, that this is an Old-Testament expression.   It
belongs to the Old dispensation, not to the New.   What,
then, is the corresponding expression in the New Testa-

ment? You will find it 2 Thess. ii. 1, "Our gathering together unto Him," unto Jesus. Yes, the great hope of the Christian Church is not death, but the coming of Christ; and the gathering to which we should look forward with greatest joy, is not to our reunion with those whom we have loved on earth, but our gathering to Jesus, our being with Christ and beholding His glory. Jesus touched the deepest chord in His people's hearts when He offered up the beautiful prayer, "Father, I will that they also whom thou hast given me be with me where I am; that they may behold my glory, which thou hast given me: for thou lovedst me before the foundation of the world."

ISRAEL'S PROGRESS

Numbers 31:6, 7

" And Moses sent them to the war, a thousand of every tribe, them and
Phinehas the son of Eleazar the priest, to the war, with the holy
instruments, and the trumpets to blow in his hand. And they
warred against the Midianites, as the Lord commanded Moses."

YOU will remember, brethren, that when Balaam found
that God would not allow him to curse Israel, a new and
awful thought occurred to his mind. He had discovered,
that so long as Israel stood in God's favour, no weapon
formed against them could prosper—curses were withheld,
and turned into blessings; their enemies were made to
lick the dust. But what if Israel could be separated from
God; if they could be led into sin, then God would no
longer protect them. Balak would gain his end, and he
himself would be enriched with Balak's gold. Such a
thought would never have entered into any but a very
corrupt heart. It did enter into Balaam's, and not only
enter but was harboured there; and not only harboured, but
divulged to Balak, who put it into immediate execution.
This puts Balaam's real character in an awful point of
view. It shews us that his regard to Jehovah's will was
not real, but apparent only; and that notwithstanding
all his professions of disregard for Balak's gold, he was
quite intent upon getting it in some way or other. It is
in this dark light that his character is always placed in the
New Testament. St Peter speaks of him, (2 Pet. ii. 15,)

as having "loved the wages of unrighteousness." And our exalted Redeemer, in the epistle to the Church at Pergamos, says (Rev. ii. 14) that "Balaam taught Balak to cast a stumbling-block before the children of Israel." We know the consequences of this temptation. Israel fell into the snare, and joined himself unto Baal-peor. The wrath of God fell on Israel, and twenty-four thousand of them were smitten by a plague and perished, and the scourge was only stayed by the courage and zeal of Phinehas a priest. In consequence of this sin of Midian, God gave the command, "Vex the Midianites, and smite them;" and in this chapter we are informed of the manner in which that command was fulfilled.

It is instructive to compare this warfare of the children of Israel with their earlier battles. There are many points of difference between them. In Egypt, when surrounded by their enemies, they were not called to fight. They were quite unprepared for war; but God fought for them, and they were still, and held their peace. Then again, subsequently they were *attacked* by the Amalekites. They did not begin the encounter, but only repelled the attacks; whereas on this occasion Moses said unto the people, (ver. 3,) "Arm some of yourselves unto the war, and let them go against the Midianites, and avenge the Lord of Midian." Their earlier encounters were all in self-defence—their later ones were *aggressive*. Here then, brethren, we cannot but discern a *mark of progress* in Israel's history. At first, when they were weak, and without experience of God's power and unchanging love, they were more *passive*. Now that they had been formed into a more compact body, and trained to arms, and still more, had experienced the power and faithfulness of God, they were called to be *aggressive*, to *attack* and destroy the enemies of God.

Now, we think, brethren, that this progress in Israel's history is typical of the *progress* in the Christian life. In the first beginnings of the spiritual life, the young Christian's mind is chiefly *passive*. God's work is to shew him his own need, and what *are* his enemies; and of the parts of the Christian armour which St Paul enumerates in Ephes. vi., he chiefly uses those which are for defence—the girdle of truth, the breastplate of righteousness, the sandals of peace, the shield of faith, and the helmet of salvation. But as he advances in the divine life, and the love of Christ more powerfully constrains his heart, he lays a firm hold of the sword of the Spirit, and feels called upon to minister, in some way or other, those precious truths to others which have come home with power to his own soul. To one in this state of mind it is not enough merely to repel temptations; he begins to be *aggressive*, and to attack the kingdom of Satan, that he may rescue his miserable captives. The very spirit of the gospel, brethren, is *aggressive*, not in a worldly sense, nor indeed in the sense in which it was true of Israel, but in a higher and holier sense; for it is a spirit of faith in God —a spirit of holy jealousy for God's glory—a spirit of deep compassion for perishing souls. Whenever a spirit of lukewarmness and deadness comes over the soul or the Christian Church, you see this to be one *sign* of it, that Satan is allowed to keep his captives, and to extend his kingdom without an effort to hinder it. There is indifference, and a too patient endurance of sins which ought through grace to be overcome. But just in proportion as we walk with Jesus and know His power and grace in

pardoning and overcoming sin in our own souls, shall we
be earnest, loving, and hopeful about others. We shall
not indeed lightly estimate the *power* of our spiritual enemies, or the strength of his kingdom, but we shall have
more faith in God—in His power, His faithfulness, and
His love—more faith in that grand scheme of redemption
which He has planned and executed.

Dear brethren, do you ever ask yourselves, What progress is my soul making ? So many years of my life have
passed away, I have been acquainted with God so long—
what progress have I made ? Perhaps you find it difficult
to answer the question ; you do not clearly see what is a
sign of progress. There are many signs ; and it is safer
not to try ourselves by one only. If you are living near
to God, you will be growing more and more dead to the
world. In tribulation you will be more *resigned* to the
will of God ; you will be more self-denying in your life
and more clothed with humility. But besides all those
marks, you will feel a deeper concern for the advancement
of Christ's kingdom ; you will join the soldiers of Christ
in their aggressive movements on Satan's kingdom.
This, brethren, is one mark of progress.

But note another mark. When Moses sent them into
the battle, a thousand of every tribe, he sent Phinehas,
the son of Eleazar the priest, with them, and the holy
instruments, and the trumpets to blow in his hand. What
these holy instruments were we are not informed, but
doubtless they were meant to be symbols of God's presence with His people. But with regard to the trumpets,
you may remember the interesting account given of them
in chap. x., where we are told that they were to be used
for the calling of the assembly, for the journeying of the
camps, and also in war, as it is distinctly stated, ver. 9,

" And if ye go to war in your land against the enemy
that oppresseth you, then ye shall blow an alarm with
trumpets, and ye shall be remembered before the Lord
your God, and ye shall be saved from your enemies ;" so
that those trumpets were closely connected with Israel's
daily life in peace and war. Some here, perhaps, may not
have forgotten, that when we were considering that passage,
we explained the two silver trumpets to be types of the
gospel—the proclamation of the gospel—as the sacrifices
were types of Christ. By all these arrangements, then,
Israel was taught some great truths. Infidels are fond of
speaking of the cruelty in war practised by the Israelites,
and of the spirit of revenge on which they were encouraged
to act ; and some, perhaps, may have referred to this very
chapter, "Avenge the children of Israel of the Midianites."
But such objections shew great shallowness of mind, and
that those who make them do not understand God's
government over the world, nor do they shew any careful
attention to the contest. This punishment of the Midianites, for instance, was not an act of private revenge or
national covetousness. In that case it would have been a
most immoral act. It was a solemn act of God's righteous
government, whereby He manifested His righteous hatred
of sin, and carried into effect that great principle of His
government, "Be sure your sin will find you out." And
thus, whilst giving the command, "Avenge the Lord of
Midian," God taught them that all success was in *His own*
hands, and not in *theirs*. The priest, and holy instruments,
and silver trumpets, were as needful as their weapons of
war. These were a practical warning against a spirit of
revenge, and an encouragement to depend wholly on God.
They must have served to impress most powerfully on the
minds of the Israelites that this war was a great *moral*

act, and that in engaging in it they should depend wholly
on God.

And these accompaniments of war shewed also *progress*
in Israel's history. Their earlier battles were always acts
of faith ; but then no priest went forth with their army,
no holy instruments were carried forth, or trumpets blown;
for it was subsequently that they were brought into covenant with God at Sinai, and had still brighter tokens of
His presence—subsequently, that the two silver trumpets
were appointed to carry terror into the hearts of their
enemies, and to make them realize that they were *remembered* before Jehovah. And this, brethren, may suggest
to us one point of difference between the earlier and later
conflicts of a Christian. When he is young and inexperi-
enced in conflict, there is generally too much confidence
in *self*. But when God has taught him deeper lessons in
the work of war, he has less confidence in self, and more
in God. Then, brethren, it is not his own courage or
skill, not his own strength or perseverance, but Christ his
eternal and ever-present Priest, the holy instruments of
the sanctuary, and the silver trumpet of the gospel, which
are his great and only hope of victory. Resting on Jesus
as his atoning Priest, and relying on the precious promises
of Scripture, though weak in himself, he can sometimes
at least use the language of the Psalmist, (Ps. xviii. 32–35,)
"It is God that girdeth me with strength, and maketh my
way perfect. He maketh my feet like hinds' feet, and
setteth me upon my high places. He teacheth my hands
to war, so that a bow of steel is broken by mine arms.
Thou hast also given me the shield of thy salvation : and
thy right hand hath holden me up, and thy gentleness
hath made me great."

Brethren, guard against *self*. *Self* is the root of infinite evil. Why is it that so many stumble? It is self-confidence. Why is it that we often need such severe discipline? It is because *self* is so entwined with all our feelings, mars so many motives, hinders lofty aims, weakens our best endeavours. Christ and self are two opposites; and Christ and victory go together,—self and defeat accompany each other. The more Christ lives in us, the more complete will be the crucifixion of self, and the greater our victories over our spiritual enemies. We wax stronger in the Lord, and in the power of His might.

But there is still another point of progress discernible in this part of Israel's history, and that is in the use that was made of the spoils of the Midianites. *Jehovah* gave them this victory. They all felt it. It was in His name that they went forth, and in His name that they triumphed. Here we find, (ver. 12,) that they "brought the captives, and the prey, and the spoil, to Moses and Eleazar, the priest, and unto the congregation of the children of Israel." And then a division of the booty took place. It was divided into two equal parts, one of which was given to those who went into the battle, and the other belonged to those who remained in the camp. Those who encountered the Midianites being but a small part of the whole of Israel, only 12,000 men, had in reality the largest share; and this was but right, as they had been exposed to the dangers and fatigues of war. But this was not the whole of the arrangement. The most important part remains to be mentioned. After this division had taken place, a part was to be consecrated to God. Of that which belonged to the warriors themselves one five-hundredth part was offered unto the Lord, as a heave-offering, as we are expressly told, (ver. 4,) "And Moses gave the tribute which was the Lord's heave-offering unto Eleazar

the priest." This portion, then, came to the priests. Of
the other part, which belonged to those who did *not* go
into battle, one-fiftieth part was consecrated to God, (ver.
30,) "And of the children of Israel's half, thou shalt
take one portion of fifty of the persons, of the beeves, of
the asses, and of the flocks, and of all manner of beasts."
This portion belonged to the Levites. And so, if we
compare together the portion of the priests with that of
the Levites, we find that was as one to ten. But even
this is not all. When those who went into battle were
numbered, it was found that there "lacked not one man,"
not one was lost. This was a wonderful proof of God's
care and protection. No less than 24,000 fell by the
plague, and not even *one* in the war with a powerful people.
This produced a strong impression on the minds of the
officers. They were thankful, as well they might be, for
God's goodness; and they shewed their gratitude by making an additional freewill-offering to God. "We have,
therefore," they say, (ver. 50,) "brought an oblation for the
Lord, what every man hath gotten, of jewels, of gold,
chains and bracelets, rings, ear-rings, and tablets, to make
an atonement for our souls before the Lord;" and this
offering was brought by Moses and Eleazar the priest into
the tabernacle of the congregation, for a "memorial for
the children of Israel before the Lord."

Now, in all this, brethren, we can discern *progress*
in Israel's history. In the earlier part of it we do
not meet with any such arrangement, but when brought
into immediate covenant union with God, He taught
them practically that they themselves, and all that they
had, belonged to Himself. He trained them to a spirit
of self-denial. This, brethren, is an important lesson, which this history impresses upon us. If we were

asked, " What are the two graces in which Christians are most wanting ?" we should answer, " charity" and " self-denial ;" *that* charity which bears long, which covers a multitude of sins, and that spirit of self-denial which leads us habitually to crucify the old man, and to place God's glory before our own comfort, ease, and pleasure. There are many Christians who are sound in doctrine, and who seem to glory that they are free from this and that error, but there is much self-indulgence in their lives. It is a striking thing how much self-denial man will undergo, if he hopes to *earn* heaven by it ; but surely, brethren, a full and free salvation, and the wonderful love of Christ, should be far more powerful in producing a spirit of self-sacrifice. Look at Jesus. His whole life was one of self-surrender and self-sacrifice, and His people ought to be like Him in this.

Let us never then, brethren, think it sufficient to hold this or that truth, however important, but let us ask ourselves this question, " What influence are those truths exciting on my heart and life ?" If they do not make us like Jesus, do not lead us to realize that we owe ourselves, and all that we have to God, and to practise daily self-denial, then they are not producing the effect in us which they ought to produce. But *self*, brethren, is a very deep and comprehensive thing, and so there are many different ways of denying it ; but this history leads our thoughts especially to *one* form of it, that denial of self which leads us to give of our substance to God, as a grateful acknowledgment that all we are and all we have is His. There are very different ways pursued by those who do consecrate of their means to God. Some give just as it may happen, according as they have few or many calls. The disadvantage of this is, that impulse may have much

to do with it. Others again, consecrate a certain portion
of their income to God. There are many advantages in
this; for, first, it is done more calmly, principle has more
to do with it than impulse; and secondly, when it is *once*
consecrated, it is usually given more *cheerfully;* and
thirdly, when once devoted, there is no fresh conflict with
self each time, but the mind has only calmly to consider
in what proportion it should be distributed. It was but a
small part, brethren, that Israel was called to consecrate
on this occasion, one five-hundredth and one-fiftieth part;
but this we must remember was not an ordinary rule,
but an exceptional case. It was given out of *spoils* of
war. The ordinary rule was one-tenth. But for Christians no rule can be laid down. Those to whom much is
given can of course give more in proportion. Zaccheus
gave one-half of his goods to the poor. This question is
one which must be left to every Christian's conscience.
It is a solemn question, one to be settled on our knees in
prayer. But one thing, brethren, may be said, "Such a
sum ought to be consecrated as involves self-denial." It
is such offerings which are acceptable to God.

One more remark. How striking was the result of the
conflict, "There lacketh not one man of us." Oh, that
it might be so in another conflict in which we are now
engaged; but this is not to be expected. But, brethren,
in Christ's army it will be so. Great as are the dangers
which beset the soldiers of Christ, and fearful as are the
conflicts through which they are called to pass, an unseen
Hand upholds and protects them, so that when every conflict is over, and the whole army meets before the throne,
and the sum is taken, it will be found that all the elect
are there, and the great Captain of our salvation will be
able to say, "There lacketh not one man of us."

THE SIN OF DISCOURAGING
OUR BRETHREN

Numbers 32:6, 7

"And Moses said unto the children of Gad, and to the children of
Reuben, Shall your brethren go to war, and shall ye sit here?
And wherefore discourage ye the heart of the children of Israel
from going over into the land which the Lord hath given them?"

THE next event in the history of Israel is an instructive
one, and full of practical importance. The children of
Reuben and the children of Gad were very rich in cattle;
and when they saw the fertile country of which the
congregation of Israel had already taken possession, they
wished to be allowed to occupy it, instead of having a
portion in the land of Canaan. There were many things
which made the request suspicious. In the first place,
it was the land of Canaan itself, which was promised to
Israel, the land which was bounded by the Mediterranean
on the one side, and by the Jordan on the other. It is
true, indeed, that the Euphrates appears in the original
grant to be fixed as the eastern boundary of Israel's dominion. Thus we read, (Gen. xv. 18,) "In the same day
the Lord made a covenant with Abram, saying, Unto
thy seed have I given this land, from the river of Egypt
unto the great river, the river Euphrates." But up to
this day that promise has not yet been fulfilled; and it
would always appear the proper order that the land of
Canaan should have been conquered and possessed first,
before any territory was occupied beyond Jordan. When

we remember too that Moses was not allowed to enter
the Land of Promise—only to see it from Pisgah—we
perceive at once that a great difference was made between
Canaan itself and the territories contiguous to it. Their
willingness to settle *without* the land of Canaan, instead
of wishing to settle within it, was itself a suspicious
thing. It might have arisen from a carelessness about
the promise, from a regard to temporal prosperity only.
And yet, brethren, it is a remarkable thing, that in dealing with the children of Reuben and Gad, Moses does
not bring forward this argument, or charge them with a
disregard of God's promise. He regards the request as
originating in another principle of corrupt human nature,
and *that* was in a desire to shun difficulties and dangers,
in a selfish consideration of their own ease and benefit,
and a disregard of the welfare of their brethren. Moses
said to them, "Shall your brethren go to war, and shall
ye sit here?" And then he dwells strongly on the evil
effect of their example, the great discouragement which
it necessarily cast on the ardour and hope of their brethren. "And wherefore discourage ye the heart of the
children of Israel from going over into the land which
the Lord hath given them?" He spoke still more
strongly to them; for, reminding them of the sins of
their fathers who had perished in the wilderness, he
added, (ver. 14,) "And, behold, ye are risen up in your
fathers' stead, an increase of sinful men, to augment yet
the fierce anger of the Lord toward Israel." But this
strong language was soon withdrawn, for the children
of Reuben and Gad said, "We ourselves will go ready
armed before the children of Israel, until we have brought
them unto their place. We will not return to our houses
until the children of Israel have inherited every man his

inheritance." Moses was satisfied, and said, (ver. 20, &c.,) "If ye will do this thing, if ye will go armed before the Lord to war, and will go all of you armed over Jordan before the Lord, until he hath driven out his enemies from before him, and the land be subdued before the Lord; then afterward ye shall return, and be guiltless before the Lord, and before Israel; and this land shall be your possession before the Lord." Moses's fears then were happily not well founded; but still the words which he spoke to them on the supposition that there was a selfish motive, are very striking, and place in an impressive point of view the sin and danger of discouraging our brethren.

The children of God are very prone to be discouraged. The truth is, that their path through the wilderness is not an easy one. There are many trials without, and still greater trials within; and so, sooner or later, seasons of discouragement will set in—seasons in which it would take but a little to " break the bruised reed." We have seen already how often Israel was discouraged because of the way; and the frequent words of encouragement which God spake to Joshua prove that he was in danger of being disheartened. So (Deut. i. 38) we read, " But Joshua the son of Nun, which standeth before thee, he shall go in thither: encourage him; for he shall cause Israel to inherit it." And again, (Josh. i. 6, 7,) "Be strong, and of good courage; for unto this people shalt thou divide for an inheritance the land which I sware unto their fathers to give them. Only be thou strong, and very courageous, that thou mayest observe to do according to all the law which Moses my servant commanded thee." The danger of discouragement being so very great, it is the duty of Christians to encourage each

other, to exhort one another in words of kindness, cheerfulness, and love, to hold on their way.   How beautiful
is the example of Jesus, in the tenderness of the sympathy wherewith He encouraged the weak.   It must have
been a season of great discouragement to the man who
was born blind, when his parents withdrew from him
their support, and the Jews excommunicated him; in the
language of Scripture, "cast him out."   But what did
Jesus do?   We read, (John ix. 35,) "Jesus heard that
they had cast him out; and when he had found him, He
said unto him, Dost thou believe on the Son of God?
He answered and said unto him, Who is He, Lord, that
I might believe on him?   And Jesus said unto him,
Thou hast both seen him, and it is He that talketh with
thee."   And again, when a woman anointed the feet of
Jesus with the ointment of spikenard, and Judas Iscariot
discouraged her by saying, "Why was not this ointment
sold for three hundred pence, and given to the poor?"
Jesus encouraged her.   "Why trouble ye the woman, for
she hath wrought a good work upon me?   For ye have
the poor always with you; but me ye have not always.
Verily I say unto you, wheresoever this gospel shall be
preached in the whole world, there shall also this that
this woman hath done be told for a memorial of her."
But Christians, brethren, are too often unlike their Master
—wanting in that gentle and encouraging sympathy.
They often wound and dishearten the weak, if not the
strong, by an inconsistent life, by careless and desponding words, and by raising unnecessary difficulties; and
so, many a holy aspiration, many an animating hope,
many a holy work, is crushed in the bud.   It may be
well, brethren, to note more carefully some of the ways
in which Christians most frequently discourage each

other's hearts. First, then, brethren, we may mention an inconsistent life.

There is nothing so beautiful on earth as a consistent life, a life entirely consecrated to God—devoted to one great object, and guided by one great principle. Such a life, brethren, makes people feel that there is something from God in true religion; and it greatly encourages those who are seeking Christ. It is to such a life that St Paul exhorts us in the words, " I therefore, a prisoner of the Lord, beseech you that ye walk worthy of the vocation wherewith ye are called."

On the contrary, the inconsistent lives of Christians are the greatest possible hindrance to the world, and to those who are weak in faith. There was great apparent inconsistency in the request of the Reubenites. They ought to have valued God's promise, and have wished to settle within the limits of the Promised Land; but the rich pastures of the territories already won, and situated without its boundaries, were a temptation to them. And Moses saw at once the effect that this example would have upon the hearts of their brethren. It would discourage them. It is just so, brethren, with those, who ought to live for heaven, who profess to be looking for it, and yet set their affections on things below,—on the creature, or the world, or on money. This contrariety between the profession and the life, cannot be otherwise than a stumblingblock to the world, and a great discouragement to those who are weak in faith. Some it hardens in their unbelief; others are led by it into painful doubt and perplexity. Brethren, it is no small sin to discourage our brethren. If we would avoid it, and help rather than dishearten them, we must endeavour to walk with God; we must pray for holiness and consistency of life, a heart dead to the world, and alive to God through faith in Christ Jesus.

But again, the natural heart is very prone to think that religion is a gloomy thing, a system of sacrifices ; and this we cannot wonder at, as it only sees what must be given up, but cannot perceive what is gained : " For eye hath not seen, nor ear heard, neither have entered into the heart of man, the things which God hath prepared for them that love Him.   But God hath revealed them unto us by His Spirit ; for the Spirit searcheth all things, yea, the deep things of God."   It cannot understand that excellency of the knowledge of Christ which makes sacrifices easy and delightful, and renders things impossible to flesh and blood altogether possible.

Now, when Christians are gloomy and desponding, when their look is melancholy and their language dissatisfied, it tends to confirm the notion that true religion does not make the heart happy, does not give it rest ; and so the wanderer, discouraged at the outset, seeks cheerfulness and pleasure elsewhere, and not in Christ.   Now why, brethren, should Christians ever give such an impression of religion ?   Surely it must be of all things the most blessed to be reconciled to God, to have the forgiveness of all sins, to be partaker of a title and a meetness for the inheritance of the saints in light, to have in Jesus a full supply for every need.   It is true that the Christian has many trials and difficulties which are unknown to the world, fightings within, as well as fears without.   But his fightings are not hopeless struggles. They are the precursors of victory ; for, says St Paul, we are made more than conquerors through Him that loved us.   In his difficulties he has a sure and faithful guide, and in his sorrows he may say to his soul, " Hope thou in God; for I shall yet praise Him for the help of His countenance." Why then should gloom and despondency overshadow his soul? There is no sufficient reason. It is true that natural temperament or physical causes may hinder a Christian rising into habitual cheerfulness of mind; but one thing it ought not to hinder, and that is calmness and peace. If we have not these, brethren, it is because we live below our privileges. We do not realize our standing in Christ Jesus, or know the things which are freely given us of God. And all this, brethren, is not natural temperament, but want of simple faith. It is most important that true Christians should not indulge in a morbid, downcast frame of mind. They should resist it, and feel it a duty to cultivate Christian cheerfulness. It is a duty on account of their own state of mind; for such feelings dishonour God. It is a duty on account of others; for such a manner tends to discourage our brethren, and gives false impressions to the world. Are you generally desponding? Search out the reason. It is that you do not walk with God, that you suffer the world, or some unsubdued affection, to dim the light of God's countenance. What you want is more decision and earnestness, more unity of heart. Seek it. There are others besides yourself prone to discouragement—do not discourage them. There is more than one of whom God says to you, " Encourage him." Will you not do so? If you ask how, we answer, by cultivating a cheerful and hopeful spirit; and the way to attain this spirit is to be much with God, to be more occupied with Him than with your own feelings.

Another way of discouraging our brethren is by shewing want of sympathy in their difficulties.

There are many difficulties, especially at the commencement of the Christian life, and they vary considerably, according to the habits and temper of the mind. If it be of a reasoning cast, its difficulties will usually be greater and more perplexing. Now it is a very wearying thing to have some difficulty which none can understand,—to be obliged to work our way through it alone, without any helping hand to unravel it, or any sympathy to soothe the spirit; and yet how many spirits, and some noble ones, are left to go on their solitary way, and thus become depressed and discouraged. This, brethren, ought not to be. We should try to enter into the difficulties, of whatsoever kind, of our brethren. If our own experience does not fully qualify us to do so, still we should *try* to do so. We should, at least, listen with patience, and shew sympathy. Even this may be made the means of removing the cloud, or at least of encouraging a desponding heart. Sympathy, brethren, is gifted by God with immense power —a look—a word—a tear—how much it will soothe and cheer. You may feel unable to produce an effective argument, or to give any good advice—but even if you cannot, kindness and sympathy will do much to encourage. Hardness and want of sympathy have much to do with making the world as full of misery as it is.

Another cause of discouragement to others is our shrinking, or appearing to shrink, from difficulties. Moses evidently thought that this was the motive of the request of the Reubenites. They wished to settle down in a land already won, instead of sharing the danger and difficulties of war with their brethren. "Shall your brethren go to war, and ye sit here?" The event proved that happily this was not the case. Moses was mistaken in his suspicions. But it is quite clear, that had this been the case scarcely anything could have discouraged the rest of the

Israelites more completely.   Now this, brethren, we fear, is not a very uncommon cause of discouragements.   There are too many Christians who shrink from difficulties. They prefer some smooth and easy course, the pastures of Jazer and Gilead to the warfare and conflicts of Canaan. If some easy work is proposed to them, which is accompanied by no great difficulties, and which involves no real self-denial, they may be ready for it.   But they do not like to take up the cross, and especially a *daily* cross— one that lasts long.   Brethren, we ought not to shrink from difficulties in doing the will of God.   It is usually God's way to surround His own work with difficulties, and often with such difficulties as His own hand alone can remove.   And this He does to try His people's faith, not to discourage them.   Viewed at a distance, like the wall of some great fortress, they appear very formidable, but when grappled with in faith, one after another they fall away.   There are beautiful promises, brethren, to encourage us under difficulties.   One you will find, Isa. xli. 14, 16, "Fear not, thou worm Jacob, and ye men of Israel ; I will help thee, saith the Lord, and thy Redeemer, the Holy One of Israel.   Behold, I will make thee a new sharp threshing instrument having teeth . thou shalt thresh the mountains, and beat them small, and shalt make the hills as chaff.   Thou shalt fan them, and the wind shall carry them away, and the whirlwind shall scatter them : and thou shalt rejoice in the Lord, and shalt glory in the Holy One of Israel."   How striking, brethren, is the expression here, "Thou *worm* Jacob."   God brings the hearts of His people very low, He shews them what they are in *themselves*, before He enables them to overcome difficulties, that they may feel that the excellency of the power is not of *themselves*, but of *Him*.   The other pas-

sage is Zech. iv. 7, " Who art thou, O great mountain ?
before Zerubbabel thou shalt become a plain." Let us,
then, brethren, settle it well in our hearts, that we *must*
have difficulties in doing the work of God,—but let not
these dismay our hearts, or lead us to discourage our
brethren.

These, brethren, are some of the most obvious ways in
which we are in danger of discouraging others, and of
casting a stumblingblock in the way of the world, or of
those who are weak in faith: Inconsistency of life—
despondency of spirit—want of sympathy with other's
difficulties—shrinking from the cross and its difficulties
ourselves, and what is connected with it—*magnifying*
difficulties. And from all this we may draw one important conclusion, that it is only by *walking* with God
that we can be kept from falling into this sin. We ought
to be *very careful* what we say ; but it is not merely our
words, and *outward* conduct, that is of consequence ; it
is the *habitual frame* of our minds. There is an influence going forth every moment from every mind ; and as
is the *entire state* of our minds, such is our influence.
What motives we have, brethren, to abide in Christ—
what obligations we are under to be conformed to His
holy image. If we content ourselves with a low standard,
we cannot be really happy ourselves—cannot glorify God,
nor can we avoid falling into the sin of hindering those
for whom Christ died. How solemn are the words of
Jesus, (Matt. xviii. 6,) " Whoso shall offend one of these
little ones which believe in me, it were better for him that
a millstone were hanged about his neck, and that he were
drowned in the depth of the sea. Woe unto the world
because of offences ! for it must needs be that offences
come ; but woe to that man by whom the offence cometh ! "

How beautiful was the spirit of St Paul, when, entering
into the subject of meats, he says, " Wherefore if meat
make my brother to offend, I will eat no flesh while the
world standeth, lest I make my brother to offend." May
God give us so to feel, and so to live, that we may ever
encourage and not discourage our brethren.

THE DANGER OF ALLOWING SIN

Numbers 33: 51-56

" Speak unto the children of Israel, and say unto them, When ye are
passed over Jordan into the land of Canaan; then ye shall drive
out all the inhabitants of the land from before you, and destroy
all their pictures, and destroy all their molten images, and quite
pluck down all their high places. And ye shall dispossess the
inhabitants of the land, and dwell therein : for I have given you
the land to possess it. And ye shall divide the land by lot for an
inheritance among your families; and to the more ye shall give
the more inheritance, and to the fewer ye shall give the less inheritance : every man's inheritance shall be in the place where his
lot falleth; according to the tribes of your fathers ye shall inherit.
But if ye will not drive out the inhabitants of the land from before you; then it shall come to pass, that those which ye let
remain of them shall be pricks in your eyes, and thorns in your
sides, and shall vex you in the land wherein ye dwell. Moreover,
it shall come to pass, that I shall do unto you as I thought to do
unto them."

THE earlier part of this chapter contains a very long, and
the most complete, list there is of the stations in the wilderness. These were *now* past. The Israelites were now
on the confines of the Land of Promise. So God speaks
to them about the future, tells them what it was His will
that they should do when they enclosed the Land of Promise, and what would be the consequence of disobedience.
These, then, are the two points which we may consider
this morning—Israel's calling; and the consequences of
neglecting it. First, then, *Israel's calling.* This was to
drive out *all* the inhabitants of the land, to dispossess

them, and themselves to dwell in it.   If we view this with
reference to the inhabitants themselves, we must regard
it as the righteous judgment of God upon them on
account of their sins.   The fearful catastrophe had been
predicted centuries before, but its execution was sus-
pended, until the iniquity of the Amorites was full, the
cup of their iniquity overflowing.   But *then* it came
with certainty.   The same awful process is still going on
both in nations and individuals ; each sin that is committed by the impenitent and hardened, adds a drop to
the cup of their iniquity.   The cup fills quite gradually
and imperceptibly, till at last it reaches a point at which
one sin more fills it.   The final sin may not be so great
and appalling ; it may be apparently less fearful than
many previously committed, but it is enough to fill the
cup, and then the righteous retribution falls.   Such has
been the history of many nations, which have now disappeared from the earth, and of many individuals who
have passed into eternity.   Is it not almost more than we
can dare to contemplate ? and yet it is full of many important lessons.

But we may also regard this visitation with reference
to *Israel,* and then it will become evident that it was
necessary for their *safety.*   The Israelites themselves were
so prone to fall away from God, that their being surrounded by many idolatrous and degraded nations would
be sure to lead them gradually away from Him.   They
would soon cease to be a separate people,—a people consecrated to Jehovah.   Hence it was that the command
was so very stringent, " Ye shall drive out *all* the inhabitants of the land."   That little word " all" is very expres-
sive.   It shews that the judgment was to be *universal.*
It proved the greatness of God's care for Israel.   It was

also the *test* of Israel's obedience; and it was a test, we
know, which they did not stand.   Man's *conscience* is
such that in many cases he cannot set God's commands
at complete defiance; but his *heart* is such that he is
disposed too often to render only a *partial* obedience to
God's commands.   He obeys not from love, but to silence
the upbraidings of conscience.   You will remember that
this was precisely the sin of Saul.   God said to him,
(1 Sam. xv. 3,) "Now, go and smite Amalek; and utterly
destroy all that they have, and spare them not."   How
did the King of Israel fulfil this command?   He smote
the Amalekites, and took Agag, the King of the Amalekites, alive, and utterly destroyed all the people with the
edge of the sword.   "But Saul and the people *spared*
Agag, and the best of the sheep, and oxen, and of the
fatlings, and the lambs, and all that was good, and would
not utterly destroy them."   And yet Saul so deceived
himself with this partial obedience that he said to Samuel,
"Blessed be thou of the Lord; I have performed the
commandments of the Lord."   Now, Israel acted in the
same way with reference to the command, "Drive out *all*
the inhabitants of the land."   They substituted a partial
for an unreserved obedience, and drove out *some*, but not
all, the inhabitants of the land.   We find a long list of
Israel's defects of obedience in Judges i. 21, "And the
children of Benjamin did not drive out the Jebusites that
inhabited Jerusalem;" and ver. 27, "Neither did Manasseh drive out the inhabitants of Beth-shean and her
towns;" ver. 29, "Neither did Ephraim drive out the
Canaanites that dwelt in Gezer;" ver. 30, "Neither did
Zebulon drive out the inhabitants of Kitron;" ver. 31,
"Neither did Asher drive out the inhabitants of Accho;"
ver. 33, "Neither did Naphtali drive out the inhabitants

of Beth-shemesh." So that here, brethren, we find, not
one will only, but many failing in their obedience. And
what followed? An angel, we read in the next chapter,
came to Bochim, and said, "I made you to go up out of
Egypt, and have brought you unto the land which I sware
unto your fathers; and I said, I will never break my covenant with you. And ye shall make no league with the
inhabitants of this land; ye shall throw down their altars:
but ye have not obeyed my voice: why have ye done this?
Wherefore I also said, I will not drive them out from
before you; but they shall be as thorns in your sides, and
their gods shall be a snare unto you."

This then, brethren, was Israel's *calling*. It was to
drive out *all* the inhabitants of the land; but we see that
they did not do so.

Now, in this, as in so many other points, Israel's calling
is typical of the Christian life. In what way? We often
take Canaan to be a type of heaven. And so in many
respects it was. Its comparative rest was a feeble shadow
of the perfect rest of heaven. Its possession was a shadow
of that inheritance, incorruptible, undefiled, and that fadeth
not away, on which the Church shall enter, when its wilderness life is over. Yet it is easy to see that there are many
other points in which Canaan was no type of heaven; and
one of these evidently was, that whereas in heaven there
will be no sin, no enemies, no temptations, in Canaan all
these existed. The Israelites had many a hard-fought
struggle with the inhabitants of the land, and were often
led away by their sinful example. In this point of view,
then, Canaan was not a type of heaven, but rather of the
Christian life *now;* and to that command, "Drive out all
the inhabitants of the land, and dispossess them," we shall
find an analogous one, descriptive of the Christian calling,

" Put off the old man with his deeds." There is a principle of evil, called in Scripture the "old man," which comprehends sinful desires and evil habits ; and this we are called to dispossess of the land. Many Christians are obscure in their views on this point. They seem to understand by "sanctification" the gradual change of the old man into the new,—the working up of old materials ; whereas, according to Scripture, it is always and utterly at variance with the new. The one can never by any power be changed into the other. There cannot be any league between them. What the Spirit of God does, is not to change the old nature into the new, but to introduce a new principle, called by St Peter the "divine nature," into our heart in defiance of it. And between these two natures, the new and the old, there is deadly and perpetual warfare ; as St Paul says, (Gal. v. 17,) "For the flesh lusteth against the Spirit, and the Spirit against the flesh, and these are contrary the one to the other." Yes, as contrary as light and darkness, the kingdom of God and the kingdom of Satan.

It is important, brethren, and very instructive, carefully to note the language of Scripture when it speaks of these two principles in the Christian. The Christian is spoken of as *one* who *has* put off the old man. So we read, (Col. iii. 9,) "Lie not one to another, seeing that ye have put off the old man with his deeds." And the "old man" cannot be put off without the "new man" being put on. And so the apostle adds, "And have put on the new man, which is renewed in knowledge after the image of him that created him." And yet, though this twofold act of putting off the one and putting on the other is a past act, he is still exhorted to put off the old man and to put on the new man, so that it is a continuing act. Thus St Paul says, (Ephes. iv. 22,) "That ye put off, concerning the former conversation, the old man, which is corrupt according to the deceitful lusts : and that ye put on the new man, which after God is created in righteousness and true holiness." So again St Paul says of *himself*, "I am crucified with Christ ; " and of *those* that are Christ's, that they "have crucified the flesh with its affections and lusts." And yet he says, (Rom. viii. 13,) "But if ye through the Spirit do mortify the deeds of the body, ye shall live." And, (Col. iii. 5,) "Mortify therefore your members that are upon the earth ; " so that it is clear, brethren, that there is something that *is* done in the Christian by the Spirit. He *is* dead, *is* crucified with Christ—his old man is nailed to the cross, yet there is something to be done by him, through the same Spirit. The old man is daily to be put off, the new man to be put on. The old man, though nailed to the cross, is never utterly extinct until the earthly house of our tabernacle is exchanged for the "building of God, the house not made with hands, eternal in the heavens." The new man requires to be constantly strengthened by fresh gifts of the Spirit of God. When, then, God says, "Drive out *all* the inhabitants of the land," it has a meaning for the Christian ; and its meaning virtually is, " Mortify the old man," crucify the whole body of sin. Do not spare any sin. Let all be resisted and overcome. Now, the old man, brethren, is in no sense the *same* in every Christian. It is the principle of sin, the principle of self. In whatever heart it is, its nature is the same ; but in other aspects it is not always the same—for instance, it is not always the same in its *power*. In one Christian it prevails much, in another more believing and watchful heart it is kept under control. Then, again, it is made up of different elements, and the elements which constitute it are not always the same in their proportions. Thus, the chief element in one case will be pride, in another self-righteousness, in another hypocrisy, in another vanity, in another temper, in another impurity. Sometimes two will appear together in intimate alliance, and those not unfrequently two very opposite evils. In endeavouring then to carry out the injunction, "Drive out all the inhabitants of the land," it is important, on the one hand, that we should be aware of the element of the old man which is most prominent in us; and, on the other, that we should never forget that our besetting sin is not the *only* evil against which we have to contend, but against the old man *as a whole*. If, for instance, you feel that temper is your besetting sin, you must endeavour by the power of the Spirit of God to dispossess it, and to put on the meekness and gentleness of Jesus; but this is not all that you have to contend against. There is a principle of sin and alienation from God, of which this is one fruit, and it is against *that* that you must wage unceasing warfare.

Let us now pass to the second point—the consequences of neglecting this *calling*.

We see it, brethren, in Israel. They did not, we have seen, fulfil the command, "Drive out all the inhabitants of the land." Most of the tribes allowed some to remain, whom they brought under tribute; in fact, with whom they made a league. The consequence was that those few inhabitants, though not powerful, caused them constant trouble; sometimes they seized an opportunity to attack them again; still oftener they proved a snare to them by leading them into sin, so that in the expresssive language of Scripture they were "pricks in their eyes, and thorns in their sides." Thus Israel's sin was made their punishment. They spared those whom they ought not to have spared, and they suffered terribly in consequence. All this bears upon the Christian's life. There is a deep mystery, brethren, in the spiritual life. How wonderful it is that there should be two principles,—two natures in perpetual warfare with each other in the Christian's heart. The one of God, the product of the Spirit; the other of Satan, the result of the fall. The one the ally of God, holding communion with Him; the other allied with the powers of darkness, an enemy in the camp ever ready to open the gates. Now there are times when Christians deeply feel this mystery of the spiritual life. They ask themselves, "How is all this?" How blessed it would be if, when brought to Christ, the principle of sin were at once and for ever destroyed; if we could walk through the world without conflict, at any rate without an enemy within us. Why is it not so? It is a difficult question to answer, brethren. We know but little of the reasons of God's ways, and it is doubtless well for us to know but a little, if we do not foolishly suppose that we know much. It should be enough for us to know that all God's ways are perfectly wise—all His purposes full of love. It is not, then, our endeavour to give a full answer to so deep a question. It is beyond our power, but one answer we may gather from Israel's history, you will find it Judges ii. 21, 22, " I also will not henceforth drive out any before them of the nations which Joshua left when he died : that through them I may *prove Israel*, whether they will keep the way of the Lord, to walk therein, as their fathers did keep it, or not." May it not, then, be to *prove* us that we carry within us up to our dying hour an enemy, a *principle* which is altogether at enmity with God. It seems, brethren, to be God's purpose not to put His people at once and for ever beyond the reach of temptation, but to exercise their faith and patience, and to shew the power of that divine principle which His own grace has put into their hearts. We often, brethren, need to be reminded that God acts for His own glory. If He were only to think of our *comfort*, doubtless it would have added much to it to have had no enemy within. But the frequent triumphs of the true Christian over this inward enemy—triumphs more difficult and more glorious than the capture of Sebastopol—triumphs which nothing but the Spirit of God and the power of Christ can accomplish within us ; these, brethren, give more glory to God, because they display His attributes and His gifts. Do not, then, be cast down when you are deeply aud painfully conscious of this inward conflict. Take it as God's appointment. Remember that it is to *prove* you, and that God proves you in mercy, to make you not only conqueror, but more than conqueror through Him that loved us. But there is another point of view in which we must look at this. There are many cases in which this severity, the painful severity, of conflict is owing, in great measure, to previous unfaithfulness to God. Suppose a person to have indulged in some sinful habit at any period of his life ; it may be a want of truth, or impurity, or in any other sin, though the power of that sin will be broken by the entrance of the Spirit of God into the heart, yet it will cast its shadow long after it. Though blotted out for ever from the book of God's remembrance, yet it will return again to the charge in times of weakness, and Satan will endeavour by means of it to enchain the soul again. The habitual sins of the unrenewed man are the snares and temptation of the renewed man.

There is much of practical warning in this solemn truth. If ever, brethren, you are tempted to indulge any sinful thought in your heart, remember that *that* indulgence will certainly find you out again. If it is forgiven, and it may be, and will be, if you turn in repentance to the fountain opened for sin and for uncleanness—the fountain of Christ's precious blood—still you will not be exactly as you were. That sinful thought, harboured in your mind, strengthened the old man, and weakened the new man; and though in Jesus you may find fresh grace and divine strength, still you will have to encounter more bitter conflicts than you would have had if you had been more faithful to God, and through His grace had "driven out *all* the inhabitants of the land." We would not, brethren, discourage any earnest souls, by announcing this solemn law of God's government, or make any sad whom God would not make sad. We would not ourselves limit, or cause others to limit the *grace* of God. Oh, no. In Christ there is the fulness of all grace, the forgiveness of all sin, and power to overcome. If you believe in Jesus, and are washed in His blood, your sins, however many, are blotted out, and will be remembered no more. Still, brethren, it is needful to point out to what unfaithfulness to God will surely lead, to point out what sad consequences, in the very nature of things, will follow all indulgence in sin, whether in thought, word, or act. Never, brethren, should a sinful thought be indulged, under the notion that God will forgive it, and that it will be easy to overcome it at some future time. God may, in mercy, forgive it; but if He does so, that act of unfaithfulness will bring bitterness into the soul, will prepare the way for new conflicts and temptations. What then, brethren, do we learn from all this, but to keep close to God, to walk with Christ, to

fly to Him as our only refuge, when the sinful thought
arises in our hearts? We should cast ourselves wholly
on Jesus for the forgiveness of all past and present sins,
and for strength to drive out "every inhabitant of the
land"—the old man, with all his deceitful lusts. If
through grace, brethren, we so walk, in constant communion with God, abiding in Christ, willingly allowing
nothing that can hide His face from us, then the new man
will grow stronger and stronger, the old man weaker and
weaker. We shall experience more and more the depth
of the beautiful assurance, "My grace is sufficient for
thee." Out of weakness we shall be made strong, victory
will crown conflict, until the last and most glorious triumph of all will place us in the presence of Jesus, where
there will be no principle of sin within us to molest, no
influences of the world to deaden, no power of Satan to
seduce us. And *there*, brethren, enjoying eternal rest,
we shall be thankful for the conflicts through which we
have passed. We shall wonder, oh, how much more than
at present, at the grace which forgave so many sins, at
the mercy which held us up, and lifted us when fallen, at
the strength which *could* give victory to such weak, sinful creatures over such mighty foes, and we shall say,
with an emphasis altogether new, "Unto Him that loved
us, and washed us from our sins in His own blood, and
hath made us kings and priests unto God, and His Father,
to Him be glory and dominion for ever and ever. Amen."

CITIES OF REFUGE

Numbers 35:10-12

" And the Lord spake unto Moses, saying, Speak unto the children of
Israel, and say unto them, When ye be come over Jordan into the
land of Canaan, then ye shall appoint you cities to be cities of
refuge for you; that the slayer may flee thither, which killeth any
person at unawares. And they shall be unto you cities for refuge
from the avenger; that the manslayer die not, until he stand before
the congregation in judgment."

WE come now, brethren, to one of the most interesting
arrangements in the whole of Israel's history, the appointment of the cities of refuge.

We are informed in ver. 7 of this chapter, that forty-
eight cities were to be made over by Israel to the Levites.
The Levites represented the spiritual Israel. They were
consecrated to the special service of God. They were not
to cultivate the land, or carry on war. The service of the
sanctuary was theirs. Hence it was that a special provision was made for them,—one suited to their calling.
They were not to dwell in the country, but to be gathered
together in cities specially set apart for them, consecrated,
as it were, for their use. And this we may regard as a type
of the power of Divine grace; for before the entrance of
Israel into the Promised Land, the cities were the centres
of corruption, and specially under the curse of God. Now
they were to be centres of blessing, and regarded as specially holy. But this was the case with six of them more
than with all the rest. The forty-two were for the *Levites'*

exclusive use.   But these six, whilst they belonged to the
Levites, were for the benefit of the manslayer, to whatsoever tribe he might belong, and even for the stranger
who dwelt in Israel, as ver. 15 proves, "These six cities
shall be a refuge, both for the children of Israel and for
the *stranger*, and for the sojourner among them, that
every one that killeth any person unawares may flee
thither;" and consequently such were selected as were
accessible from any point, so that there should be no
place in Canaan so far removed from them that the manslayer could not reach them.   This point is specially mentioned, Deut. xix. 6, "Lest the avenger of blood pursue
the slayer, while his heart is hot, and overtake him,
because the *way is long*, and slay him."   Three, therefore,
of these cities were on the one side Jordan, and three on
the other.   Their names are given, Josh. xx. 7, 8, "And
they appointed Kedesh in Galilee in mount Naphtali,
and Shechem in mount Ephraim, and Kirjath-arba (which
is Hebron) in the mountain of Judah.   And on the other
side Jordan, by Jericho eastward, they assigned Bezer in
the wilderness upon the plain out of the tribe of Reuben,
and Ramoth in Gilead out of the tribe of Gad, and Golan
in Bashan out of the tribe of Manasseh."

You will remember, brethren, that we have already
seen again and again that the history of Israel is a typical
history.   Christ was proclaimed to them and to us in
numberless arrangements and gifts.   The manna in the
wilderness set Him forth as the food of our souls.   The
tree thrown into the waters of Marah was a prophecy of
the transforming power of His grace.   But no arrangement or gift is more full of Christ than these six appointed
cities.   They point us to Jesus as the refuge, and the only
refuge, for our souls.

Let us trace the points of resemblance between the two, the temporary and the eternal refuge.

And, first, we may notice that a very wide distinction was made here between the murderer and manslayer. Whensoever, and under whatever circumstances, a person's life was taken, the homicide might fly to a city of refuge; but in every case he was afterwards brought up before the congregation in judgment, and a careful examination took place as to whether it was a case of murder or manslaughter. Minute rules were laid down by God himself to guide this examination. There were three outward and three inward marks, any one of which proved him to be a murderer. The outward marks had reference to the way in which life was taken. The 16th and two following verses shew what these were. If an instrument of iron was made use of, or a stone was thrown by the hand, or he was smitten with a hard weapon of wood, then the perpetrator was judged to be a murderer; or if any other instrument was used, and it could be shewn that he had perpetrated the deed under feelings of hatred, or intentionally, or in enmity, then also he was judged to be a murderer; and this point proved, the city could afford him no refuge. He was delivered up to the avenger of blood, who took his life. But if there was proof that the act was unpremeditated, then he remained in the city of refuge, and the avenger of blood could not touch him. Of what, then, shall we say that the manslayer was a type? We may say, "of sinners;" but taken more accurately, we should say, "of those who sin in ignorance." If we read Scripture with care, we shall see that whilst it speaks of every sin as deadly in its nature, of every sin as deserving God's wrath, it nevertheless makes a distinction between sins which are ignorantly and those which are

wilfully committed. If you will turn, for instance, to
Lev. iv., you will find special offerings prescribed for those
who sin *ignorantly*. The words of St Paul, too, will
doubtless occur to you, " But I obtained mercy, because I
did it ignorantly in unbelief."   And then there are those
awful words, Heb. x. 26, " For if we sin wilfully after
that we have received the knowledge of the truth, there
remaineth no more sacrifice for sins." There are, then,
wilful sins,—that is, not only sins in which the will has
a part, for it has this in every sin, but those which are
intentional, deliberate, and premeditated, committed with
the knowledge that they *are* contrary to the will of God ;
and there are sins which may be very great in God's sight,
which may not be known as sins at the time, either
because ignorance is great and the conscience is not
awakened, or because the particular sin is of a refined
and subtle kind.   Now, it is of sins which we commit in
ignorance of which the manslayer is more properly a type.
And it is an important lesson which this arrangement
rivets on our hearts.   It tells us, brethren, that sins of
ignorance *are sins* in the sight of God ; and that even
from these there is only one way to escape, and that is by
fleeing to a city of refuge.   Supposing that we had never
committed any *deliberate* sin, had never indulged in anything which we knew to be wrong, even then we should
need the blood of Jesus.   Our sins of ignorance alone are
enough to ruin us, and would infallibly ruin us if we did
not hasten to Christ.   And if, brethren, our sins committed in ignorance are *such*, oh, what shall He think of
our wilful sins,—deliberate sins committed in the hour of
temptation.   We may well bless God that there is a contrast here, as well as a resemblance, between the type and
the antitype.   The six appointed cities afforded a refuge

to the manslayer only,—to the man who had taken another's life at unawares. They cast out the man who had
committed the act deliberately. But it is not so, brethren,
with Christ. His precious blood cleanseth from all sin,
deliberate as well as unpremeditated. It may be, brethren,
that in looking back on your past lives, you may see
many things which you did, not knowing them to be
wrong at the time. Since *then* you have got more light;
you look at them now as God looks at them. Perhaps
you have taken, and can take, these to the fountain opened
for sin and for uncleanness. But there may be *other* sins
which burden you more,—sins which you know to have
been *deliberate*. For these you may sometimes fear that
there is no forgiveness. But there is, brethren. The
antitype exceeds the type. On the cross of Christ is this
beautiful inscription : "Though your sins be as scarlet,
they shall be white as snow ; and though they be red like
crimson, they shall be as wool." On the gate of our City
of Refuge you may read the encouraging words, "Him
that cometh unto Me, I will in no wise cast out."

And now, brethren, imagine the manslayer on his way
to his city of refuge. His hand is stained with blood.
He cannot return to his home, his family, and his employ-
ments. He must leave all, and go out literally empty to
save his life. The avenger of blood, his heart burning
with revenge, his steps quickened by the loss of some dear
relative, and his work appointed and sanctioned by God,
is on his track. To return home, or to pause, is death.
One thought occupies his mind, " Where can I be safe ? "
One answer is given, " Fly to the city of refuge." He flies to
the nearest city along the road, which, according to Jewish
tradition, was said to have been forty-eight feet wide, and
always kept in good repair. Wearied he may be before he

reaches it. Still he goes on, and great indeed is his joy
when it comes in sight. Deeply he feels the mercy of
God in this appointment. He summons all his remaining strength, and almost feels himself within the city
gates. There he is safe. He can *dare* to think over his
past perils, for he knows he is safe. The appointment
of God protects him. He who gave authority to the
avenger of blood to pursue him, and to shed his blood,
if caught outside the city, will not let a hair of his
head be injured within it. He feels that he is safe—
the avenger of blood knows that he is safe—all who
witness with anxiety the flight and the pursuit, know that
he is safe. One word describes his condition while fly-
ing, "danger;" one word describes it within the city
walls, "safety."

All this, brethren, is a type of that which takes place
in a man's heart when the Spirit of God visits his soul.
Then he begins to see the true nature of sin, and to perceive his own great danger. The danger is not at a distance. It is immediate and imminent. The avenger of
blood is upon him. You know, brethren, what it is. It
is the law, that law which is holy, just, and good. It
is terrible to be pursued by it; to be conscious of its
breadth and strictness, and to have its curse ringing in
our ears. No enemy is more dreadful to the awakened
conscience than the law of God. The avenger of blood
was armed with the authority of God; so also is the law.
It is God's voice of righteousness, His uplifted arm of
vengeance; it pursues the convicted sinner through all
his subterfuges. He wishes to find rest in his home, his
family, and his calling; but no; he is pursued still; no
arm of flesh, no creature can give him rest,—can afford
him safety. He must give up everything, and fly to the

City of Refuge. He must go forth utterly empty, that he may find safety and all he wants in Christ Jesus. He does go. He flies from the avenger of blood along the appointed path, but the broken law follows him. His danger appears to get greater and greater, and his heart often sinks into despondency. Then perhaps some encouraging promise cheers him. Its adaptation to his wants makes him exclaim, "Is it not for me?" Its *certainty* makes him trust it. He presses forward until Jesus, the one and only Refuge for sinners, appears in view; he casts himself at the foot of the cross, and there he is safe. The law cannot accuse him there; for it is satisfied by the righteousness and blood of Jesus. His conscience is purged from dead works to serve the living God; his heart is at rest.

Dear brethren, has this great and important process gone on in your heart? Have you ever realized the appalling danger of your soul? and felt the law as the avenger of blood pursuing you? Many, oh how many! rest in the creature; their home, their relations, their occupations, are their all. The love of some creature fills their hearts, and yet can never satisfy it. Oh remember, brethren, if you value your souls, that there is no resting-place in all these. Death will remove them all from you, and you from all. What you want is something that cannot die; it is Christ you need. Give up all, everything without exception, for Him. His own words prove the necessity, (Luke xiv. 26, 27,) "If any man come to me, and hate not his father and mother, and wife and children, and brethren, yea and his own life also, he cannot be my disciple; and whosoever doth not bear his cross, and come after me, cannot be my disciple." You must forget your own people, and your father's house, forget your own righteousness, forget the creature, so as not to idolize it, and come utterly *empty* to Christ; and that not once only, but every day. Oh, it is a great and deep truth to learn that we *are nothing*, and *have nothing*. Nothing but the grace of God can make us feel our own utter emptiness, can make us *content* to be empty in ourselves, that we may have all things in Christ.

But if, brethren, this work is going on, perhaps all unknown to any but God, in the depth of your hearts, and you are on your way to the City of Refuge, though agitated with many fears, remember how very encouraging the Bible is to all who are seeking Jesus, the true City of Refuge. Think of the mercy which has provided such a refuge,—one so all-sufficient, and of the promises which point you to it. St Paul, in a beautiful passage in which there is probably an allusion to the cities of refuge, reminds us, that "God, willing more abundantly to shew unto the heirs of promise the immutability of his counsel, confirmed it by an oath, that by two immutable things in which it was impossible for God to lie, we might have a strong consolation who have fled for refuge to lay hold upon the hope set before us, which hope we have as an anchor of the soul, both sure and steadfast, and which entereth into that within the vail." Why, then, brethren, with such a refuge provided, and such promises, should we ever despond, even though the avenger of blood does pursue. With our faces towards the city of refuge, and our feet hastening thither, we shall not fall or perish. But we have still another point to notice, and that is the provision made for the manslayer within the city of refuge. He was not only safe from the avenger of blood, but also amply provided for. "They shall give him a place," we read, (Josh. xx. 4,) "that he may dwell among them ;" and this gift of a place probably involved a supply for his necessities, as he entered the city destitute of everything. Here again, brethren, we have a picture of what Christ is, and of what the Christian has in Him. The first great want, the first pressing need of his soul is safety ; and there is safety in Christ. When we are one with Him, we are safe; and we may be conscious of our safety. For it is written, (Rom. viii. 1,) "There is no condemnation to them that are in Christ Jesus, who walk not after the flesh, but after the Spirit;" "Who shall lay anything to the charge of God's elect ?" Is there any avenger of blood who shall do so ? Oh no. "It is God that justifieth." But there is more than safety in Christ. When rescued from danger, snatched from the avenger's hands, he wants something more. He wants a supply of all his wants. He has not, and never can have anything of his own. He must live on another. And this he can do ; for in Christ there is a full supply for all his wants. Hear what St John says, "Out of His fulness have all we received, and grace for grace." And St Paul says, "My God shall supply all your need according to His riches in glory by Christ Jesus." Yes, if we are Christ's all things are ours, "life and death, things present, and things to come;" everything that is God's is Christ's, and everything that is Christ's is ours. If, dear brethren, you have reason to believe that you have passed from death unto life, if you have proofs that you are one with Christ, endeavour to *realize* it, to realize your safety in Him, and still more to realize what there is in Him; to live, not to yourself, or in yourself, but upon Him. This gives strength to endure trial, it produces devotedness in

God's service, and it sustains perseverance and peace. To live upon Christ's fulness is our duty and our privilege, and it gives glory to God.

But again we read, (ver. 26, &c.,) "But if the slayer shall at any time come without the border of the city of his refuge, whither he has fled, and the revenger of blood find him without the border of the city of his refuge, and the revenger of blood kill the slayer, he shall not be guilty of blood. Because he should have remained in the city of his refuge until the death of the high priest; but after the death of the high priest the slayer shall return into the land of his possession." From this it appears, that it was absolutely necessary that the manslayer should remain in the city of refuge; to leave it was to expose himself again to the danger of death, to the hand of the avenger of blood. One thing only relaxed this rule, and that was the death of the high priest "which was anointed with holy oil." In that case he was allowed to return to his home and relatives. But why, it may be asked, did the death of the high priest produce this change in the position of the manslayer? It is a difficult question to answer, nor can we venture to answer it with much confidence. The reason, however, may be this. The manslayer, though safe in the city of refuge, was in many respects in a state of imprisonment. He was away from his home and family, and unable to venture beyond the walls of the city. Now the high priest anointed with the holy oil was a type of Jesus; and as the death of Christ effected a real redemption, a real deliverance from bondage for all who believe on Him—so did the death of the high priest effect a typical redemption, and restore the manslayer to his home and friends; all consequences of his deed were done away. But our great

High Priest never dies. There is no imprisonment in our city of refuge. We must be willing to give up every thing to enter it; but it does not separate us from those whom we love. There, in that city, we belong to a new family, we feel the power of new bonds,—that holy, unseen, and yet powerful bond which unites together all who are in Jesus. From that city and that family the true Christian never more goes out; no, not when he dies, for death does not separate him from Christ; death cannot rend the bonds which unite the "whole family in heaven and in earth." No. Christ's life is an eternal life. Union with Him is an eternal union, our refuge is an eternal refuge; and the golden cord which unites all who love Christ to each other, is so strong that death cannot rend it. Its duration is the lifetime of our High Priest. It is eternity.

THE SCARLET LINE

Joshua 2:17-19

" And the men said unto her, We will be blameless of this thine oath
which thou hast made us swear.   Behold, when we come into the
land, thou shalt bind this line of scarlet thread in the window
which thou didst let us down by : and thou shalt bring thy father,
and thy mother, and thy brethren, and all thy father's household,
home unto thee.   And it shall be, that whosoever shall go out of
the doors of thy house into the street, his blood shall be upon his
head, and we will be guiltless : and whosoever shall be with thee
in the house, his blood shall be on our head, if any hand be upon
him."

WE hear, brethren, very much of war. England—and,
we may say, Europe—waits with almost breathless expectation for tidings from the East.   War is always awful,—
one of the very worst of judgments.   The loss of life, the
thousands that it plunges into mourning, the demorali-
zation which it produces,—all these are very sad.   Yet,
brethren, in this great struggle there is much to comfort.
It is a noble struggle.   England is in the path of duty ;
for it is not for herself, for her own purposes, but in
behalf of great principles, in behalf of righteousness, in
defence of the oppressed against the oppressor, that she
sheds the blood of her sons, and clothes her daughters
with mourning.   And there is comfort not only in its
being a righteous cause, but in that which God may
accomplish by it.   It is a comfort to think that in the
hardships of war, and the sufferings of sickness and of

wounds, the grace of God may be accomplishing a mighty
work in many hearts. Seed long sown, and often watered
by tears, may be springing up. Many a mother's and
sister's prayers for a son or brother may be answered in
this unexpected manner. An hospital, and most of all a
military hospital, must always be an affecting place. But
viewed in this light, brethren, is it not in the highest
sense the house of God? There our great High Priest is
present,—there the penitent is pouring out his soul to
God in bitter remembrance of past forgetfulness,—there
the dying believer can say, "Though far away from home
and country, yet there is One with me. I know that my
Redeemer liveth."

The portion of Israel's history to which we now come,
speaks of war. It tells us of the entire destruction of a
large town, the slaughter of its inhabitants, the destruction of its property. What an amount of woe must have
been there! Yet, brethren, we must remember that it was
destroyed at God's express command. And we should notice in how remarkable a manner the grace of God shone
forth in the very midst of this terrible judgment.

We know not, brethren, whether you may have noticed
in Scripture that we find there the blessing of God and
the curse of God concentrated not only in *individual*
souls, but also in *cities*. Thus Jerusalem is constantly set
forth in Scripture as the city of blessing. Take, for instance, Ps. xlviii. 1–3, "Great is the Lord, and greatly to
be praised in the city of our God, in the mountain of his
holiness. Beautiful for situation, the joy of the whole
earth, is mount Zion, on the sides of the north, the city of
the great King. God is known in her palaces for a
refuge." Or again, Ps. l. 2, "Out of Zion, the perfection
of beauty, God hath shined." On the other hand, Jericho is

the city of the curse. "The city," it is said, (Josh. vi. 17,) "shall be accursed, even it, and all that are therein, to the Lord;" and ver. 18, "And ye, in any wise keep yourselves from the accursed thing, lest ye make yourselves accursed, when ye take of the accursed thing, and make the camp of Israel a curse, and trouble it." And then afterwards we find a curse pronounced on the man who shall attempt to rebuild it, (Josh. vi. 26,) "And Joshua adjured them at that time, saying, Cursed be the man before the Lord that riseth up and buildeth this city Jericho: he shall lay the foundation thereof in his first-born, and in his youngest son shall he set up the gates of it." For five hundred years the city of the curse disappeared. At the expiration of that time an attempt was made to rebuild it by Hiel the Bethelite. But the slumbering curse awoke, and Hiel's eldest and youngest sons died, the one when the foundation was laid, the other when the gates were set up. These two cities, then, are evidently *representative* cities. Jerusalem, the city of blessing, represents the Church of God, destined to eternal life. Jericho, the city of the curse, represents the world, alienated from God, and destined to destruction. And then, brethren, what will Rahab represent but those who are gathered out of the one into the other, not on account of anything good in themselves, any natural excellencies or attainments, but by the *grace* of God, and according to His good pleasure. And specially, brethren, does she, herself a Gentile, seem to represent those of the Gentiles who are brought to God. You remember the words of James when addressing the council of Jerusalem, (Acts xv. 14,) "Simeon hath declared how God at the first did visit the Gentiles, to take out of them a people for his name." Of the people gathered out of the world by grace for the name and glory of God, Rahab was a type. Israel's camp was now at Shittim ; and Joshua, intending to lay siege to Jericho, sent two spies to view the land. They went accordingly ; and the providence of God, which orders each step in the pathway of His people, guided them to the house of Rahab, and there they lodged. Danger soon threatened them. Their entrance into the city was made known to the king of Jericho, and he sent to Rahab, and required that the two men should be given up. Then it was that by her acts and her words she shewed that she had a true and living faith. For, dangerous as it was to herself, she hid the two spies upon the roof of the house ; for she entered into God's purpose concerning Israel and Jericho. There is a remarkable force of conviction in her words, as well as consistency in her acts. She said unto the men themselves, (ver. 9–11,) " I know that the Lord hath given you the land, and that your terror is fallen upon us, and that all the inhabitants of the land faint because of you. For we have heard how the Lord dried up the water of the Red Sea for you, when ye came out of Egypt ; and what ye did unto the two kings of the Amorites, that were on the other side Jordan, Sihon and Og, whom ye utterly destroyed. And as soon as we had heard these things, our hearts did melt, neither did there remain any more courage in any man, because of you : for the Lord your God, he is God in heaven above, and in earth beneath." All the inhabitants of the land trembled. But Rahab's faith shewed itself in this, that she recognised God. She looked above *second* causes. It was not Israel's power and prowess, but *God's hand*, which she saw. " I know that the Lord hath given you the land. The Lord your God, he is God in heaven above, and in the earth beneath."

All this, brethren, throws *much* light on the nature of
true faith. It shews us, in the first place, that living
faith carries us *straight* to *God.* Our hearts are very
prone to get entangled in *second* causes,—to look at the
hand of man, and forget the hand of God. Too often,
also, we say in our hearts, "If such a thing had not happened, I should not have had this or that trial." We
ought never for a moment to indulge such thoughts.
Once give way to such reasonings, and Satan is sure to
get advantage, and you will be led to dishonour God, and
your own heart will be *miserably* restless. The language
of faith is, "It is the Lord." It elevates the heart above
second causes, and enables it to rest, not, it may be, without many struggles, on the *will* and *arm* of God.

Again, we see in this history that faith is the principle of a new life. Rahab's life had been an unhallowed
one, and she had sunk lower than many others in Jericho. But now through Divine grace she rises higher
than all. She, and she alone, welcomes the messengers
of God, shews them kindness, and is anxious to secure a
refuge from the awful destruction which she saw approaching. That kindness to the two spies,—that disregard to
danger in the path of duty,—that consciousness of the
doom now at hand,—that earnest wish to escape it,
shewed that there was a new principle of life in her soul.
She acted differently from her former self, and differently from all the inhabitants of Jericho, just because
she *believed.* "By faith," says St Paul, (Heb. xi. 31),
"the harlot Rahab perished not with them that believed
not, when she had received the spies with peace." And
faith, brethren, is always the same ; the same in its object,
which is God,—the same in its principle, which is His
grace,—the same in its results, which is holiness of life.

Rahab believed in the approaching doom of Jericho; she felt that its days were numbered. The true Christian now believes that a more awful and universal judgment is coming upon the world, and he flees from the wrath to come—flees to the only Refuge from the storm. "All men," says St Paul, "have not faith." No, indeed. But have *you* it, dear brethren, such faith as Rahab had—a faith which sees God's hand, which receives His word, whatever the world may think, which acts upon it, which looks forward to the great day approaching so fast, and upward to Jesus, as an all-sufficient Saviour? Without such faith, one which leads to holiness, watchfulness, and prayer, there can be no salvation; without it, a doom may be approaching of which Jericho's is but a faint shadow, and yet we perceive it not. We may slumber on, or tremble, as many of Jericho's inhabitants appear to have done, and yet not get within a shelter, and so, when it actually comes, all its foreshadows being overlooked, it will find us unprepared.

But Rahab went further. She wished to have some assurance that her life, and the life of her family, would be spared. "Give me," she says, (ver. 12,) "a true token, that ye will save alive my father, and my mother, and my brethren, and my sisters, and all that they have, and deliver our lives from death." She wanted a true token, but did not decide what that token should be. This, however, the two spies did, and a very instructive one it was, (ver. 18.) "Behold, when we come into the land, thou shalt bind this line of scarlet thread in the window which thou didst let us down by." She gladly accepted the token, and, without loss of time, "she bound the scarlet line in the window." It is not wonderful that she should have desired this token; and we may well imagine

what comfort she must have felt when the scarlet line
was floating in the air at her window. Very solemn
thoughts must often have weighed upon her heart—
thoughts of the awful destruction which awaited her
fellow-townsmen; but she felt no anxiety about herself
and family. The scarlet line silenced every fear.

And if it was natural in Rahab to desire a token of her
safety, is it not even more natural in the true Christian
to desire it? Should he rest satisfied without a *pledge* of
his safety? Ought he not to desire, and how fervently!
to say with the apostle, "We know that if our earthly
house of this tabernacle is dissolved, we have a building
of God, an house not made with hands, eternal in the
heavens?" If Rahab was not content to rest uncertain
about her safety, why, brethren, should we? If a token
was granted to her, why should not one be granted to us?
And *one* there is, brethren, which is granted sooner or
later to those who walk with God. It is not always given
at once; often it grows up by degrees. But yet, sooner
or later, it is given. What is it, brethren? It is something of which that scarlet line was a shadow and a type,
—the blood of Jesus sprinkled upon the heart. The blood
of Jesus secures pardon, and also produces assurance.
But you will notice that there is a wide difference between
the two. Forgiveness is one thing; the knowledge of
forgiveness is another. Whenever the blood of Jesus is
sprinkled upon the heart, *then* there is the full and free
forgiveness of all sin. But, perhaps, for some considerable
time there may be no assurance of it. Forgiveness of
sin we must have, to be Christians. Assurance is a privilege which Christians should seek, and seek until they
find, and then watch, that they may retain it. This distinction may be traced in the Old Testament types. For

instance, some of the sacrifices were propitiatory. They were means typically of procuring forgiveness; and in this they were foreshadows of the blood of Christ, which cleanses from all sin. Others, again, went beyond this. They served two purposes, and represented the putting away of sin, and also assurance of safety. This was the case with the passover lamb. Its shed blood represented the blood of Jesus shed for us, whereby alone we can obtain remission of sins. The blood sprinkled upon the door-posts of the Israelites was a token of safety. The one set forth the forgiveness of sins; the other, assurance of God's favour. The scarlet line is typical of the blood of Jesus likewise, but not in *procuring* forgiveness, only as *assuring* us of pardon and salvation; for Rahab *believed* first, and the scarlet line was given as a token rather to crown her faith. It had nothing to do with producing it. Dear brethren, is this scarlet line hanging out at your window, visible to Him who sees in secret, and to your own dim eyes? Are you firmly assured of the love of God? and can you trust entirely to His faithfulness? We have observed already, that assurance of God's love, and of our standing in Christ, does not always spring up at once; often it is the *result* of a close walk with God. It crowns some act, or many acts, of faith. We have an indication of this in this very history, for the scarlet thread was hung out of the very window through which she had let down the two spies—an act of faith and love on her part. If, then, brethren, you would have the scarlet line floating at the window of your hearts, you must trust simply in Christ. This of itself is enough to bring, and does often bring, assurance; but if not, endeavour to walk with God. Be diligent in doing His will and work, and perhaps God will meet you then, and will

crown some act of faith and self-denial and devoted service with a true token, a scarlet line of His assurance love.
Having proceeded thus far with the history of Rahab, we
must say a few words about its conclusion, although it
will carry us forward into another chapter. When Jericho's
day of visitation came, she was spared; and it is evident
that she was miraculously spared, for we are distinctly
told (Josh. ii. 15) that "her house was upon the town
wall, and she dwelt upon the wall." One wall of the
house in which she dwelt was the continuance of the town
wall. When, then, the walls of Jericho fell down at the
blast of the trumpets and Israel's shout, if it had not
been for the power and watchful care of God, she and her
family would have been buried in the ruins of the house.
That part of the wall in which it was built must have
been miraculously spared. God interposed to spare her.
What a difference that little piece of scarlet line made!
It was not a mere token arranged between man and man;
it was sanctioned in heaven. God's eye as well as man's
was fixed upon the scarlet line, and Rahab was protected.
And if that scarlet line made so great a difference in her
case, and secured her protection, oh, how much more shall
the blood of Christ secure that of the true Christian! Is
it sprinkled upon your heart? Does God's eye see it
there? Then all your sins, however many, are forgiven;
all your enemies, however strong, will be overcome.
"Who," says St Paul, "shall lay anything to the charge
of God's elect? It is God that justifieth, who is he that
condemneth? It is Christ that died, yea rather, that is
risen again, who is even at the right hand of God, who
also maketh intercession for us. Who shall separate us
from the love of Christ? Shall tribulation, or distress, or
persecution, or famine, or nakedness, or peril, or sword?

Nay, in all these things we are more than conquerors through him that loved us." The true Christian, many as are his fears and conflicts, is safe in the hands of Christ. When the flood came, Noah was preserved; and when the earth shall again undergo judgment, and in one sense be destroyed, in another purified by fire,—when many a voice will be heard crying to the mountains and rocks to fall upon them, and hide them from the wrath of the Lamb, then will the true Christian be quite safe. The scarlet line of Christ's precious blood sprinkled upon his heart is his true token and security; and the beautiful words of the Psalmist will have an exact fulfilment, (Ps. xci. 4–7,) "He shall cover thee with his feathers, and under his wings shalt thou trust: his truth shall be thy shield and buckler. Thou shalt not be afraid for the terror by night; nor for the arrow that flieth by day; nor for the pestilence that walketh in darkness; nor for the destruction that wasteth at noon-day. A thousand shall fall at thy side, and ten thousand at thy right hand; but it shall not come nigh thee."

But there is still one other point to be noticed in Rahab's history. You will find it stated in Josh. vi. 25, where it says, "She dwelleth in Israel unto this day." So that from that time forth, though she had been a sinner of the Gentiles, she was put among God's children, reckoned as one of His own Israel; and even, we learn from Matt. i. 5, so honoured of God as to be one of the line from whom Jesus was descended. And do we not learn from this, brethren, how completely the blood of Jesus cleanses from all sin? how *real* a thing is the forgiveness of sins? how great and entire is the change which the grace of God makes in the heart? "If any man be in Christ," says St Paul, "he is a new creature: old things are passed away; behold, all things are become new." Never, brethren, can we bend our heads too low in the remembrance of our past sins, and in the consciousness of the deep depravity of our own hearts. Yet this humiliation need not prevent us from joining in the song, (Rev. i. 5, 6,) "Unto him that loved us, and washed us from our sins in his own blood, and hath made us kings and priests unto God and his Father; to him be glory and dominion for ever and ever. Amen."

"YE HAVE NOT PASSED THIS WAY BEFORE"

" For ye have not passed this way heretofore."

WE now come to a most interesting event in Israel's history,—the passage of the river Jordan. We have seen the variety of the trials which they had to undergo in their journey from Egypt to the Land of Promise, along with the corresponding variety of the blessings shed on their path. In Egypt, they endured a crushing bondage, and yet, to the astonishment of their oppressors, they increased in the very midst of it. They were delivered from it only after the infliction of the most terrible plagues, which plunged every Egyptian family into mourning, throughout the length and breadth of the land. They marched forth, but had made little progress before their enemies overtook them, at a place where there was no way of escape. But the hand of God miraculously delivered them, by dividing the waters of the Red Sea, and thus making a new path for His people. Yet this deliverance was no pledge of freedom from future trials. In the wilderness of Shur they found no water, at Marah it was bitter. In the wilderness of Sin their food failed, but God fed them with bread from heaven; at Rephidim they thirsted again, and the smitten rock yielded them water. But it is needless to repeat all their sufferings, their disappointments, their chastisements, and, parallel with these, all

their mercies and privileges—the manifestations of God's
presence among them. They are familiar to us all. But
so great was the variety of their experience, even at the
earlier part of their journeyings, and so condensed with
sufferings and mercies into that period of their history,
that we might almost suppose that no *new* circumstance,
or *combination* of circumstances, could await them on
their onward progress ; that their experience was ex-
hausted ; and that their future would not be the evolu-
tion of any new events, but the repetition of what they
had previously passed through. This, however, was far
from being the case. At the period of which we read in
this chapter, they had arrived at the banks of Jordan.
The promised land was stretched out before them—the
object of their hopes, the end of their journeyings. But
the waters of Jordan divided them from it, and at this
season of the year it overflowed its banks, so that the
passage was one of difficulty and danger. After all their
past history, there was much that was *new* in their position,—their nearness to the Land of Promise—their station on the bank of a swollen river—the untried way
across it. And thus we find that He who had led them,
and was leading them still, distinctly presented to them
the *novelty* of their situation, in the words, " Ye have not
passed this way heretofore." Hence there was to be a
solemn preparation before they began to cross. The
command to them was, " Sanctify yourselves ; " and
arrangements were prescribed by God himself for the
passage of His people through this their last hindrance.
The ark of the covenant, the symbol of the Divine Presence, was ordered to be carried by the priests and Levites
into the midst of Jordan. No sooner did the soles of the
feet of the priests touch the waters of Jordan, than the

stream would divide. Then the children of Israel were to follow, but not close after the ark,—there was to be a space between them of about three thousand feet, that they might know the way that they should go ; and it was a very instructive arrangement, that the ark, which preceded them into the midst of Jordan, followed them out of it; for thus we are distinctly told, (chap. iv. 11,) "And it came to pass, when all the people were clean passed over, that the ark of the Lord passed over, and the priests, in the presence of the people." The symbol of God's presence went down before them, to make a pathway through the divided waters ; and it stayed behind them, to keep back the threatening stream. And thus there was an anticipation of that beautiful promise, "When thou passest through the waters, I will be with thee." They passed in safety, and set up on the other side a memorial of this last wilderness-miracle of God's power and love. It is easy to see how striking is the typical meaning of this part of Israel's history. *We* are travelling onward, but the future is hidden from our eyes. We are not as those whose path lies across an extensive plain, and the boundary of whose vision is far away, but rather like those who are journeying in a deep valley, and who cannot see the storms that may be gathering behind the mountains. Our horizon is very limited. What Jordans we may have to cross, we know not. But we *have* an ark, of which that which accompanied Israel is but a faint and feeble shadow—an ark that is a stronger pledge of God's faithfulness, a deeper manifestation of His love and power. The Christian's ark is Christ. Jesus journeys with him through all the wilderness into the land of promise.

Every congregation is made up of a number of minds,

no two of which would probably be found to be exactly
alike. There are, indeed, many points. of resemblance,
which ought not to be overlooked. All are alike naturally infected with the deadly disease of sin ; and God is
dealing with every one of us for the gracious purpose of
restoring us to Himself. With this view, He has admitted us into covenant with Himself. He has made
known to us the mystery of His holy will in the Bible.
He has appointed sacraments, as means of grace. He
speaks solemnly to our consciences. He pleads perse-
veringly with our hearts, by the influences of His Spirit,
to promote the great end, the salvation of our souls.
Trials, losses, disappointments, sufferings, are dispensed
at different times, and in different measures, to arouse
and solemnise us, and to make us yield ourselves up,
through the teaching of the Spirit of God. But with all
this resemblance there is much diversity. There is something peculiar to each mind, something in which it is
unlike its fellows. Each has some peculiar adjustment of
its natural powers ; and this necessarily causes a peculiar
and distinctive history. Just so far as our minds are
similarly constituted, and we are infected with the same
awful disease, and united to the same Saviour, and influenced by the same Spirit, we can sympathise with each
other. Just so far as there is something distinctive in
our minds, modifying our experiences, and stamping a
peculiar character upon our history, will our path be
lonely ; and we shall feel that there is one only who
" knoweth the way that we take." But He does know it,
and adapts His dealings to our need. Some are comparatively free from trial, others are called to bear their
yoke in their youth. Some are just reached by the wave,
the spray only seems to reach them ; others are immersed

in its depths, the waves and billows pass over them. And the history of these last bears greater resemblance to the varied experience of Israel; and yet, brethren, even concerning these, with whom God has already dealt so mysteriously, (and if with them, how much more with those who have had but little trial?) it may come true in the future, "Ye have not passed the way heretofore."

There may be some who are already entering a way that is new and mysterious to them. There was perhaps a time when they felt no anxiety or alarm about the great subject of their acceptance with God, and when the pleasures and enjoyments of the world filled up their thoughts; but a new impression has been made upon their minds, and they are beginning to be sensible that there is a great purpose for which they have been created, and, alas! they have not yet fulfilled it. Some trial or preservation, some word spoken, or secret influence of the Spirit, has aroused them to feel that God claims their hearts; and that His will, and not their own, should be the rule of their lives. They endeavour to fulfil that great purpose; and hope, by obedience to God's law, to obtain peace and rest. But the more earnest and sincere they are in their endeavours to walk in complete obedience, the more conscious they become of alarming failure. Hence they experience dreadful alternations of hope and fear; and, on the whole, hope decreases, and fear makes sad advances upon them. Their prayers are sometimes cold, and still more frequently distracted; their thoughts confused, and often vain; their resolutions are broken as easily by the force of temptation as the withs that bound Samson; and the commandment, which is holy, just, and good, and which was ordained unto life, they find to be unto death. They once hoped to find peace and rest by obedience to the law. They

grasped its apparently friendly hand, that they might be
led by it into the presence and enjoyment of God. But
now it stands before them with a threatening aspect; and,
like the cherubim placed at the east entrance of the
garden of Eden with a flaming sword, it guards the way
to the tree of life. And thus, like St Paul, they find the
commandment to be " unto death." " The law worketh
wrath." How can this Jordan, which separates them with
its overflowing waters from the land of peace, be crossed?
There is but one path across it, and that path is Christ.
Jesus, the ark of our covenant, is gone before us. He
fulfilled the law for us, and in His own body bore the
penalty of our transgressions. And *thus* having, by His
doing and suffering, obtained everlasting salvation for us,
He offers it to us, not as the reward of obedience to the
law, but a free gift to be received by faith. Thus St Paul
says, (Rom. iii. 20–22,) " Therefore by the deeds of the
law there shall no flesh be justified in his sight: for by
the law is the knowledge of sin. But now the righteousness of God without the law is manifested, being witnessed
by the law and the prophets; even the righteousness of
God which is by faith of Jesus Christ unto all and upon
all them that believe: for there is no difference." And
again, (chap. iv. 16,) " Therefore it is of faith, that it might
be by grace." The waters, then, of this terrible Jordan are
divided for those who are in Christ Jesus. The law does
not condemn them, for in Christ they are justified from
all things. The enemy that once barred their way to
Canaan has now become their friend. Its hostile and
condemning voice is hushed. It no longer threatens them
with death, but as a friend points out to them the way of
holiness. It has been their schoolmaster to bring them
to Christ; and now that they are in Christ, it becomes

the rule of a holy and happy life. And thus, "what the law could not do, in that it was weak through the flesh, God sending his own Son in the likeness of sinful flesh, and for sin, condemned sin in the flesh : that the righteousness of the law might be fulfilled in us, who walk not after the flesh, but after the Spirit."

But there is another period in our lives of which the passage of Israel through Jordan is a more exact type. We must acknowledge, brethren, that there is something extremely awful in such a conclusion to our earthly pilgrimage as *death;* and the real wonder is, not that there are some, who through fear of death are all their lifetime subject to bondage, but that there are such multitudes to whose thoughts this solemn and mysterious event is scarcely ever present, and on whose minds it makes no lasting impression. We will not dwell now on its fearful origin or its universality, for "death passed upon all men, for that *all* have sinned;" and again, "death *reigned* by one." Nor will we pause to consider all the things which make it so mysterious and awful,—either the fact that it introduces us into the presence of Him who will judge the quick and the dead, or that it fixes for ever that moral and spiritual state in which it finds us. These two great realities would of themselves be quite sufficient to invest death with a tremendous awfulness.

But there is another element in it more immediately suggested by our text, which should certainly deepen that impression, and that is its *novelty*. It lies quite beyond the bounds of our present experience. We may perfectly realize all the circumstances of death up to the moment of the separation of the soul from the body: the weakness, weariness, and pain of sickness—the tenderness and love of relations and friends in watching over us, and in

smoothing our dying pillow; because in all this we have
past experience to go upon, and we have only to imagine
an increase of that which we have already felt. We have
known what weakness and suffering are. We have felt
the support and consolation of the love and sympathy of
relations and friends; and it requires no great effort of
mind to suppose all these increased in degree, and thus to
obtain beforehand some impressions of that solemn hour.
But when we endeavour to advance a step beyond this,
and to realize the mysterious separation of the soul from
the body, the loosening and snapping asunder of that
invisible bond which unites them, we feel that we have
stepped into a new region. Our past experiences fail us;
and after trying much to realize it, we cannot but feel,
" Ye have not passed this way heretofore."

And then we may add to this the *loneliness* of death.
None of us can be said to live altogether alone. There
are, we have said, peculiarities in the constitution of our
minds, and consequently in our history, in which others
cannot sympathise, and thus far we are conscious of a
loneliness in this world. But there are always so many
points in which we can sympathise with our brethren,
and they with us, that if there be not some great fault
in our minds, we may have the consolation of sympathising with others, and of meeting with sympathy. And
who can calculate the relief which this affords in the
sorrows of life? But in death this fails. We have to
cross our Jordan, not in company, like Israel of old, but
alone—one by *one*. The presence, and sympathy, and
love of relations and friends reach only up to that point
where the unknown region begins. The separation of
the soul from the body, which the dying man cannot
realize, they have no more power to realize. Where the

actual passage begins *they* cannot accompany him.   As far as man is concerned, *each one* must step down into Jordan *alone;* and in reference to this loneliness of death it may be truly said, "Ye have not passed this way heretofore."

And yet both the unknown mystery of death and its loneliness have been fully provided for in Him who "through death destroyed him that had the power of death, that is the devil."

For Jesus, the ark of our covenant, has gone down before us into Jordan.   There has been a space between His death and ours, that we might know the way that we should go; but His soul was not left in hell, neither was the Holy One suffered to see corruption.   He rose from the depths of Jordan, and marched along the path of life, leading captivity captive, and by His glorious resurrection He gave abundant proof that He has made an ever-enduring pathway for His people through the waters of Jordan.   And even along this opened pathway they do not walk alone.   He who once for all overcame death, accompanies each of His members through the valley of the shadow of death.   The brightness of His presence lightens it up.   The dark stream of Jordan manifests His power and reflects His light.   And thus the loneliness of death is overcome.   Just there where friends are found to leave the dying Christian, does Jesus become more distinctly present to his mind and heart.   He places His foot beside the Christian's, and divides Jordan's stream, and the holy angels who minister to the heirs of salvation accept the charge of the ransomed spirit, and bear it triumphant to Abraham's bosom, the meeting-place of the company of the redeemed.   And thus it is that so many believers have not only been willing to depart, the friend to leave friends, the mother to leave her

children, but have even longed to depart. The valley of
death has not presented itself to the eye of faith as a
dreary, lonely path, but all-resplendent with the rays of
the Sun of righteousness ; and the dying Christian has
again and again taken up the words of the Saviour, "Ye
shall leave me alone, and yet I am not alone, because the
Father is with me." And the unknown mystery of death,
from which our inmost being so naturally recoils, is overcome, no less than its *loneliness*. We should not venture
to cross a high mountain pass, abounding in chasms and
terrible precipices, when a thick fog has settled on its
top, or when night has cast its shadows upon it. We
should shrink from venturing upon the unknown and
dangerous way *alone*. But if a mountain guide of experience and intelligence direct our steps, we can venture
forth into the unknown path without apprehension. And
thus it is with the Christian. Every step of the path after
death is unexperienced and unknown. We have not
been that way heretofore. But the Christian has a Guide,
One who is perfectly familiar with every step of the way,
and who has proved Himself a faithful guide, not only to
others, but to ourselves, if we have placed ourselves under
His guidance. When it is necessary to employ an unknown guide, it is a comfort to hear abundant testimony
as to his competency and faithfulness. But we have a
cloud of witnesses to proclaim the all-sufficiency and
wisdom of our heavenly Guide. Patriarchs, prophets,
psalmists, apostles, evangelists, martyrs, all bear witness
to His love and faithfulness. But more precious to us
than all these is our own experience of His gentle and
faithful guidance ; and, therefore, if our past and present
experience is like that of the Psalmist, " He maketh me
to lie down in green pastures : he leadeth me beside the

still waters. He restoreth my soul : he leadeth me in the paths of righteousness for his name's sake ;"—we need not shrink from the language of bolder confidence and more exalted hope, " Yea, though I walk through the valley of the shadow of death, I will fear no evil : for thou art with me ; thy rod and thy staff they comfort me."

But let us not forget, brethren, that it is presumptuous to expect this blessed hope and confidence to arise in our hearts in the immediate prospect of death, if we are neglecting and slighting the ark of our covenant at this moment. The symbol of God's presence *did not* meet the Israelites for the first time at the brink of Jordan, but accompanied them throughout all their journey in the wilderness. Let us take heed, then, to the impressive words, " Sanctify yourselves." As we have been " set apart" for God in our unconscious infancy, let us set ourselves apart for Him through faith in Christ in our conscious manhood. Let us dedicate ourselves to Him wholly, unreservedly, body, soul, and spirit. Let us endeavour to walk with God daily, ever looking to the ark of our covenant ; in heartiness of heart, looking to Him for a broken and contrite spirit, under a sense of guilt for forgiveness, in doubtfulness and fearfulness for clearness and quietness of mind, in weakness for strength, in sorrow for joy, in suffering for patience, in temptations for a way to escape, that we may be able to bear them, in conflicts for victory, in the daily duties of life for simplicity of spirit, that "whatsoever we do, in word or deed, we may do all to the glory of God." Then will our path shine more and more unto the perfect day, and when we arrive at the brink of Jordan we shall find its streams divided for us by the presence of the ark of our covenant, and we shall have " an abundant entrance into God's everlasting kingdom."

THE CAPTURE OF JERICHO

Joshua 6:20

" So the people shouted when the priests blew with the trumpets : and
it came to pass, when the people heard the sound of the trumpet,
and the people shouted with a great shout, that the wall fell down
flat, so that the people went up into the city, every man straight
before him, and they took the city."

ONE great miracle had just been wrought. Israel had
passed through the waters of Jordan as on dry ground,
and now they were standing on the very Land of Promise,
the end of all their journeyings. But another miracle
ceased. The manna, wherewith their daily wants had
been supplied for the space of forty years, no longer descended from above. Their faith was no longer tried in
this way, nor had they any more this peculiar proof of
God's loving-kindness and care. The period of miracle
was in great measure, though not altogether, over, and
they were to live, as others, from the fruit of the land.
Thus we read, (chap v. 12,) "And the manna ceased on
the morrow after they had eaten of the old corn of the
land ; neither had the children of Israel manna any more;
but they did eat of the fruit of the land of Canaan that
year."

But though this miracle, this exercise of faith, ceased,
there was still another miracle, another exercise of faith,
before them ; and that was the capture of Jericho. All
the preparations and all the arrangements of the siege
were of a very peculiar kind, and shewed, in a most

striking manner, that it was not by might or by power, but by the Spirit of God, and through faith, that this walled city was to be destroyed. It is these preparations and arrangements, spoken of in chap. v. and vi., that we wish to notice this morning. The first act of preparation was one which, to the world, would appear very strange. It was not provisions of weapons of war, or the collection of material; it was the circumcision of the people. Those who now stood before Jericho, with one or two exceptions, had all been born in the wilderness; and it appears that, during their journeyings, this important rite, the token of the covenant, had been neglected. Taking into account the time and circumstances, we can scarcely doubt but that the administration of this rite had a twofold reference,—a reference to the past, and a reference to the future. With regard to the past, it was the rolling away of Israel's sins. Even though this generation had not come out of Egypt, it had, doubtless, received some of its evil by tradition from its fathers; and, in consequence of its uncircumcised state, was regarded by God as under its reproach; for we are told (ver. 9) that, when circumcised, God said, "This day have I rolled away the reproach of Egypt from off you." Such was its retrospective force and value. And if we look at it with regard to the future, we cannot but regard it as a preparation for the siege of Jericho, and for that new life which Israel was to live in the Land of Promise, and this was still one of faith and dependence on God. The walls of Jericho were to fall, not by the power of man, but by the power of God, and of faith, clinging to the power and faithfulness of God.

Now, all this is evidently typical of the Christian life. We have already remarked, on a former occasion, that, in one point of view, Canaan is typical of heaven, as the place of perfect rest from all the trials and weariness of our pilgrimage life. In another point of view, it must be typical of the Christian's life on earth—of that rest which we have in Christ now—a rest, however, not free from conflict; for though Israel found rest in Canaan from its journeyings, it found no entire deliverance from conflict. According to this twofold view of Canaan, the administration of this rite at Gilgal will have a twofold typical meaning. Now, we know that circumcision under the old covenant, occupied the same place as baptism does under the new; and both virtually have the same meaning. One passage of Scripture is sufficient to prove this point, (Col. ii. 11, 12,)—" In whom also ye are circumcised with the circumcision made without hands, in putting off the body of the sins of the flesh by the circumcision of Christ : buried with him in baptism, wherein also ye are risen with him through the faith of the operation of God, who hath raised him from the dead." Both signified the putting away of the sins of the old and natural life, and the reception of a new principle of life into the soul ; circumcision, however, being typically connected with the birth of Jesus, " in putting off," says St Paul, " the body of the sins of the flesh, by the *circumcision of Christ*." Baptism being sacramentally connected, not with the birth of Jesus, but with His death and resurrection, and thus he goes on to speak of Christians being "buried and rising with Jesus." If, then, brethren, we take Canaan to be typical of heaven, what can be the meaning of this administration of the rite to the whole people, their feet now standing in the Land of Promise? It cannot, *then*, mean the *first* circumcision of the heart —the first putting away of sin ; because this takes place at the first dawn of the Christian life. It must rather signify the *completion* of that life—the full and final removal of all sin from the heart, when the Christian crosses Jordan, and enters into the rest of God. We may grow in grace, brethren, and we ought to " press after the mark of the prize of our high calling in Christ Jesus ; " but so long as we are in this world, there will be a principle of evil in our hearts, even though they have been circumcised by the Spirit of God. There will be conflict. It is only when we lay down our mortal bodies, and our spirits pass into the presence of God—it is only then that the circumcision of the heart will be so consummated, that there will be no remainder of sin, and every vestige of this sinful world, this Egypt, will disappear for ever.

Such seems to be the meaning of this event in Israel's history, when Canaan is taken as a type of heaven. But if we take Canaan to be a type of the Christian life on earth, and connect the circumcision of Israel with the siege and capture of Jericho, then, brethren, we shall learn from it this important truth, that we can gain no victory without the circumcision of *our hearts*. If you understand aright what it is to which God calls you, you will see that it is to overcome sin by the blood of the Lamb. The strongholds of Satan must be broken down. But this cannot be unless our hearts are changed by the Spirit of God. It is only before the heart that is circumcised by the Spirit, and endued with the Divine principle of faith, that the walls of Jericho will fall. " Whatsoever," says St John, (1 Ep. v. 4, 5,) " is born of God overcometh the world : and this is the victory that overcometh the world, even our faith. Who is he that overcometh the world, but he that believeth that Jesus is the Son of God ? "

Have you realized, brethren, this simple but great truth?
It may be that you are conscious of some evils within.
If they are such evils as in their nature break forth outwardly, such as temper and the varied sins of the tongue,
there is no doubt but that self-control can effect much.
It can restrain such outbreaks. But this, though a moral
duty, is not a victory over Satan. To be a real victory,
they must be overcome in the heart; and to effect this,
the introduction of a new principle is necessary. As
Scripture says, we must be circumcised with the circumcision made without hands, made by the Spirit of God.
If, then, brethren, you feel that your heart is not altogether
right yet,—if you feel that there is still sin there to be
overcome, idols to be cast out, then cast yourselves on
God; pray earnestly for the Holy Spirit to give you a
strength which by nature you have not. Then difficulties
will be surmounted, besetting sins will not have dominion,
the walls of Jericho, however strong, will fall. This, then,
brethren, was the first act of preparation for the destruction of Jericho. What was the second? It was one of a
very different kind,—one not of duty, but of encouragement. When the hosts of Israel were near Jericho, Joshua
had a remarkable vision. We are not told what he was
doing. He was probably surveying the walls of Jericho,
and may have been lifting up his heart to God for success
in this their first siege. On lifting up his eyes from the
ground, there stood, as we read, (chap. v. 13,) "a man
over against him, with his sword drawn in his hand."
Joshua fearlessly went up to him and said, "Art thou for
us, or for our adversaries?" An answer which must have
been altogether unexpected was given, one which shewed
that he who spoke was one greater than Joshua, "Nay,"
he said, "but as Captain of the host of the Lord am I now

come." We cannot doubt for one moment who this was. It must have been the Son of God, who afterwards, as the Son of man, is called the "Captain of our salvation." As St Paul says, (Heb. ii. 10,) "For it became him, for whom are all things, and by whom are all things, in bringing many sons unto glory, to make the Captain of their salvation perfect through sufferings." Of Him, too, Isaiah prophesies, "Behold, I have given him for a witness to the people, a leader and commander to the people." Joshua felt the dignity of the person who thus spoke to him, "He fell on his face to the earth, and did worship, and said unto him, What saith my Lord unto his servant?" And the Captain of the Lord's host said unto Joshua, "Loose thy shoe from off thy foot, for the place whereon thou standest is holy ground." It is easy, brethren, to see what great encouragement this must have given to Joshua. We do not know what were his feelings at that moment. He may have been feeling somewhat desponding,—may have been thinking how unskilled he was in conducting operations of this kind ; some doubts about the issue may have crossed his mind. If so, how completely must this appearance of the Captain of the Lord's host have met and overcome all his doubts and fears. From that moment he could not but feel, "Unskilled as I am, we need not fear. Another, and he the Lord himself directs our arms, guides all our operations, will give us strength in the day of battle, and strike terror into the hearts of our enemies." What follows corresponds exactly to this beginning. Never was there any battle or siege in which there was so much of God and so little of man. It was not Israel or Joshua, but the Captain of the Lord's host who secured the victory, and gave Jericho into their hands.

And this, brethren, is what is continually taking place in the experience of God's people. They know what it is to be discouraged at times. It may be the conflict with some besetting sin, and with the great enemy of souls, which tries them sore ; or it may be some work which they have in hand which appals them by its difficulties. In a moment of unbelief, they look at themselves, at their own strength, their own resources, and their hearts fail them. Then, whilst they are thus disheartened, Jesus draws near to their souls. He draws their thoughts away from themselves, their own weakness and insufficiency, and shews them His power and faithfulness. Their hope rises, and they return to the siege of the high-walled Jericho full of courage and expectation, because they do not look to themselves, but to Christ, the power of God unto salvation, the Captain of the Lord's host.

There was, then, brethren, a twofold preparation for the siege of Jericho. The one was the administration of the rite of circumcision, followed by the passover. The other was the appearance of the Son of God as Captain of the Lord's host.

We have now to look at the remarkable arrangements whereby, as means, very remarkable means, Jericho was taken. They were commanded, we must all remember, to compass the city once a-day on six successive days, seven priests bearing before the ark of the covenant seven trumpets of rams' horns ; and on the seventh day they were to compass the city seven times. They did so. "The people shouted when the priests blew with the trumpets : and it came to pass, when the people heard the sound of the trumpet, and the people shouted with a great shout, that the wall fell down flat, so that the people went up into the city, every man straight before him, and they

took the city." Now, amongst the many things which
must strike us here, we cannot fail to observe, not only
the utter inadequacy of the means used, but, more than
this, the want of connexion between the blowing of
the trumpets and the shout of the people, and the falling
of Jericho's walls. But God made a connexion. The
reason why He commanded such *inadequate* means to be
used, was simply to shew that the power was His; and
the reason why He commanded any means to be used at
all, was simply to try the faith of the Israelites. Had
they had some great thing to do, they might have im-
puted success to it, instead of to God; or, had they had
nothing to do, there would have been no exercise of faith.
We see from all this how jealous God is of His own glory
—how evidently it is His will that we should feel that *all*
the power is His, and also how in everything He purposes
to try His people's faith. The general lesson, then, which
we may learn from this is, to use means in full faith,
however inadequate they may appear, if only they are
appointed of God, but never to rest in them. It is on
God alone that we must rest; on His love and power that
we must lean, and we must give all the glory to Him, and
not to man, for everything effected by His power in the
use of means.

But there is much more in this into which we ought to
go. We have seen more than once of what the ark of the
covenant was a symbol and type. It was a symbol of
God's presence, and it was a type of Jesus, God manifest
in the flesh. We have also met more than once with
these silver trumpets, and have remarked that, as the
sacrifices were typical of Christ, so the silver trumpets
were typical of the gospel, whose sound is gone forth in
all the world. Here, then, brethren, we have represented

to us in vivid manner the great conflict in which true
Christians are now engaged, and those all-sufficient means
of defence and victory. Jericho, the city of the curse, is
a type of the *world*, and of Satan's kingdom, which we
have to overcome. And what are the weapons of our warfare? Christ, brethren, represented by the ark of the
covenant—Christ without us, on whom alone we must
lean—Christ within us, the only hope of glory. Let
Jesus go before us, as our Captain, our skilful and all-
powerful leader and commander. Let Him be in the
midst of us as our ark and covenant. Let us blow
aloud the gospel trumpet, which speaks of a full and
free salvation—all in Christ. Let us lift up the trumpet
in faith, full faith, in the power of God, and then
the walls of our Jericho, however strong, must and will
fall. Men of the world may distrust this instrumentality.
It may appear to them altogether weak—yea, even foolishness. This is nothing new; for St Paul says, (1 Cor.
i. 18,) "For the preaching of the cross is to them that
perish foolishness." Yes; but what does he add? "But
unto us which are saved the *power* of God." The *power*
of God! Moral arguments may possibly make here and
there a moral man, though it is very rare that they can
accomplish even this. Wise laws may contribute to the
orderly behaviour of a population, though there will
always be sad disorder; but let all this happen. What
then? "The walls of Jericho still stand." Satan will
still keep possession of his palace and his goods in peace.
Nothing but the gospel of Jesus Christ can destroy
Satan's kingdom, can translate souls out of darkness into
marvellous light; and it is no less the truth as it is in
Jesus which causes the enemy to flee when he assaults
us. All the saints now before the throne of God were

washed in the blood of Jesus. They had no inherent goodness. What they now are in the rest above, free from all sin, beautiful in the robe of Christ's righteousness, *that* the grace of God made them; all the victories which they gained on earth were won by the blood of the Lamb, and the power of the truth. Jesus triumphed for them, and in them. Brethren, let us cleave to Jesus, even as they did. Let us go forth to each conflict with our foes, having Christ near and within us. He has given us the promise, "Lo, I am with you always, even to the end of the world,"—"with you in conflict as your captain, in danger as your shield, in sorrow as your comforter, in bereavement as your brother and unchanging friend." He is too patient to give us up, wayward as we are, too faithful to forsake us; and, strengthened by His strength, we shall be enabled to triumph over every difficulty, and shall be borne onward to the promised rest.

THE ACCURSED THING

Joshua 7:13

" Up, sanctify the people, and say, Sanctify yourselves against to-
morrow : for thus saith the Lord God of Israel, There is an
accursed thing in the midst of thee, O Israel : thou canst not stand
before thine enemies, until ye take away the accursed thing from
among you."

THE siege of Jericho was soon followed by that of Ai, a
small and less important place.   As in the case of Jericho,
Joshua sent spies to examine the city.   They reported that
the people were but few, and that two or three thousand
men might easily take it.   These were accordingly sent,
but instead of taking the city, to the utter astonishment
and grief of Joshua and the men of Israel, they fled before
the men of Ai, and lost a few of their men.   Although
the loss was in reality small, nothing could well exceed
the discouragement to Joshua and Israel.   It was not the
actual loss so much as the utter disappointment, and the
consequent difficulties of their position, which depressed
them so deeply.   The feelings and conduct of Joshua on
this occasion clearly shew how little strength of character
he had as compared with Moses.   He did not know the
reason of this discomfiture, and so wished that they had
never crossed the Jordan.   " Alas," he says, ver. 7, " O Lord
God, wherefore hast thou at all brought this people over
Jordan, to deliver us into the hand of the Amorites, to
destroy us ?   Would to God we had been content, and
dwelt on the other side Jordan !"   There was unbelief

in this, for it was not a mere question of contentment. The command, the promise, and the power of God had brought them over Jordan. Then, too, Joshua imagines the greatest dangers as likely to arise out of this defeat. He pictured to himself all the tribes of Canaan in league against them, and Israel cut off, (ver. 8, 9,) "O Lord, what shall I say, when Israel turneth their backs before their enemies! For the Canaanites and all the inhabitants of the land shall hear of it, and shall environ us round, and cut off our name from the earth: and what wilt thou do unto thy great name?" It shewed Joshua's faith when he went to God in the time of trouble; but it shewed the power of unbelief when, instead of calmly finding out the cause of the disaster, he wished the dealings of God to be otherwise than they were, and allowed his imagination to picture all the possible consequences of his failure. When difficulties and disappointments come, we ought not, brethren, to be too much cast down. We ought not to allow ourselves to imagine the worst; we should stay our hearts on God, believing that there is a needs-be for the difficulty and trial. It is meant for the exercise of our faith. The cause of this defeat was soon brought to light in a most striking manner. "Get thee up," God said to Joshua; "wherefore liest thou thus upon thy face? Israel hath sinned, and they have also transgressed my covenant which I commanded them: for they have even taken of the accursed thing, and have also stolen, and dissembled also, and they have put it even among their own stuff." Measures were immediately taken for the discovery of the transgressor. God appointed the measures. First of all the tribe was taken to which the sinner belonged—taken, we suppose, by lot. This was the tribe of all others the most privileged,—the tribe of Judah,—out of which eventually, according to the flesh, came salvation. Then the family was selected. This was the family of the Zarhites. The household of Zabdi was taken, and when the household came forward, man by man, Achan was taken. There must have been something deeply solemn in this gradual approach to the sinner, the cause of Israel's calamity. It must have brought home to every heart with overwhelming conviction that God was in the midst of Israel. Achan then was discovered ; but mark the wisdom with which Joshua dealt with him. Something concerning his sin was already known; yet Joshua did not *charge* him with it, but tried to get him to *confess* it. " My son, give, I pray thee, glory to the Lord God of Israel, and make confession unto him : and tell me now what thou hast done ; hide it not from me." Notice, brethren here the expression " Give glory to the Lord." We often meet with it in Scripture, and in more than one passage it seems to be connected with repentance. Take, for instance, 1 Sam. vi. 5, " Ye shall give glory unto the God of Israel : peradventure he will lighten his hand from off you, and from off your gods, and from off your land." So again, Mal. ii. 2, "If ye will not hear, and if ye will not lay it to heart, to give glory to my name, saith the Lord of hosts, I will even send a curse upon you, and I will curse your blessings :" and this is expressed still more clearly, Rev. xvi. 9, " And men were scorched with great heat, and blasphemed the name of God, which hath power over these plagues : and they repented not to give him glory." You see then, brethren, one way in which you may give glory to God. It is by true repentance. You see also the attribute, if we may use the expression, of true repentance ; it gives glory to God, for the penitent condemns himself, and acknowledges the truth, the righteousness, and the love of God. In two other passages of Scripture it is, however, connected with the confession of sin. One is the chapter from which our text is taken, the words which we have just read to you. The other you will find, John ix. 24, " Give God the praise : we know that this man is a sinner." The Pharisees did not mean by this, " Give the glory of your cure to God, and not to this sinful man ;" for they did not believe that any cure had been effected. What they believed was, that it was all a *trick*. And when they said, " Give God the praise," they meant to insinuate that they had discovered it all,—that it was better for him now to confess that it was all a cheat, and no miracle. Here, therefore, the expression, "Give God the praise," is connected with the confession of sin. Let us remember, then, brethren, that we cannot give glory to God whilst we continue impenitent and conceal our sins. Our hearts must be deeply humbled before God. There must be unreserved confession of sin to God, and of crime to man as well as God, in order to give Him glory.

Achan *did* confess his sin. " Indeed," he said, (ver. 20, 21,) " I have sinned against the Lord God of Israel, and thus and thus have I done when I saw among the spoils a goodly Babylonish garment, and two hundred shekels of silver, and a wedge of gold of fifty shekels weight, then I coveted them, and took them ; and, behold, they are hid in the earth in the midst of my tent, and the silver under it." Judgment followed. Achan and all his possessions were brought forth into the valley, called from that day the valley of Achor, or trouble, and here he was stoned with stones. Then the fierceness of God's anger was turned away. Words of encouragement were spoken to Joshua. The Lord said unto Joshua, (chap. viii. 1,)

"Fear not, neither be thou dismayed;" and Ai was soon taken and reduced to ashes. There are many important lessons in this chapter of Israel's history. Let us gather up some of them. First, then, brethren, we have here a striking illustration of the great law of God's kingdom,— "Be sure that your sin will find you out." There is nothing more certain than that sin is sure to find out the sinner, either in this world or the world to come. With regard to some of the more refined sins which are deeply sinful in God's sight—such as pride, some forms of selfishness, and unbelief—this will take place in the world to come. The parables of the rich man and the rich fool present impressive examples of this result of sin. The life may be all smooth and easy. The praise of man may resound on every side; and yet the soul may be hastening downward to a dark and dreary doom; and some sin, condemned by God's Word, but unseen to every eye but' God's, tracks the impenitent and unbelieving soul onward, follows him day by day, never leaves him, and finds him out with all its awfulness beyond the grave.

Achan's sin was, however, one of those which find the sinner out in this world. Yet to him it must have seemed very improbable that it would ever be discovered. In all the hurry and bustle of a siege, he could take what he would, all unobserved. He did so. It was not the eye of man, it was the eye of God that detected him, the hand of God which arrested him. The disaster at Ai probably cost him little anxiety. He could not connect it in any way with the wedge of gold. But when at God's command an inquiry was instituted,—when a gradual approach was made, and first the tribe, then his family, then his father's house, and then he himself was taken, he must have felt how sin had deceived him, how the eye of God was upon him, and how the righteousness of God was following him with unerring grasp.

Brethren, the same solemn process is still going on in many different ways. It is not *safe*, brethren, to cherish any sin, even the most hidden sin of the heart. The Scripture says, (Gal. vi. 7, 8,) "Whatsoever a man soweth, *that* shall he also reap. For he that soweth to his flesh shall of the flesh reap corruption ; and he that soweth to the Spirit shall of the Spirit reap life everlasting." There are some who live only for the world, who sow only to the flesh. They are under the power of some besetting sin,—it may be Achan's, or some other; and that sin unrepented of finds them out in everlasting death. But those who sow to the Spirit, who know what it is to live by faith, should take heed lest they *sometimes* sow to the flesh, lest they do anything which gives strength to the corrupt principle within, and which weakens the new man. Hezekiah usually walked in the Spirit ; but, though the recipient of so much grace, he sowed to the flesh when he received the messengers of the King of Babylon, and shewed them all that was in his house. " God left him," we read, (2 Chron. xxxii. 31,) "to try him, that he might know all that was in his heart." And just so, brethren, if God leaves us but one moment, we should begin at once to sow to the flesh,—we should cease to sow to the Spirit. Peter, again, usually sowed to the Spirit ; but he sowed to the flesh when he denied his Master, and when he acted towards the Gentile Christians in such a way as to require the rebuke of another apostle ; and in each case sin found him out. It requires, brethren, much prayer, much close and circumspect walking with God, to sow *always* to the Spirit, to avoid worldliness of heart, all conformity to its ways, all recompense of evil by evil ; and still more, the doing things, good things, in our own spirit, instead of the Spirit of God. It is not enough to do things generally good, and approved by others. Even such things may be done to self,—done in our own spirit. The way to walk in the Spirit is to do all things to God, all things in dependence on Him, all things to His glory.

But there is another consequence of besetting sins which this history strikingly illustrates, and that is the *weakness* which it produces in the whole spiritual life. This one sin of Achan's would appear to many no very great sin; yet not only was it productive of fearful consequences to himself and family, but it weakened the forces of Israel. Those who had passed through Jordan on dry ground, and before whom the walls of Jericho fell down, were forced to fly before a small force of the enemy. One sin weakened Israel, brought confusion and discouragement into their camp, and seemed to bring everything to nought. How great is the power, how terrible the consequences, of one sin, and that, observe, not of a great national sin, but of the sin of *one* man! Yet all Israel seemed to be held guilty of it. " Therefore the children of Israel could not stand before their enemies, but turned their backs before their enemies, because they were accursed: neither will I be with you any more, except ye destroy the accursed from among you. Up, sanctify the people, and say, Sanctify yourselves against to-morrow: for thus saith the Lord God of Israel, There is an accursed thing in the midst of thee, O Israel: thou canst not stand before thine enemies, until ye take away the accursed thing from among you."

Now, we, brethren, have enemies against whom we ought to *stand*. We " wrestle not against flesh and blood, but against principalities and powers, against the rulers of the darkness of this world, against spiritual wickedness in high places;" and these enemies are so powerful, that it is only in God that we can stand against them. When we rest wholly on the atonement of Jesus —when our desire is to live wholly to God—when nothing is allowed to come between us and Him—then we are bold and very courageous. Childlike confidence in God makes us strong and hopeful in God's work. We are conscious that His presence is with us giving power, however feeble we are; and this, brethren, is the great secret of prosperous work. It is a close walk with God, a walk in which, and out of which, springs up cheerful and holy confidence. But if any sin is allowed, any duty is wilfully neglected, then estrangement follows; prayer is hindered, all the graces of the Spirit are weakened, and the old and corrupt nature gains greater power. Then, brethren, we cannot stand against our enemies. How can we? How, if God is displeased? How, if Jesus is crucified afresh? How, if the Spirit is grieved, how can we do the work of God with *power?* It is His *felt* presence which is its life and power, its joy and consolation. The nearer we live to God, the more power we shall have in conflict, and in work. Let us keep, then, our hearts, dear brethren, with all diligence, for out of them are the issues of life. Whatever our besetting sin may be, let us watch against it. If it be *pride,* let us pray for humility. If *vanity,* let us endeavour to esteem others better than ourselves. If *worldliness,* let us remember God's command, not to touch the " accursed thing." " Be not conformed to this world : but be ye transformed by the renewing of your mind, that ye may prove what is that good, and acceptable, and perfect will of God." (Rom. xii. 2.) If *temper,* put on, through grace, the meekness and gentleness of Christ. The only way to overcome a besetting sin, to put away the accursed thing, is to live near to God, to walk with Him. If we grow careless and hurried in our devotions—if we cease to meditate on God's Word, and to examine our own hearts —sin, even the sin which seemed to be subdued, will gain fresh power, and the whole spiritual life will be weakened, all the graces of the Spirit will fade and languish. The words of the prophet are but too appropriate, (Isa. i. 22,) " Thy silver is become dross, thy wine mixed with water."

There is one more thought, brethren, and one of consolation, which strikes us here. We have seen that the valley in which these painful events happened was called the valley of Achor, or trouble. It was ever after remembered in Israel, and became proverbial amongst them. Now, if you turn to Hosea ii. 15, you will find these beautiful and striking words :—" And I will give her her vineyards from thence, and the valley of Achor for a door of hope : and she shall sing there, as in the days of her youth, and as in the day when she came up out of the land of Egypt." Here, then, we are reminded of the words of St Paul, " Where sin abounded, grace did much more abound." It lightens up with the rays of hope even the valley of trouble and discouragement.

There are some, doubtless, here who have found this in their own experience. Some heavy and much dreaded cross has been laid upon you. You shrunk from it. It filled you at first with dismay ; your heart was faint, and the future seemed charged with trouble. But when the hand of God had brought you into the very gorge of the valley, the narrowest and darkest part of all, just that which you dreaded most, light unexpectedly sprung up, and hope arose in your heart; and so, even in the valley of Achor, you could sing the Lord's song, sing as in the days of your gladness, only with a more calm and subdued voice. It is no small blessing, brethren, to realize that the grace of God is a transforming power. It can bring good out of severe and bitter conflicts. It can lighten up the valley, however dark—the valley of Achor —yea, more than that, the valley of the shadow of death. What follows from this, but that we should walk by faith? Let us leave, brethren, the future in God's hand—"Sufficient for the day is the evil thereof." What we want to know is simply this,—Is Christ mine, and am I His? For if so, we have an all-sufficient promise,—"All things work together for good to them that love God." We have a refuge which can never fail—a Captain, who *can* and will bring us into our promised Canaan, "the rest that remaineth for the people of God."

We here close, dear brethren, our somewhat long course of sermons on Israel's history, as typical of the Christian life. We commenced with Egypt, and have followed them through the wilderness into the Land of Promise, where, after the sieges of Jericho and Ai, they gained a firm footing. Interesting as much of the subsequent history is, this seems the best place to pause, and make way for another course. When we look back on the past one, how much cause we see for humiliation before God— humiliation for the feeble and imperfect manner in which we have touched on so great and beautiful a subject! Many things have contributed to this imperfection,—the increasing pressure of work, the frequent interruptions so perpetual in a place like this. But what we want most of all, brethren, is, a deeper *teaching* of the Spirit of God —yea, to be *filled* with the Spirit of God. We have often thought, that if our affectionate flock knew how painful it is never to reach beyond one step towards that which we conceive a sermon ought to be, they would be more earnest in prayer for their ministers—they would pray that they might have a deeper teaching of the Spirit of God. Meanwhile, brethren, if our report has not been made helpful to any other soul, it is one consolation, that it has been a blessing to our own; and whilst it has been our longing and our prayer that it might be helper of your joy, God has graciously increased our own joy in Him. Usher in, dear brethren, the new course of our beloved brother and fellow-labourer with your earnest prayers.